ALLEGORY AND REPRESENTATION

Selected Papers from the English Institute
New Series

Allegory and Representation

Selected Papers
from the English Institute, 1979–80

New Series, no. 5

Edited, with a Preface, by Stephen J. Greenblatt

THE JOHNS HOPKINS UNIVERSITY PRESS
BALTIMORE AND LONDON

The Johns Hopkins University Press, Baltimore Maryland 21218
The Johns Hopkins Press Ltd., London

Library of Congress Cataloging in Publication Data

English Institute.
  Allegory and representation.

  (Selected papers from the English Institute ;
1979–80, new ser., no. 5)
    1. Allegories—Addresses, essays, lectures.
2. Arts—Addresses, essays, lectures.
I. Greenblatt, Stephen Jay. II. Title. III. Series:
Selected papers from the English Institute ; new
ser., no. 5.
NX650.A44E5   700   81–47595
ISBN 0-8018-2642-X   AACR2

Contents

Preface

These seven papers were read at the 1979 and 1980 annual meetings of the English Institute: the papers by Paul de Man, Joel Fineman, and Robert Durling in a program on "Allegory"; the papers by Michael Fried, Hugh Kenner, Leo Bersani, and Michael Holquist in a program on "Mimesis and Representation." The latter program was conceived in part as a response to the former, for all of the speakers in the "Allegory" program raised questions that bore powerfully on the status of representation.

This questioning of representation is clearest perhaps in Paul de Man's provocative essay "Pascal's Allegory of Persuasion"; here allegory and mimesis are initially set against each other, but in the course of the essay they are seen to touch in the shared impossibility of a just, stable, and direct representation. "Why it it," de Man writes of allegory, "that the furthest reaching truths about ourselves and the world have to be stated in such a lopsided, referentially indirect mode?" The answer, at least as suggested by Pascal's "Réflexions sur le géométrie," is that the target toward which signs are turned remains finally unknown, that there is, in consequence, no possibility of direct signification, that "the notion of language as sign is in fact dependent on and derived from a different notion in which language functions as rudderless signification and transforms what it denominates into the linguistic equivalent of the arithmetical zero."

Allegory in this view then is quite the opposite of what it often pretends to be: the recovery of the pure visibility of the truth, undisguised by the local and accidental. Allegory may dream of presenting the thing itself—not particular instances of sin or goodness, but Sin and Goodness themselves directly acting in the moral world they also constitute—but its deeper purpose and its actual effect is to acknowledge the darkness, the arbitrariness, and the void that underlie, and paradoxically make possible, all representation of realms of light, order, and presence. Insofar as the project of mimesis is the direct representation of a stable, objective reality, allegory, in attempting and always failing to present Reality, inevitably reveals the impossibility of this project. This impossibility is precisely the foundation upon which all representation, indeed all discourse, is constructed. I might add that in the question period, which forms an integral part of English Institute programs, de Man responded to one objection by remarking, perhaps not altogether in jest, "If you want to talk about men, you are in the wrong field. We can only talk about letters." Our words are permanently cut off from what we dream of signifying, and criticism, like allegory itself, must acknowledge this condition.

This conception of allegory and, more generally, of representation as built upon its own undoing is reiterated in a different theoretical register and with different consequences in Joel Fineman's "The Structure of Allegorical Desire." For Fineman, to talk about letters— here, quite literally, the primal /p/ and /m/—is inevitably to talk about men as well as literature, but this conjunction does not signal the consummation devoutly wished by allegory, that is, the perfect, authoritative representation of the Truth. On the contrary, one discovers that allegory arises in periods of loss, periods in which a once powerful theological, political, or familial authority is threatened with effacement. Allegory arises then from the painful absence of that which it claims to recover, and, as in de Man, the paradox of an order built upon its own undoing cannot be restricted to this one discursive mode; indeed for Fineman, the longing for an origin whose loss is the necessary condition of that longing is the character not only of all discourse but of human existence itself.

The language of the two initial essays—"the synechdocal totalization of infinitude," "the hypothesised intersection of paradigmatic synchrony and syntagmatic diachrony," and so forth—will at times seem strange and difficult to readers unfamiliar with the linguistic and philosophical influences upon recent critical theory, but the central concerns here are highly traditional questions of the relation between literary form and literary content, persuasion and truth, and representation and reality. So influential and pervasive are these questions in our culture that artistic practice from the time of Plato may be said to have evolved at least in part as a complex set of responses to them. That is, not only do the questions that these essays pose arise from the contemporary interpretation of works of art, but works of art have for centuries been generated out of these questions. The essays in this volume sketch a variety of such responses and suggest above all else what we may call the cunning of representation: the resiliency, brilliance, and resourcefulness with which artistic practice has responded to an unappeasable craving for reality and truth and a recurrent fear that these forever lie just beyond our grasp.

Thus, for example, Dante is, as Robert Durling argues, deeply sensitive to the gap between the sign and the signified and hence to the possibility that *The Divine Comedy* itself could be regarded as a magnificent version of the counterfeiting that is punished in the *Inferno*. The gap cannot be merely wished away in a magical return to a simple and natural relation between representation and reality, but Dante's allegory is, Durling suggests, a complex and shifting attempt to focus and interrelate religious, metaphysical, cosmic, social, and moral dimensions in representations of the human body and of human speech. The disturbing sense of negation and void—the contamination of natural meanings, the loss of origins, the fraudulence of signs—is then located in Satan's body, which is a demonic parody of the mystical body of God, and the representation of these bodies, along with the body politic, is a poem in which Dante's own human body is as fully engaged as possible.

The presence in the work of art of the artist's own body—the representation of live bodily being—is also the subject of Michael Fried's brilliant chapter. Indeed, I think we may see the radical project of Gustave Courbet's realism, as Fried describes it—the systematic effacement of a theatrical distance between creator and art object, the representation of absorptive states and the full implication of the beholder in these states—as the heir to the mystical absorption of Dante's allegory. But, of course, the modern representation utterly transforms the medieval religious vision by placing the artist's body, both in its potency and its sense of loss, where God's body and Satan's body once reigned. With this transformation, Courbet attempts to do something that Dante, with his intense faith in a transcendent divinity, would have resisted as much as desired—namely, to fuse to an unprecedented degree representation with what it represents so that there is ideally no longer *anything* outside of the human creation, not the body as object, not landscape, certainly not God.

In this attempt, Courbet's realism paradoxically anticipates the achievements of seemingly antirealist contemporary painting; both meet in a will to seize upon the deepest resources of the visible, resources that are not so much set *against* representation as set beneath or prior to it, just as vision in each of our lives is prior to the acquisition of speech. Indeed, Fried suggests, Courbet's art strives to probe beneath vision itself to reach a still deeper stratum of primordial embodiedness. Hence Courbet seems to go as far as possible toward a healing of the loss or undoing out of which, as we have said, most great representational art in our culture seems to be generated. He does so by pursuing representation to the point of its own extinction, the point at which the gap that made representation necessary and desirable is all but closed. I think that the extraordinary power of Courbet's art may lie in his grappling with this "all but": the distance he cannot ignore and that his painting must forever seek to destroy.

The power of vision is found in a different form in Hugh Kenner's eloquent "The Possum in the Cave," in which the sense of sight functions not to collapse mimetic distance, but to guarantee the rightness or integrity of representation. The gaps, the loss of origins, the effacement of a natural relation between sign and signified are all conceded, but only to a logocentric "poetics of the cave," the poetics exemplified by T. S. Eliot's "post-symbolist signification of ineffabilities, controlled by allusion and acoustic nuance." Against this rich, melancholy echo-chamber of self-referentiality and self-deconstruction, Kenner holds up Ezra Pound's "poetics of sunlight" where words "point, and the arranger of the words works in trust that we shall find their connection validated outside the poem."

Pound's words "send us out toward the verifiable," and we can gauge their accuracy by means of a map, a photograph, or the testimony of our own eyes. Nothing could be more straightforward. But perhaps we may suggest that there is, in the midst of this apparently untroubled and empirical affirmation of the physical, an oddly utopian element that is signalled by the interplay of the historical and the visual. After all, as Kenner observes, Pound visits and writes of Montségur not only for the quality of its light and line but also for its history, a history that is linked to Pound's larger and, we may well say, darker historical vision. This vision too may be tested, of course, against history books and our own experience, against our present understanding of the Albigensian heresy or of modern politics, but this test will surely not have the crisp, satisfying resolution of the appeal to the photograph. Indeed, the historical dimension will, I think, cast a shadow on the "poetics of sunlight" and reintroduce those doubts that such a poetics should have laid to rest. I should add that such doubts are subtly intimated by Kenner himself when he observes that the mimetic verses he quotes from Canto 38 comprise a "topos of loss"; inseparably mingled with what can be verified are things and feelings that cannot submit to ocular proof: a sense of devastation, a vanished civilization.

Let us return to the central motif of Kenner's chapter—the contrast of opposing modes of representation—for it will lead us to Leo Bersani's disturbing and suggestive "Representation and Its Discontents." Against "an art of entrapped realism," sado-masochistic and hence fixated upon reiterated, narrative scenes of violence and pain, Bersani opposes "an art of happily mobile fantasies." There is, as in Kenner's chapter, a utopian element in this alternative representational practice, or better still a recollection of the Land of Cockayne, for in contrast to a mimesis organized so as to produce a violent closure, a mode of representation that consists of sexual and ontological floating is described by Bersani. This psychoanalytic reading is, we might note, in some sense the reverse of Fineman's, for where Fineman sees representation as a compensation for the *absence* of the father and the *loss* of union with the mother, a loss necessarily prior to representation's mimetic appropriation of the world, Bersani sees that appropriation as the child's response to the mother's *kiss,* and the father's presence brings such representation to a violent close.

The "art of happily mobile fantasies," we may be tempted to conclude, is fatherless representation, but Bersani knows that the drive for control, closure, and the "shared commotion" produced by violence does not simply and miraculously vanish. The paternal figure must be transformed so that he no longer plays "the role of inhibiting law," but rather provides "the opportunity for a socializing of the traumatic loving initially experienced at the mother's breast." This transformation is not achieved by turning away from the representation of violence, Bersani suggests, but rather by an erotic submission to it, and this submission, at once passive and ironic, has the effect of transforming violence into dream, memory, and project. Actual sado-masochistic violence can be eschewed or sublimated because exuberantly ironic representations always assure one that such violence is occurring, with our complicity, somewhere else.

This brings us finally to Michael Holquist's superb chapter, "The Politics of Representation," in which irony and submission also function, but in a strikingly different way, to accomodate, deflect, and subvert historical repression and violence. Here, too, an alternative model is opposed to representation as a fixed imprisonment of the self, but the central interest of this alternative is not mobility as sexual and ontological floating, but as a strategy: a way to survive, to insinuate oneself into a system of monolithic power, to create dialogue where there was only monologue, to generate a more capacious and decent social meaning. It might seem at first that Mikhail Bakhtin's cunningly indirect representations of his convictions are a special case, and Holquist himself is particularly insistent upon the specifically Slavic circumstances and meaning of this story, rooted as it is in the pressures of Stalinist censorship, the traditional Aesopian indirection in Eastern European intellectual and artistic discourse, the precise and for us peculiar cast of Bakhtin's Russian Orthodoxy. Holquist argues convincingly, however, that Bakhtin's beliefs about representation and his representation of these beliefs provide a model whose implications extend far beyond the borders of the Eastern Bloc.

Paul de Man's question with which we began—"Why is it that the furthest reaching truths about ourselves and the world have to be

stated in such a lopsided, referentially indirect mode?"—is thus re-
stated as a question about the politics of representation, and an
answer is sought not in the logic of the sign or in the universal
psychogenesis of the subject, but in the particular social circumstances that both shape and inhibit representation in a given culture.
For, if I may add my own terms here, all discourse is improvisation,
both an entry into and a deflection of existing strategies of representation. The improviser never encounters the theoretical origins of
signification, whether they lie in pure presence or absence. All
artists enter into representations that are already under way and
make a place for themselves in relation to these representations
which are, we might add, never fully coordinated. Even in the most
oppressive or, alternatively, the most happily unified of cultures,
there are always conflicts of interest, strategy, and desire, so that the
artist's task includes a substantial element of choice or tact or
struggle. This task is shaped by the fact that the improvisor is himself
in part the product of these prior representations. But only in part,
for were there a perfect fit, there would no longer be that craving
for reality that forever generates ironic submission and disguised
revolt.

STEPHEN J. GREENBLATT
University of California–Berkeley

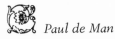 *Paul de Man*

Pascal's Allegory of Persuasion

Attempts to define allegory keep reencountering a set of predictable problems, of which the summary can serve as a preliminary characterization of the mode. Allegory is sequential and narrative, yet the topic of its narration is not necessarily temporal at all, thus raising the question of the referential status of a text whose semantic function, though strongly in evidence, is not primarily determined by mimetic moments; more than ordinary modes of fiction, allegory is at the furthest possible remove from historiography. The "realism" that appeals to us in the details of medieval art is a calligraphy rather than a mimesis, a technical device to insure that the emblems will be correctly identified and decoded, not an appeal to the pagan pleasures of imitation. For it is part of allegory that, despite its obliqueness and innate obscurity, the resistance to understanding emanates from the difficulty or censorship inherent in the statement and not from the devices of enunciation: Hegel rightly distinguishes between allegory and enigma in terms of allegory's "aim for the most complete clarity, so that the external means it uses must be as transparent as possible with regard to the meaning it is to make apparent."[1] The difficulty of allegory is rather that this emphatic clarity of representation does not stand in the service of something that can be represented.

The consequence, throughout the history of the term *allegory,* is a recurrent ambivalence in its aesthetic valorization. Allegory is frequently dismissed as wooden, barren (*kahl*), ineffective, or ugly, yet the reasons for its ineffectiveness, far from being a shortcoming, are of such all-encompassing magnitude that they coincide with the furthest reaching achievements available to the mind and reveal boundaries that aesthetically more successful works of art, because of this very success, were unable to perceive. To remain with Hegel a moment longer, the aesthetic condemnation of allegory, which becomes evident in the assumed inferiority of Vergil with regard to Homer, is outdone, in Hegel's own allegory of history, by its assignation to the meta-aesthetic age of Christianity, thus making the triadic procession from Homer to Vergil to Dante characteristic for the history of art itself as the dialectical overcoming of art.[2] The theoretical discussion of the uncertain value of allegory repeats, in the *Aesthetics,* the theoretical discussion of the uncertain value of art itself. In the wavering status of the allegorical sign, the system of which the allegorical is a constitutive component is being itself unsettled.

Allegory is the purveyor of demanding truths, and thus its burden is to articulate an epistemological order of truth and deceit with a narrative or compositional order of persuasion. In a stable system of signification, such an articulation is not problematic; a representation is, for example, persuasive and convincing to the extent that it is faithful, exactly in the same manner that an argument is persuasive to the extent that it is truthful. Persuasion and proof should not, in principle, be distinct from each other, and it would not occur to a mathematician to call his proofs allegories. From a theoretical point of view, there ought to be no difficulty in moving from epistemology to persuasion. The very occurrence of allegory, however, indicates a possible complication. Why is it that the furthest reaching truths about ourselves and the world have to be stated in such a lopsided, referentially indirect mode? Or, to be more specific, why is it that texts that attempt the articulation of epistemology with persuasion turn out to be inconclusive about their own intelligibility in the same manner and for the same reasons that produce allegory? A large number of such texts on the relationship between truth and persuasion exist in the canon of philosophy and of rhetoric, often crystallized around such traditional philosophical topoi as the relationship between analytic and synthetic judgments, between propositional and modal logic, between logic and mathematics, between logic and rhetoric, between rhetoric as *inventio* and rhetoric as *dispositio,* and so forth. In order to try to progress in the precise formulation of the difficulty, I turn to what I find to be a suggestive example, one of the later didactic texts written by Pascal for the instruction of the pupils at Port Royal. The text, which dates from 1657 or 1658 (Pascal died in 1662), remained unpublished for a long time, but did not pass unnoticed, since Arnauld and Nicole incorporated parts of it in the *Logique* of Port Royal. It has since been mentioned by most specialists of Pascal and has been the object of at least one learned monograph.[3] The text is entitled *Réflexions sur la géométrie en général; De l'esprit géométrique et de l'Art de persuader*,[4] a title rendered somewhat oddly, but not uninterestingly, in one English edition of Pascal as *The Mind of the Geometrician*.[5] It is an exemplary case for our inquiry, since it deals with what Pascal calls, in the first section, "l'étude de la verité" or epistemology and, in the second, "l'art de persuader" or rhetoric.

Ever since it was discovered, *Réflexions* has puzzled its readers. Arnauld's and Nicole's way of excerpting from it to make it serve the more narrowly traditional Cartesian mold of the *Logique* considerably simplified and indeed mutilated its Pascalian complexity; the Dominican Father Touttée, who was the first to unearth it from among Pascal's papers, expressed great doubts about its internal coherence and consistency.[6] Despite strong internal evidence to the contrary, the text has often not been considered as a single entity divided in two parts, but as two entirely separate disquisitions; Pascal's early editors, Desmolets (in 1728) and Condoret (in 1776), gave it as separate fragments, and not until 1844 did it appear more or less in the now generally accepted form of one single unit divided into two parts.[7] The history of the text's philology curiously repeats the theoretical argument, which has compulsively to do with questions of units and pairs, divisibility, and heterogeneity.

The argument of the *Réflexions* is digressive, but not at all lacking in consistency. If it indeed reaches dead ends and breaking points, it does so by excess of rigor rather than for lack of it. That such breaking points are reached, however, cannot be denied. Recent commentators have valiantly tried to patch up the most conspicuous holes by attributing them to historical indeterminations characteristic of Pascal's time and situation.[8] In a text that is historically as overdetermined as this one—and that contains echoes of an almost endless series of disputations which, in the wake of such philosophers as Descartes, Leibniz, Hobbes, and Gassendi, mark the period as one of intense epistemological speculation—the temptation is great to domesticate the more threatening difficulties by historicizing them out of consciousness. Even after this operation has been performed, some anomalies remain that pertain specifically to the nature rather than the state of the question. The most conspicuous break occurs in the second part, in the section on persuasion (356). Pascal has asserted the existence of two entirely different modes by which arguments can be conducted. The first mode has been established in the first section, in polemical opposition to the scholastic logic of syllogisms, as the method of the geometricians, and it can be codified in the rules that Arnauld and Nicole incorporated in the *Logique*. When these rules are observed, it is the only mode to be both productive and reliable. Because of the fallen condition of man, however, it cannot establish itself as the only way. Though man is accessible to reason and convinced by proof, he is even more accessible to the language of pleasure and of seduction, which governs his needs and his passions rather than his mind. In their own realms, the language of seduction (*langage d'agrément*) and the language of persuasion can rule or even cooperate, but when natural truth and human desire fail to coincide, they can enter into conflict. At that moment, says Pascal, "a dubious balance is achieved between truth and pleasure (*vérité et volupté*), and the knowledge of the one and the awareness of the other wage a combat of which the outcome is very uncertain" (356). Such dialectical moments are, as the readers of the *Pensées* well know, very common in Pascal and function as the necessary precondition for insights. No such resolution occurs at this crucial moment, however, although the efficacy of the entire text is at stake. Pascal retreats in a phraseology of which it is impossible to say whether it is evasive or ironically personal: "Now, of these two methods, the one of persuasion, the other of seduction (*convaincre . . . agrées*), I shall give rules only for the former . . . [the geometrical persuasion]. Not that I do not believe the other to be incomparably more difficult, more subtle, more useful, and more admirable. So, if I do not discuss it, it is because of my inability to do so. I feel it to be so far beyond my means that I consider it entirely impossible. Not that I do not believe that if anyone is able to do so, it is people whom I know, and that no one has as clear and abundant insight into the matter as they do" (356). The reference appears to be to Pascal's friend the Chevalier de Méré, who had already been present by

polemical allusion at an earlier and delicate moment in the first part
of the treatise,[9] thus enforcing the impression that, at the moment
in the demonstration when we are the most in need of clear and explicit formulation, what we get is private obfuscation. For, as is clear
from many testimonials and, among many other instances, from the
prose of the *Lettres provinciales,* Pascal's claim at being incompetent
in the rhetoric of seduction is certainly not made in good faith. The
concluding paragraphs of the text never recover from this decisive
break in a by no means undecisive argument. What is it, in this argument, that accounts for the occurrence of this disruption? What is
it, in a rigorous epistemology, that makes it impossible to decide
whether its exposition is a proof or an allegory? We have to retrace
and interpret the course of the argument, as it develops in the first
section of the *Réflexions* and as it finds its equivalent in the underlying logical and rhetorical structure of the *Pensées,* in order to
answer this question.

"De l'esprit géométrique," part 1 of the *Réflexions,* starts out
from a classical and very well known problem in epistemology: the
distinction between nominal and real definition, *definitio nominis*
and *definitio reo.* Pascal insists at once that the superiority and reli-
ability of the geometrical (i.e., mathematical) method is established
because "in geometry we recognize only those definitions that logi-
cians call *definitions of name (définitions de nom),* that is to say,
giving a name only to those things which have been clearly designated
in perfectly known terms" (349). Nothing could be simpler, in Pascal's exposition, than this process of denomination, which exists
only as a kind of stenography, a free and flexible code used for
reasons of economy to avoid cumbersome repetitions, and which in
no way influences the thing itself in its substance or in its properties.
Definitions of name are, says Pascal, "entirely free and never open
to contradiction" (349). They require some hygiene and some polic-
ing. One should avoid, for example, that the same signifier designate
two distinct meanings, but this can easily be assured by public convention. Real definitions, on the other hand, are a great deal more
coercive and dangerous: they are actually not definitions, but axioms

or, even more frequently, propositions that need to be proven. The confusion between nominal and real definitions is the main cause of the difficulties and obscurities that plague philosophical disputation, and to keep the distinction between them clear and sharp is, in Pascal's own terms, "the (real) reason for writing the treatise, more than the subject with which I deal" (351). The mind of the geometrician is exemplary to the extent that it observes this distinction.

Can it really do so? As soon as it is enunciated, the apparently simple definition of definition runs into complications, for the text glides almost imperceptibly from the discussion of nominal definition to that of what it calls "primitive words," which are not subject to definition at all, since their pretended definitions are infinite regresses of accumulated tautologies. These terms (which include the basic topoi of geometrical discourse, such as motion, number, and extension) represent the natural language element that Descartes scornfully rejected from scientific discourse, but which reappear here as the natural light that guarantees the intelligibility of primitive terms despite their undefinability. In geometrical (i.e., epistemologically sound) discourse, primitive words and nominal definition are coextensive and blend into each other: in this "judicious science . . . all terms are perfectly intelligible, either by natural light or by the definitions it produces" (351).

But things are not quite so simple. For if primitive words possess a natural meaning, then this meaning would have to be universal, as is the science that operates with these words; however, in one of the sudden shifts so characteristic of Pascal and which sets him entirely apart from Arnauld's trust in logic, this turns out not to be the case. "It is not the case," says Pascal, "that all men have the same idea of the essence of the things which I showed to be impossible and useless to define . . . (such as, for example, time). It is not the nature of these things which I declare to be known by all, but simply *the relationship between the name and the thing,* so that on hearing the expression *time,* all turn (or direct) the mind toward the same entity . . . (*tous portent la pensée vers le même objet)*" (350). Here the word does not function as a sign or a name, as was the case in the nominal definition, but as a vector, a directional motion that is manifest only as a turn, since the target toward which it turns remains unknown. In other words, the sign has become a trope, a substitutive relationship that has to posit a meaning whose existence cannot be verified, but that confers upon the sign an unavoidable signifying function. The indeterminacy of this function is carried by the figural expression "porter la pensée," a figure that cannot be accounted for in phenomenal terms. The nature of the relationship between figure (or trope) and mind can only be described by a figure, the same figure that Pascal will use in the *Pensées* in order to describe figure: "Figure *porte* absence et présence, plaisir et déplaisir." (265–677, 534);[10] this is a sentence to which we will have to return later on. This much, at least, is clearly established: in the language of geometry, nominal definition and primitive terms are coextensive, but the semantic function of the primitive terms is structured like a trope. As such, it acquires a signifying function that it controls neither in its existence nor in its direction. Another way of stating this is to say that the nominal definition of primitive terms always turns into a proposition that has to, but cannot, be proven. Since definition is now itself a primitive term, it follows that the definition of the nominal definition is itself a real, and not a nominal, definition. This initial complication has far-reaching consequences for the further development of the text.

The discussion of denomination and of definition leads directly into Pascal's more fundamental and systematic statement about the intelligibility and coherence of mind and cosmos: the principle of double infinity, which also underlies the theological considerations of the *Pensées*. From a traditional point of view, the interest of the *Réflexions* is that it spells out, more explicitly than can be the case in the apologetic and religious context of the *Pensées*, the link between this central principle, so often expressed, in Pascal himself and in his interpreters, in a tonality of existential pathos, and the geometrical or mathematical logic of which it is actually a version. The text helps to undo the tendencious and simplistic opposition between knowledge and faith which is often forced upon Pascal. The *logos* of the world consists of the "necessary and reciprocal link" that exists between the intrawordly dimensions of motion, number, and space (to which Pascal also adds time), the principle asserted in the only quotation from Scripture to appear in the text: *Deus fecit omnia in pondere, in numero, et mensura.*[11]

Pascal is indeed in conformity with his age of science in making the cohesion of arithmetic, geometry, and rational mechanics the logical model for epistemological discourse. He is also in essential conformity with that age, the age of Leibniz and the development of infinitesimal calculus, in designating the principle of double infinity, the infinitely large and the infinitely small, as the "common property (of space, time, motion, and number) where knowledge opens up the mind to the greatest marvels in nature" (351). Thus, when the burden of Pascal's text becomes the assertion of the infinite divisibility of space and of number (it being assumed that infinite expansion is readily granted, but that the mind resists the notion of infinite divisibility), one is not surprised to find the first four of the five arguments designed to overcome that resistance to be traditional assertions that do not stand in need of development. They reiterate such fundamental principles of calculus as the impossibility of comparing finite and infinite quantities and, in general, move between spatial and numerical dimensions by means of simple computation (as in the instance of the irrational number for the square root of two), or by experimental representations in space, without the intervention of discursive language (353). The text starts to proliferate and to grow tense, however, when it has to counter an objection that is to be attributed to Méré and that compels Pascal to reintroduce the question of the relationship between language and cognition. Méré argued that it is perfectly possible in the order of space to conceive of an extension made up from parts that are themselves devoid of extension, thus implying that space can be made up of a finite quantity of indivisible parts, rather than of an infinity of infinitely divisible ones, because it is possible to make up numbers out of units that are themselves devoid of number. Méré uses the principle of homogeneity between space and number, which is also the ground of Pascal's cosmology, to put the principle of infinitesimal smallness into question. Pascal's retort (353) marks the truly Pascalian moment in the demonstration. It begins by dissociating the laws of number from the laws of geometry, by showing that what applies to the indivisible unit of number, the *one,* does not apply to the indivisible unit of space. The status of the *one* is paradoxical and apparently contradictory: as the very principle of singleness, it has no plurality, no number. As Euclid said, *one* is not a number. It is a mere name given to the entity that does not possess the properties of number, a nominal definition of nonnumber. On the other hand, the one partakes of number, according to the principle of homogeneity enunciated by the same Euclid who decreed the one not to be a number. The principle of homogeneity ("magnitudes are said to be of the same kind or species, when one magnitude can be made to exceed another by reiterated multiplication") is mathematically linked to the principle of infinity implicit in this proposition. *One* is not a number; this proposition is correct, but so is the opposite proposition, namely, that *one is* a number, provided it is mediated by the principle of homogeneity which asserts that *one* is of the same species as number, as a house is not a city, yet a city made up of houses that are of the same species as the city, since one can always add a house to a city and it remains a city. Generic homogeneity, or the infinitesimal, is a synechdocal structure. We again find in the fundamental model of Pascal's cosmos, which is based on tropes of homogeneity and on the notion of the infinite, a system that allows for a great deal of dialectical contradiction (one can say $1 = N$ as well as $1 \neq N$), but one that guarantees intelligibility.

The interest of the argument is, however, that it has to reintroduce the ambivalence of definitional language. The synechodocal totalization of infinitude is possible because the unit of number, the *one,* functions as a nominal definition. But, for the argument to be valid, the nominally indivisible number must be distinguished from the *really* indivisible space, a demonstration that Pascal can accomplish easily, but only because the key words of the demonstration—indivisible, spatial extension (*étendue*), species (genre), and definition—function as real, and not as nominal, definitions, as "définition de chose" and not as "définition de nom." The language almost forces this formulation upon Pascal, when he has to say: "cette dernière preuve est fondée sur la *définition* de ces deux *choses,* indivisible et étendue" or "Donc, il n'est pas de même genre que l'étendue, par la *definition* des *choses* du même genre" (354; italics mine). The reintroduction of a language of *real* definition also allows for the next turn in the demonstration, which, after having separated number from space, now has to suspend this separation while maintaining it—because the underlying homology of space and number, the ground of the system, should never be fundamentally in question. There exists, in the order of number, an entity that is, unlike the *one,* heterogeneous with regard to number: this entity, which is the *zero,* is radically distinct from one. Whereas one is and is not a number at the same time, zero is radically not a number, absolutely heterogeneous to the order of number. With the introduction of zero, the separation between number and space, which is potentially threatening, is also healed. For equivalences can easily be found in the order of time and of motion for the zero function in number: instant and stasis *(repos)* are the equivalences that, thanks to the zero, allow one to reestablish the "necessarily and reciprocal link" between the four intrawordly dimensions on which divine order depends. At the end of the passage, the homogeneity of the universe is recovered, and the principle of infinitesimal symmetry is well established. But this has happened at a price: the coherence of the system is now seen to be entirely dependent on the introduction of an element—the zero and its equivalences in time and motion—that is itself entirely heterogeneous with regard to the system and is nowhere a part of it. The continuous universe held together by the double wings of the two infinites is interrupted, disrupted *at all points* by a principle of radical heterogeneity without which it cannot come into being. Moreover, this rupture of the infinitesimal and the homogeneous does not occur on the transcendental level, but on the level of language, in the inability of a theory of language as sign or as name (nominal definition) to ground this homogeneity without having recourse to the signifying function, the real definition, that makes the zero of signification the necessary condition for grounded knowledge. The notion of language as sign is dependent on, and derived from, a different notion in which language functions as rudderless signification and transforms what it denominates into the linguistic equivalence of the arithmetical zero. It is as sign that language is capable of engendering the principles of infinity, of genus, species and homogeneity, which allow for synechdocal totalizations, but none of these tropes could come about without the systematic effacement of the zero and its reconversion into a name. There can be no *one* without zero, but the zero always appears in the guise of a *one*, of a (some)thing. The name is the trope of the zero. The zero is always *called* a one, when the zero is actually nameless, "innomable." In the French language, as used by Pascal and his interpreters, this happens concretely in the confusedly alternate use of the two terms *zéro* and *néant*. The verbal, predicative form *néant*, with its gerundive ending, indicates not the zero, but rather the one, as the *limit* of the infinitely small, the almost zero that is the one. Pascal is not consistent in his use of *zéro* and *néant*; nor could he be if the system of the two infinites is to be enunciated at all. At the crucial point, however, as is the case here, he knows the difference, which his commentators, including the latest and most astute ones, always forget.[12] At the end of the most systematic exposition of the theory of the two infinites, at the conclusion of part 1 of the *Réflexions*, we find once again the ambivalence of the theory of definitional language, which we encountered at the start.

The unavoidable question will be whether the model established in this text, in which discourse is a dialectical and infinitesimal system that depends on its undoing in order to come into being, can be extended to texts that are not purely mathematical, but stated in a less abstract, more phenomenally or existentially perceivable form. One would specifically want to know whether the principle of homogeneity implicit in the theory of the two infinites, *as well as* the disruption of this system, can be retraced in the theological and subject-oriented context of the *Pensées*. Since this would involve an extensive reading of a major and difficult work, we must confine ourselves here to preliminary hints, by showing first of all how the principle of totalization, which is implicit in the notion of the infinite, underlies the dialectical pattern that is so characteristic of the *Pensées*. Once this is done, we should then ask whether this pattern is at all interrupted, as the numerical series are interrupted by zero, and how this disruption occurs. As a general precaution, we should be particularly wary not to decide too soon that this is indeed the case, not only because the consequences, from a theological and an epistemological point of view, are far-reaching but also because the remarkable elasticity of the dialectical model, capable of recovering totalities threatened by the most radical contradictions, should not be underestimated. The Pascalian dialectic should be allowed to display the full extent of its feats, and, if a disjunction is to be revealed, it can only be done so by following Pascal in pushing it to its eventual breaking point.

What is here called, for lack of a better term, a rupture or a disjunction, is not to be thought of as a negation, however tragic it may be. Negation, in a mind as resilient as Pascal's, is always susceptible of being reinscribed in a system of intelligibility. Nor can we hope to map it out as one topos among topoi, as would be the case with regular tropes of substitution. It is possible to find, in the terminology of rhetoric, terms that come close to designating such disruptions (e.g., *parabasis* or *anacoluthon*), which designate the interruption of a semantic continuum in a manner that lies beyond the power of reintegration. One must realize at once, however, that this disruption is not topical, that it cannot be located in a single point—since it is indeed the very notion of point, the geometrical zero,[13] that is being dislodged—but that it is all-pervading. The anacoluthon is omnipresent, or, in temporal terms and in Friedrich Schlegel's deliberately unintelligible formulation, the parabasis is permanent. Calling this structure ironic can be more misleading than helpful, since *irony*, like *zero*, is a term that is not susceptible to nominal or real definition. To say then, as we are actually saying, that allegory (as sequential narration) is the trope of irony (as the one is the trope of zero) is to say something that is true enough but not intelligible, which also implies that it cannot be put to work as a device of textual analysis. To discover, in the *Pensées*, the *instances de rupture*, the equivalence of the zero in Pascal's theory of number, we can only reiterate compulsively the dialectical pattern of Pascal's own model or, in other words, read and reread the *Pensées* with genuine insistence. Pascal himself has formulated the principle of totalizing reading, in which the most powerful antinomies must be brought together, in the Pensée headed "Contradiction" (257-684, 533): "One can put together a good physiognomy only by reconciling all our oppositions. It does not suffice to follow a sequence of matched properties without reconciling contraries: in order to understand an author's meaning, one must reconcile all the contradictory passages" (*pour entendre le sens d'un auteur il faut accorder tous les passages contraires*). Applied to Scripture, which Pascal here has in mind, this reconciliation leads directly to the fundamental opposition that underlies all others: that between a figural and a true reading. "If one takes the law, the sacrifices, and the kingdom as realities, it will be impossible to coordinate all passages (of the Bible); it is therefore necessary that they be mere figures" (533). The question remains, of course, whether the pair figure-reality can or cannot be itself thus reconciled, whether it is a contradiction of the type we encountered when it was said that one is a number and is not a number at the same time, or whether the order of figure and the order of reality are heterogeneous.

For all the somber felicity of their aphoristic condensation, the *Pensées* are also very systematically schematized texts that can be seen as an intricate interplay of binary oppositions. Many of the sections are, or could easily be, designated by the terms of these oppositions, as is the case for our first and simplest example, two of the *Pensées* (125-92 and 126-93, 514), which could properly be entitled "Nature" and "Custom": "What are our natural principles if not the principles we have grown accustomed to? In children, they are the principles they have learned from the customs of their fathers, like the hunt in animals. A different custom will produce different natural principles. This can be verified by experience, by observing if there are customs that cannot be erased. . . . Fathers fear that the natural love of their children can be erased. What kind of nature is this, that can thus be erased? Custom is a second nature that destroys the first. But what is nature? Why is custom not natural? I am very much afraid that this nature is only a first custom, as custom is a second nature." This passage turns around a saying of common wisdom (*La coutume est une seconde nature*), as is frequently the case in Pascal, and it thus sets up a very characteristic logical or, rather, rhetorical pattern. A set of binary oppositions is matched in a commonsensical order in terms of their properties: here, custom and nature are matched with the pairs first/second and constant/erasable (*effaçable*), respectively. Nature, being a *first* principle, is constant, whereas custom, being second or derived from nature, is susceptible to change and erasure. The schema, at the onset, is as follows:

nature	first	constant
custom	second	erasable

The pattern is put in motion by a statement (also based, in this case, on common observation) that reverses the order of association of the entities and their properties. It is said that fathers fear, apparently with good reason, that natural feelings of filial affection can be erased, thus coupling the natural with the erasable and, consequently, with secondness. A first (nature) then becomes a first second, that is, a second; a second (custom) becomes in symmetrical balance, a second first, that is, a first:

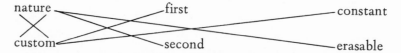

The properties of firstness and secondness have changed places, which results in the undoing or the deconstruction of the binary opposition from which we started. It has now become impossible to decide whether a given experience can be called natural or customary. Since they are able to exchange or cross over, in a chiasmic reversal, their properties, nature and custom have been brought together to the extent that their opposition has been inscribed into a system of exchange which is structured like a trope (chiasmus). Nature and custom are united within a single system, which, although experienced as negative by the author ("I am afraid that . . ."), is nevertheless a cognition.

The same pattern, with increased complications, reappears time after time and underlies some of the most famous and thematically suggestive of the Pensées. Consider, for example, the section on the nature of man (131-*434*, 514-15). It starts out from an opposition that, this time, is historical and, to that extent, empirical: the philosophical debate—to which Pascal has gained access through his closest predecessors, Montaigne and Descartes—between sceptical and dogmatic philosophy, *pyrrhoniens* and *dogmatistes*. The establishment of the original grid, which was obvious in the case of nature and custom as first and second, is more complex in this case, in which scepticism and dogmatic faith have to be matched with truth and nature, respectively. The argument goes back to the example and the logic used by Descartes in the first two meditations.[14] It established the claim for the cognitive value of doubt by reference to the polarity of sleeping and waking, of dream and reality. One normally assumes that the condition of waking is the true condition of man, the first norm from which sleep and dream are derived and displaced, secondary versions. Sleep is grafted upon the condition of awakeness like a secondary upon a primary quality. The original pattern is as follows:

wake	perception	first
sleep	dream	second

Since we think that we are awake when we dream, it follows that the properties can be ordered according to the same symmetrical pattern we encountered in the Pensée on nature and custom. Like Keats at the end of the "Ode to a Nightingale," we should each ask: Do I wake or sleep? For it is no longer certain that our primary consciousness is awake at all, that consciousness is not a palimpsest of dreams, some of them individual, some shared with others, all grafted upon each other. "Is it not possible that this half of our life (day) is itself a mere dream on which the other dreams are grafted, and of which we will awake at death?" (514). This suspicion, which undoes the natural polarities of day and night, wake and sleep, is clearly the product of the sceptical mind and justifies the pairing of scepticism with knowledge. The sceptical position always had knowledge on its side, and the only thing the dogmatists can oppose to this knowledge is the natural conviction that infinite doubt is intolerable. "What will man do in this condition? Will he doubt of everything, doubt that he is awake, that he is being pinched or burned, will he doubt that he doubts, doubt that he is? One cannot reach this condition, and I assert as a fact that there never has been a perfectly consistent and actual sceptic. Nature supports our feeble reason and shelters it from such extravagance" (515). Scepticism and dogmatism are now firmly paired with truth and nature, respectively.

Scepticism   Truth

Dogmatism   Nature

But this original configuration is not a stable one. As is clear from the preceding quotation, one cannot be consistently sceptical, but it is just as impossible to be consistently natural, for however "extravagant" the sceptical position may be, it is nevertheless the only mode of truth accessible to us, and it deprives all claims to natural truth of authority. To the belief "that one cannot doubt natural principles," the sceptics counter "that the uncertainty of our origin includes that of our nature." This argument cannot be refuted: "The dogmatists have been trying to refute it ever since the world began."

The situation is not only unstable, but coercive as well. At this point in the *Pensées,* one moves from the logic of propositions, statements as to what is the case, to model logic, statements of what should or ought to be the case. For one cannot remain suspended between the irreconcilable positions: it is clear that, by not choosing between the two poles of the polarities, one is adopting the sceptical position. The predicament is that of the undecidable: propositional logic is powerless to decide a conflict that has to find a solution, if this logic is to survive.

In a first dialectical reversal, the answer will be to give the predicament a name, which, in this case, will be "man," the being who stands in that predicament. "Man" is then not a definable entity, but an incessant motion beyond itself. "L'homme passe l'homme" says Pascal, in a phrase that has received many pseudo-Nietzschean interpretations of existential transcendence and transgression. Perhaps more important is the numerical formulation of the "definition" of man, which takes us back to the *Réflexions*. For it follows, says Pascal, that man is double, that the one is always already at least a two, a pair. Man is like the *one* in the system of number, infinitely divisible and infinitely capable of self-multiplication. He is another version of the system of the two infinites; immediately after having stated that man surpasses man, and that man is double, Pascal can add that Man *infinitely* surpasses man, "l'homme passe *infiniment* l'homme." As a metaphor of number, man is one and is not one, is a pair and is infinite all at the same time.

The dialectic of the infinite, which starts in the initial doubt, is thus able to unfold itself consistently. For the double, and hence infinitesimal, condition of man, this becomes the key to the knowledge of man's nature. "For who fails to see that without the knowledge of this double condition of nature man was in an irrevocable ignorance of the truth of his nature?" (515). This ruse of reason is purely Cartesian: doubt is suspended by the knowledge of doubt. One sees that the original structure, pairing scepticism with truth and dogmatism with nature, has been chiastically crossed, since now the true knowledge of radical scepticism is paired with nature, through the mediation of the concept of man, standing by implication for the system of double infinitude. The rhetorical pattern that underlies this system is the same as in the previous example.

It is legitimate to "pair" this Pensée with another and more rigorously schematized one, which states the same tension, but empties it of the existential pathos of totalization (122–*416*, 514). It is headed by the binary opposition "Grandeur et misère": "Since misery is derived from greatness, and greatness from misery, some have decided in favor of misery all the more decisively, since they have taken greatness to be the proof of misery, and others have decided for greatness with all the more power, since they derive it from misery itself. All they were able to say in support of greatness has served as an argument for the others to demonstrate misery, since the higher the station from which one falls the more miserable one will be, and vice versa. They are carried upon each other (*portés les uns sur les autres*) in a circle without end, it being certain that as men

gain in enlightenment, they find both greatness and misery in themselves. In a word: man knows he is miserable. He is therefore miserable, since that is what he is, but he is also great because he knows
it." (En un mot, l'homme connait qu'il est misérable. Il est donc
misérable puisqu'il l'est, mais il est bien grand puisqu'il le connait.)

The end of the text telescopes the chiasmus in a particularly con-
densed form, starting from the pairing of misery with (self-) knowledge and of greatness with being: "Man *is* great because man *knows*
misery" (*l'homme connait qu'il est misérable*). The final sentence has
reversed the pattern: misery is paired with being, in the tautology "il
est misérable puisqu'il l'est," and greatness with knowledge, the self-
knowledge of misery. The mediation is carried out by the apparently
deductive prepositions in the sentence: "il est *donc* misérable *puisqu'*il
l'est," where the cognitive power is carried by the logical articula-
tions *donc* and *puisque,* and the ontological power by the tautology
of the assertion. The dialectic has been flattened out into tautology,
in the endlessly circular repetition of the same, and the teleological
form of infinite transcendence has been replaced by this monotony.
All the same, despite the thematic and tonal difference between the
two Pensées on man, the rhetorical pattern remains the same, grounded
in the infinitesimal symmetry of the chiasmic reversal. Here, in one
of the bleakest of the *Pensées,* this pattern appears perhaps in the
purest form.[15]

The transition from self-knowledge and anthropological knowledge to teleological knowledge often passes, in Pascal, through the
dimension of the political. Louis Marin is right to insist on the close
interconnection between epistemology, political criticism, and
theology, in the sequence of *Pensées* entitled "Raison des effets."[16]
This sequence deals primarily with a distinction between popular
and scientific knowledge and thus returns to the question that underlies the *Réflexions* as well: the antinomy between natural language
and metalanguage. The polarities in Pensées 90–101 (510–11)[17] oppose the language of the people (vox populi) to that of the mathe-
maticians; moreover, *Pensée* 91 (*–336*) contains a good description of
Pascal's own writing style, in its peculiar mixture of popular, non-
technical diction with redoutable critical rigor: one must have what

Pascal calls "une pensée de derrière" (which sees behind the apparent evidence of things), yet speak like the people. Whereas the man of science possesses true knowledge (*epistème*), the people follow the vagaries of opinion (*doxa*). The starting position, then, will be:

people   doxa   false

geometrician   episteme   true

It would be a mistake, however, to dismiss popular opinion as simply false. In a way, the (popular) saying "Vox populi, vox dei" is sound, as are, according to Pascal, the various popular opinions of which he enumerates a rather baffling catalogue of examples. This being the case, a first chiasmic reversal takes place, in which popular opinion has some claims to truth, and the mind of the geometrician, in his scorn for popular wisdom, some taint of falsehood.

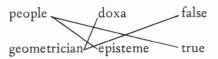

people   doxa   false

geometrician   episteme   true

This first chiasmus, however, is only the beginning. Although it is true that the people have sound opinions, it is not really true that they possess the truth. For the people can be counted on to provide the wrong reasons for their sound opinions. "They believe" says Pascal, "that truth is to be found where it is not. There is truth in their opinions, but not where they imagine it to be." This knowledge of error, which is true, is no longer a popular knowledge, but the privileged knowledge of the man who has benefited from the critical rigors of scientific reasoning. A second reversal now associates popular opinion, which to some extent is true, with epistemological falsehood, whereas the knowledge of this falsehood is again true. "We have shown that men are vain in their respect for trivial matters; this vanity reduces all their opinions to nought. We have then shown these opinions to be altogether sound; consequently, the self-esteem of the people is quite legitimate, and the people are not at all as inestimable as one believes. And thus we have destroyed the opinion that destroyed the opinion of the people. But we must now destroy this final proposition and show that it remains true that the people are in error, although their opinions are sound, because they don't locate their truth where it belongs, and by thus locating it where it is not, their opinions are again very erroneous and very unsound" (511).

Many more instances could be listed in an order than would cover the thematic scale of topoi taken up in the *Pensées,* from the most trivial to the most sublime. The same structure, the same "continual reversal from pro to contra" (*renversement continuel du pour au contre*) (511) would reappear in an endless set of variations on chiasmic crossings of binary oppositions. In the process, a wealth of thematic insights would indicate the universal effectiveness of what is a fundamentally dialectical pattern of reasoning, in which oppositions are, if not reconciled, at least pursued toward a totalization that may be infinitely postponed, but that remains operative as the sole principle of intelligibility. Our question remains whether some of the texts from the *Pensées* explicitly refuse to fit this pattern—not because they are structured along a different tropological model (which would diversify but not necessarily invalidate the dialectical model), but because they disrupt the motion of what is demonstrably the same pattern. Consider the Pensée (103–*298,* 512) headed "Justice, Power" (Justice, force).

> "It is just that what is just should be followed; it is necessary that what has the most power should be followed.
>
> Justice without power is impotent, power without justice is tyrannical.
>
> Justice without power is open to contradiction, because there always are wrongdoers. Power without justice stands accused. Justice and power must therefore be brought together, by making the just strong and the strong just.
>
> Justice is subject to dispute. Power is easily recognizable and without dispute. [Thus it has been impossible to give power to justice, because power has contradicted justice and said that it is unjust, and said that it is itself just.
>
> And thus, not being able to make the just strong, one has made the strong to be just.]
>
> [Ainsi on n'a pu donner la force à la justice, purce que la force a contredit la justice et a dit qu'elle était injuste et a dit que e'était elle qui était juste.
>
> Et ainsi ne pouvant faire que ce qui est juste fût fort, ou a fait que ce qui est fort fût juste.]

It is at once clear, on hearing the passage, that, although the chiasmic structure is the same as before, the crossing is no longer symmetrical, since it takes place in one direction but not in the other. A new complication has been introduced and is observable in an opposition that gives each of the key words a double register that is no longer, as in the previous passages, an opposition between two modes of cognition. The opposition is stated at the start in the contrast between "il est juste" and "il est nécessaire," in which the first assertion depends on a propositional cognition, but the second on sheer quantitative power, as in the proverb "La raison du plus fort est toujours la meilleure" or, in English, "Might makes right." Propositional statements line up on the side of cognition, model statements on the side of performance; they perform what they enunciate regardless of considerations of truth and falsehood. Consequently, all words used in the demonstration acquire this ambivalent status: the verb *suivre,* for instance, can be read in its deductive and cognitive sense, in which the necessity is the necessary deductiveness of reason, but it can also be read in the sense of pure coercive power, as in the phrase "la femme doit suivre son mari."

"Suivre" is thus distributed in its double register in the first two sentences of the Pensée. The same is true of justice, which can on the one hand be read as cognitive *justesse,* as the precision of rational argument, but which is clearly also to be read in the sense of the judicial praxis of a court of law. In this latter capacity, it clearly lacks the persuasive power of sheer argument which it possesses in the first sense; it is open to uncertainty and contradiction and therefore lacks power. For the proper of justice to be power, and for the proper of power to be justice, they must be able to exchange the attributes of necessity and of innocence which characterize them. Justice must become necessary by might, might innocent by justice. This would accomplish and demonstrate the homogeneity of propositional statements as cognition and of modal statements as performance. But, unlike all other previous examples from the *Pensées,* the exchange does not take place. Justice refuses to become justesse; it remains pragmatic and inconsistent, "sujet à dispute," unable to fulfill the criterium of necessity as cognitive persuasion. Might, however, has no difficulty whatever satisfying the criterion of necessity; it is "sans dispute" and can therefore *usurp* the consistency of cognition without giving anything in return. The usurpation occurs in the double register of the locution "sans dispute," a quality that pertains to mathematical proof as an indication of epistemological rigor, but which, as in "right makes might," also pertains to force by sheer intolerance and tyranny. Force, which is pure performance, usurps the claim to epistemological rightness. It does so because it can become the subject of the sentence of enunciation and can be said to speak: "la force a contredit . . ." and "la force a dit . . ."; it can pronounce on the lack of epistemological "rightness" of justice, and it can proclaim its own epistemological infallibility. The performative declares itself declarative and cognitive. The "on" in the final sentence: "on a fait que ce qui est fort fut juste" can only be "might," which belongs indeed to the order of the "faire" and not of "savoir." But the unilateral victory of force over justice, if it is to be enunciated, as is the case in this passage, still can only be stated in the mode of cognition and of deduction, as is evident from the use of the deductive "ainsi" coupled with "faire" in the sentence "ainsi on a fait . . ." The status of this "ainsi" is now very peculiar, however, for the pure act of force is entirely arbitrary and not cognitively consequential at all. The "ainsi" does not belong to Descartes, but to any despot who happens to be in power.

The discomfort one should experience on the reading of this final sentence is the same one should experience on hearing the zero assimilated to the one and thus being reinscribed into a system of cognition in which it does not belong. For at the very moment that might has usurped, by imposition and not by transgression, the authority of cognition, the tropological field of cognition is revealed to be dependent on an entity, might, that is heterogeneous with regard to this field, just as the zero was heterogeneous with regard to number. The break is immediately reinscribed as the knowledge of the break in the "ainsi on a fait . . . ," but this "ainsi" must now be said to be ironical, that is to say disruptive of its own deductive claim. The dialectic starts again, but it has been broken in a way that is essentially different from the transgressive reversals we encountered in the other instances. It is in the realm of practical and political justice, and not of Christian charity, that the equivalence of the mathematical zero reappears in the text of the *Pensées*. What is of considerable importance, from a linguistic point of view, is that the break that in the *Réflexions* was due to the complications of definition is now seen to be a function of the heterogeneity between cognitive and performative language. Language, in Pascal, now separates in two distinct directions: a cognitive function that is right (*juste*) but powerless, and a modal function that is mighty (*forte*) in its claim to rightness. The two functions are radically heterogeneous to each other. The first generates canonical rules of persuasion, whereas the second generates the eudaemonic values that are present as soon as one has to say that the claim to authority is made "at the *pleasure* of" the despot. The first is the language of truth and of persuasion by proof, the second the language of pleasure (*volupté*) and of persuasion by usurpation or seduction. We now know why it is that, in the second half of the *Réflexions*, Pascal had to dodge the question of the relationship between these two modes. To the extent that language is always cognitive and tropological as well as performative at the same time, it is a heterogeneous entity incapable of justice as well as of *justesse*. Even in the transcendental realm of revealed language in Holy Writ, the necessary choice between seduction and truth remains undecidable. Pascal's "definition" of figure retains this complication: when it is said that "Figure porte absence et présence," we recognize the infinitesimal structure of cognitive dialectics, but when it is also said that "Figure porte plaisir et déplaisir," it will be impossible to square, to inscribe the four terms *présence/absence* and *plaisir/déplaisir* into a homogeneous "geometrical" structure. The (ironic) pseudo-knowledge of this impossibility, which pretends to order sequentially, in a narrative, what is actually the destruction of all sequence, is what we call allegory.

NOTES

1. G. W. F. Hegel, *Vorlesungen über die Ästhetik,* Theorie Werkausgabe (Frankfort: Suhrkamp, 1970), 1:511. All translations are my own.

2. Ibid., p. 512.

3. Jean-Pierre Schobinger, *Kommentar zu Pascals Reflexionen über die Geometrie im allgemeinen* (Basel: Schwabe, 1974). The work consists of a translation into German of the original text, but contains an extensive line-by-line commentary, particularly valuable with regard to the history of the relationships between mathematical theory and epistemology in the seventeenth century.

4. The text appears in most current editions of Pascal's works. References are to Pascal, *Oeuvres complètes,* ed. Louis Lafuma (Paris: Editions du Seuil, Collection l'Intégrale, 1963), pp. 348-59.

5. *Great Shorter Works of Pascal,* trans. Emilie Caillet (Philadelphia: Westminster Press, 1948), pp. 189-211.

6. In a letter of 12 June 1711 to Pascal's nephew Louis Périer, Father Touttée writes: "I have the honor to return the three manuscripts you were kind enough to send me. . . . I have one general observation to make, namely that this text, which promises to discuss the method of the geometricians, indeed begins by doing so without, in my opinion, saying anything very remarkable, and then embarks on a long digression that deals with the two infinites, the infinitely large and the infinitely small that can be observed in the three or four things that make up nature. One fails to understand how this relates to the main topic of the text. This is why I think it opportune to cut the text in two and make it into two separate pieces, for they hardly seem to go together" (Quoted in Schobinger, *Kommentar zu Pascals Reflexionen,* p. 110).

7. On the history of the edition of the text, see Pascal, *Oeuvres complètes,* ed. J. Mesnard (Paris: Desclée de Brouwer, 1964 and 1970), summarized in Schobinger, *Kommentar zu Pascals Reflexionen,* pp. 108-14.

8. As one instance among many, J.-P. Schobinger confronts the problem of the discrepancy between mathematical knowledge and belief, in Pascal, as it finds expression in the fluctuations of a terminology that is, at times, derived from the language of proof (in terms such as *raison, entendement, esprit*) and, at other times, from the language of affectivity (in terms such as *coeur, sentiment, instinct*). The topic, as is well known, leads to the famous opposition between "esprit de géométrie" and "esprit de finesse." He explains the difficulty as an evolution in Pascal's attitude toward Descartes. In the *Réflexions* (except for the theological section) Pascal still adheres to a dualism of mind and the senses, or of discursive and intuitive knowledge, that goes back to Descartes. Later, "in the *Pensées,* he refines this opposition into a new model for discursive thought. The *Réflexions* therefore correspond to a Cartesian phase in Pascal's thought whereas the *Pensées* are the result of a change and represent a move away from Descartes." (Schobinger, *Kommentar zu Pascals Reflexionen,* pp. 402-4) What is striking about a statement such as this (of which many equivalences can be found in the literature on Pascal) is not that it is right or wrong, but that, by stating an epistemological tension in terms of a historical narrative, it creates an appeasing delusion of understanding.

9. On the relationship between Antoine Gombaud, Chevalier de Méré and Pascal, see J. Mesnard, *Pascal et les Roannez,* vols. 1 and 2 (Paris, 1965); F. Strowski, *Pascal et son temps* (Paris, 1907/8) vol. 2 (292-317) and also Schobinger, *Kommentar zu Pascals Reflexionen,* p. 330.

10. Pascal's *Pensées* exist in different editions with different identifying numbers. I quote the number of the Lafuma classification in the Editions du Seuil volume, followed by the number of the Brunschwieg classification in italics, and the page number in the Editions du Seuil volume.

11. Sap. 11, 21. The assimilation of space to measure (*mensura*) and especially of motion

to weight (*podere*) raises questions leading into Pascal's scientific and experimental concerns with the problems of gravity.

12. Louis Marin, in his outstanding book on Pascal and on the *Logic* of Port Royal (*La critique du discours* [Paris: Editions de Minuit, 1975]), makes a considerable contribution to Pascal's philosophy of language and its relationship to theology. Chapter 8, "De la définition de nom" (239-69) is particularly relevant to our topic and constitutes one of the best expositions of the link between nominal definition and the theory of the two infinites, culminating in the following conclusion: "The group of elements that 'ground' scientific discourse in a principle of certainty that is not absolutely convincing . . . are the same as those which provoke this discourse to transgress its limitations, because they are its limits as illimitation. By obeying the law of double infinity, magnitudes can be accurately determined by means of computation and measure but, at the same time, they point toward something other than what they are, the transcendental limits of the magnitude which orders all magnitudes." When Marin then quotes § 3 of *Pensée* 418-*233*, 550, which states that "the addition of the *one* to the infinite does not augment it" and concludes that "in this deprivation (*dénuement*) the totalization of the infinite signified = 0 fulfills itself," this would be a classical instance of the confusion of "néant" (or *one* as the infinitely small) with zero. In Pascal's number system it is possible to say that néant = ∞ (or 1 = ∞), but never that 0 (zero) = ∞.

13. On the concept of "point," see Schobinger (*Kommentar zu Pascal's Reflexionen*, p. 365) who gives interesting quotations from Simon Stevin and from Mersenne discussing the assimilation of the geometrical "point" to the arithmetical zero.

14. René Descartes, *Oeuvres philosophiques,* ed. F. Alquié, 3 vol. (Paris: Garnier, 1967) 2:406.

15. See also Pensée 514-*397*, 513.

16. Marin, *La critique du discours,* 369-400.

17. The equivalent numbers in the Lafuma classification are 337-336-335-328-313-316-329-334-80-536-467-324.

Joel Fineman

The Structure of Allegorical Desire

Μῆνιν ἄειδε, Θεά, Πη

I mean my title to be read backwards and forwards, its "of" taken as objective and subjective genitive. On the one hand, I am concerned with the ways allegories begin and with the ends towards which they tend. In general, this is the problem of allegorical narrative, primarily a temporal issue regarding the way allegories linearly unfold, but also, as has often been pointed out, a symbolic progress that lends itself to spatial projection, as when the Temple translates the Labyrinth, or the music of the spheres sounds the order of the stars. On the other hand, I am concerned with a specifically allegorical desire, a desire *for* allegory, that is implicit in the idea of structure itself and explicit in criticism that directs itself towards the structurality of literature. This is to say not only that the notion of structure, especially of literary structure, presupposes the same system of multiply articulated levels as does that of allegory, but also that the possibility of such coherently polysemic significance originates out of the same intention—what I call desire—as does allegorical narrative.

I speak of desire in deference to the thematics of allegory and to describe the self-propelling, digressive impulse of allegorical movement: for example, the way the meandering *Canterbury Tales* begins by setting the scene and establishing the atmosphere in which folk properly "longen" to go on pilgrimages, that longing being motivation for each pilgrim's journey to Canterbury, but also the way the tales themselves set off towards the equally sacred center of their own allegorical space. I therefore psychoanalytically assume that the movement of allegory, like the dreamwork, enacts a wish that determines its progress—and, of course, the dream-vision is a characteristic framing and opening device of allegory, a way of situating allegory in the *mise en abyme* opened up by the variety of cognate accusatives that dream a dream, or see a sight, or tell a tale. On the other hand, with this reference to psychoanalysis, I mean also to suggest that analysis itself, the critical response to allegory, rehearses the same wish and therefore embarks upon the same pilgrimage, so that psychoanalysis, especially structural psychoanalysis, by which today we are obliged to mean Lacan, is not simply the analysis of, but the extension and conclusion of, the classic allegorical tradition from which it derives—which is why psychoanalysis so readily assimilates the great archetypes of allegorical imagery into its discourse: the labyrinths, the depths, the navels, the psychomachian hydraulics.

I want to argue that there is, for literary criticism, an historical importance in the fact that psychoanalysis founds its scientificity on the hermeneutic circle traced by its own desire to know, as in the dream that begins psychoanalysis, Freud's dream of Irma's injection, whose wish is that its own interpretation be correct.[1] To the extent that psychoanalysis is the prevailing paradigm for critical inquiry today, it is precisely because *The Interpretation of Dreams* in this way develops itself as the dream, and therefore as the desire, of interpretation itself. In thus basing itself on its own critical reflection, however, desire becomes in psychoanalysis, as in allegory, both a theme and a structuring principle, and its psychology, its theory of the human, thus becomes, in the words of another and famously ambiguous genitive, the allegory of love, whereas its metapsychology, its theory of itself, becomes the allegory of allegory. I am concerned with the logic, presumably the psycho-logic—etymologically, the logos of the soul—that in our literary tradition links allegory, interpretation, and desire each to each, and with what happens to interpretation when its desire is no longer controllable by a figure.

That there should be formal reciprocity between allegory and its criticism is not surprising. Theoretical discussions of allegory regularly begin by lamenting the breadth of the term and relating its compass to the habit of mind that, as it is irritatedly put, sees allegory everywhere. Thus generalized, allegory rapidly acquires the status of trope of tropes, representative of the figurality of all language, of the distance between signifier and signified, and, correlatively, the response to allegory becomes representative of critical activity *per se*. As Frye says, "it is not often realized that all commentary is allegorical interpretation, an attaching of ideas to the structure of poetic imagery"—as, indeed, Frye's comment demonstrates, in its presumption of global, archetypal structure, which is already allegoricization whatever purely literary claims he may make for it.[2] Often, allegory will internalize this critical mood that it evokes, and this is what gives it its characteristically didactic and sententious tone, as in Spenser's emblematic stanzas, or the way Chaucer's pilgrims, however ironic the context, draw the exemplary morals of their own and each other's tales, or the relation of the second half of the *Roman de la Rose* to the first, or, even more patently, the way EK's appendixes to *The Shepheardes Calender* or Eliot's pedantic footnotes to *The Waste Land* seem integral parts of the poems rather than gloss. This tendency on the part of allegory to read itself, for its theme to dominate its narrative, or, as Frye says, to prescribe the direction of its commentary, suggests the formal or phenomenological affinities of the genre with criticism.[3]

More historically, we can note that allegory seems regularly to surface in critical or polemical atmospheres, when for political or metaphysical reasons there is something that cannot be said. Plutarch is generally instanced as the first to substitute ἀλληγορία for the more usual ὑπόνοια, and he does so in the double context of defending poetry and demythologizing the gods.[4] In this he picks up the protoallegorical tradition of euhemerism which goes back to the third century B.C., or to Plato, or beyond that to the Pythagoreans, and whose importance for literary theory is not so much its dismantling of the pagan pantheon as, rather, the defensively recuperative intention it displays towards authoritative texts whose literalism has failed.[5] The dignity of Apollo is deflated, but the prestige of Homer preserved, when the licentious intrigues of the gods are reinterpreted as philosophic, naturalistic, or scientific parables.

This deployment of allegory in the service of established literary tradition, a way of reviving prior literary authorities by making them new through critical revision—for example, *Ovid moralisée*—forms the basis of Edwin Honig's theory of allegorical conception,[6] which has itself been forcefully revived and redeveloped in Harold Bloom's more psychoanalytical (allegorical?) *Anxiety of Influence.*[7] In this context, and relating more directly to the historical development of

our own exegetical tradition, it is significant that Philo, who was the
first to employ an extensively allegorical mode of scriptural criticism,
was also the first to introduce the terms of negative theology into
theological discourse.[8] Here there is a kind of euhemerism in reverse,
with a God whose ineffability and incomprehensibility—knowable
as existent but not in essence—answers His embarrassingly anthropomorphic involvement in history, just as His essentially mysterious
divinity explains the necessity for a revelation expressed through
figural extravagance. Again, with Philo we note a self-conscious and
sacralizing nostalgia in response to authoritative but in some sense
faded origins, whether they be historical (the disturbingly unphilo-
sophical account of the creation of the universe presented in Scripture) or textual (the way Philo's commentary works at one inspired
and translated remove from its original source).[9] It is as though
allegory were precisely that mode that makes up for the distance, or
heals the gap, between the present and a disappearing past, which,
without interpretation, would be otherwise irretrievable and foreclosed, as, for example, the pseudo-hieroglyphology of Horapollo,
whose magic, hermetic graphesis is developed just at that moment
when the legibility of hieroglyphs is lost.[10]

With the Patristics (leaving aside the exact proportion of Philonic
and Stoic influence) these allegoricizing perspectives and purposes
turn into the dogma that lies at the base of all medieval and renaissance
critical theory. Again allegory is directed to critical and polemical
ends, and again the motive to allegoricize emerges out of recuperative
originology. The Old Testament is revived when interpreted as
typologically predictive of the New Testament, and the Gospels
themselves receive the benefit of spiritualizing exegesis when the
apocalypse they prophesy is indefinitely deferred. Here, allegory
acquires what will be in our tradition its primarily intermediate position between interpretative extremes: more figural than Montanist
literalism, for which the arrival of the Paraclete is already officially
announced by Scripture, and less recursively allusive than doceticiz-
ing Gnosticism, for which history, Christ, and Truth itself are but
discrete moments in an infinite series of suggestively unstable images
of images.[11] This is the major strain of allegoricizing sensibility in

our tradition: the second and third century legacy on which the four- or three-fold medieval schemes will depend. Between a literalism pure and simple and what today might be called an exegesis of the free-floating signifier, allegory becomes, for literature as for theology, a vivifying archaeology of occulted origins and a promissory eschatology of postponed ends—all this in the service of an essentially pietistic cosmology devoted to the corroboration of divinely ordered space and time, precisely the two matrices against which, as Auerbach showed, the connotative nuances of "figure," formal and chronic, develop.[12]

That allegory should organize itself with reference to these spatial and temporal axes, that, as it were, it should embody *figura,* follows directly from the linguistic structure attributed to the figure by classic rhetorical theory. The standard formulation, of course, is Quintilian's, which characterizes allegory as what happens when a single metaphor is introduced in continuous series.[13] For grave Quintilian this is more often than not a defect, an excess of metaphor likely to lead to enigma, but whether avoided as a vice of style or assiduously "invented" for the sake of decorous amplification, allegory will be defined up through the Renaissance as the temporal extension of trope (Thomas Wilson: "An Allegorie is none other thing, but a Metaphore used throughout a whole sentence or oration").[14] As such, the procedure of allegory, and the relations that obtain between its spatial and temporal projections, are strictly circumscribed. Metaphor is the initial equivocating insight into the system of doubly articulated correspondences and proportions upon which depends the analogizing logic of any troping proposition. As the shepherd to his flock, so the pilot to his boat, the king to his realm, the priest to his congregation, the husband to his wife, the stomach to the body—metaphor will select from such a system of hierarchically arranged ratios (*logoi*) the particular similarity that, as Aristotle puts it, it chooses to see in differences.[15] Developed at length, in narrative succession, the continued metaphor will maintain the rigor of the original conceit by appealing to the overall structure that governs each term in the series, with the result that narrative logic directs itself towards introducing the fox, the tempest, the

cuckold, or the canker as specifically structural, predetermined consequences of the first metaphorization (Abraham Fraunce: "The
excellencie of tropes is then most apparent, when either manie be
fitlie included in one word, or one so continued in manie, as that
with what thing it begin, with the same it also end: and then it is
called an Allegorie or Inversion").[16]

Thus there are allegories that are primarily perpendicular, concerned more with structure than with temporal extension, as, say,
illustrations of Fortune's wheel, or Fludd's famous diagram of the
great chain of being, or the emblem as a general literary genre, or
pastorals like *The Shepheardes Calender,* which make only the slightest gestures towards full-scale narrative progress. And, on the other
hand, there is allegory that is primarily horizontal, such as picaresque
or quest narrative, where figurative structure is only casually and
allusively appended to the circuit of adventures through time. Finally, of course, there are allegories that blend both axes together in
relatively equal proportions, as in *The Canterbury Tales,* where each
figurative tale advances the story of the pilgrimage as a whole. Whatever the prevailing orientation of any particular allegory, however,
up and down through the declensions of structure, or laterally developed through narrative time, the allegory will be successful as
allegory only to the extent that it can suggest the authenticity with
which the two coordinating poles bespeak each other, with structure
plausibly unfolded in time, and narrative persuasively upholding the
distinctions and equivalences described by structure. In Roman
Jakobson's linguistic formula, which here simply picks up classic
rhetorical theory (along with the awkward metaphoricity of the
definition of metaphor itself), allegory would be the poetical projection of the metaphoric axis onto the metonymic, where metaphor is
understood as the synchronic system of differences which constitutes
the order of language (*langue*), and metonymy as the diachronic principle of combination and connection by means of which structure is
actualized in time in speech (*parole;* cf. Taleus: "continued *met-
onymia* is also allegory").[17] And while Jakobson goes on to associate
metaphor with verse and romanticism, as opposed to metonymy,
which he identifies with realism and prose, allegory would cut across

and subtend all such stylistic categorizations, being equally possible in either verse or prose, and quite capable of transforming the most objective naturalism into the most subjective expressionism, or the most determined realism into the most surrealistically ornamental baroque.[18]

Thus defined, allegory fully deserves the generalization that renders it representative of language employed for literary ends, and at the same time we can see why, for contemporary structuralism, allegory would be the figure of speech *par excellence.* No other figure so readily lays itself out on the grid constructed out of the hypothesised intersection of paradigmatic synchrony and syntagmatic diachrony, which is to say that no other figure so immediately instances the definition of linguistic structure which was developed by Jakobson out of Saussure and the Russian Formalists, and that has since been applied to all the so-called "sciences of man," from anthropology (Lévi-Strauss) to semiotics (Barthes) to psychoanalysis (Lacan).

Several paradoxes, however, or apparent paradoxes, follow from this curiously pure structurality possessed by allegory, though taken singly none is at odds with our basic literary intuitions. On the one hand, as does structuralism itself, allegory begins with structure, thinks itself through it, regardless of whether its literary realizations orient themselves perpendicularly or horizontally, that is, as primarily metaphoric or primarily metonymic. At each point of its progress, allegory will select its signifying elements from the system of binary oppositions that is provided by what Jakobson would call the metaphoric code, that is, the structure, and, as a result, allegory will inevitably reenforce the structurality of that structure regardless of how it manipulates the elements themselves. For Jakobson and for allegory, "The poetic function projects the principle of equivalence from the axis of selection into the axis of combination,"[19] and so it is always the structure of metaphor that is projected onto the sequence of metonyny, not the other way around, which is why allegory is always a hierarchicizing mode, indicative of timeless order, however subversively intended its contents might be. This is why allegory is "the courtly figure," as Puttenham called it, an inherently

political and therefore religious trope, not because it flatters tact-
fully, but because in deferring to structure it insinuates the power of
structure, giving off what we can call the structural effect.[20] So too,
this is what leads a theoretician such as Angus Fletcher to analogize
the rhythm of allegory to that of obsessional neurosis: it is a formal
rather than a thematic aspect of the figure, deriving directly from the
structure that in-forms its movement.[21]

On the other hand, if allegorical themes are in a sense emptied of
their content by the structure that governs them, if the particular
signifiers of allegory become vehicles of a larger structural story
that they carry but in which they play no part, they are at the same
time ostentatiously foregrounded by the very structurality that becomes immanent in them. There is no clearer example of this than
that of rhyme, which is precisely the poetic feature with which
Jakobson illustrated his definition of the poetical as the superimposi-
tion of structural similarity on syntagmatic continuity. With rhyme
we do indeed have "equivalence in sound, projected into the sequence," such that the principle of equivalent selection does indeed
govern syntax;[22] and the resulting literary effect is exactly that we
hear the sound of the sound rather than the meaning of the meaning.
The same holds for the other metrical and intonational means of
marking poetic periods as isochronic, all of which render "the time
of the speech flow experienced."[23] Thus, if before we saw signifiers
lose their content when they were subsumed in a metaphoric structure to which they only obliquely referred, we here see them lose
that content once again when they stagily embody that structure in
sequential movement. We hear the sounds but not the sense when the
signifiers, graded as similarity superinduced on continuity, point to
themselves as signifiers rather than to what they signify: poetic sense
is exchanged for poetic sensuousness when the palpability and texture of the *signans* takes precedence over, and even, as in doggerel,
occludes the *signatum* altogether. With regard to Jakobson's famous
typology of the six communicative functions—the referential, which
stresses the context; the emotive, which stresses the addresser; the
conative, which stresses the addressee; the phatic, which stresses the
contact between addresser and addressee; the metalinguistic, which

stresses the code in which the message is couched—allegory would be exemplary of Jakobson's purely poetic function, namely, the message that, charged with reflexive poeticality, stresses itself as merely message.[24] This leaves us, however, with the paradox that allegory, which we normally think of as the most didactic and abstractly moral-mongering of poetic figures, is at the same time the most empty and concrete: on the one hand, a structure of differential oppositions abstracted from its constituent units; on the other, a clamor of signifiers signifying nothing but themselves. Remembering the sententiousness of allegory, we are entitled to ask whether with such a structuralist description the thematic has not been "structured" out of court.

The paradox is, of course, only an apparent one, but I draw it out in this way so as to point to a real difficulty in structuralist poetics: namely, that in order to maintain any thematic meaning at all, structuralism, like allegory, must assume a meaningful connection between metaphoric and metonymic poles. That meaning is either what permits the two to join or it is the consequence of their juncture. What this means in practice is that Jakobson will pick up the tradition of Pope and of Hopkins, or, for that matter, of Wimsatt, and argue that sound is echo to sense. Of course, Jakobson does not intend the naïve claim that there are different phonemes for different qualities—the notorious murmuring of innumerable bees—though he does accept studies that support Mallarmé's discriminations of dark and light vowels. Rather, Jakobson wants to say that the structure of poetic sounds functions in relation to the structure of its poetic signifieds as a kind of Peircean index, a *little* like that to which it points, or, in negatively contrapuntal fashion, conspicuously, but equally indicatively, unlike.[25] In pointing to themselves, therefore, as in rhyme, the sounds thus also point beyond themselves to the structure of their signifieds, and the same goes for the signifieds themselves, which at a semantic and thematic level are again a structure of signifiers pointing both to themselves and to a structure of signifiers beyond themselves, all of them, alone or together, eventually pointing to the structure of language itself. This is the essentially Hegelian assumption that lies behind Jakobson's claim that "The history of a system is in turn also a system," that is, that historical diachrony, the evolution of a language, reacts structurally upon the synchronic linguistic code.[26] Once the signifier's relation to the signified, that is, the sign as a whole, is in this way understood to be relatively motivated, rather than utterly arbitrary as in Saussure, it is possible to make the sign itself into an index pointing to the structure it embodies and supports, and thus all the levels of allegory, up through and including the thematic, will display themselves and each other with resoundingly poetic and emphatically structural effect.[27]

But this harmonious, now Leibnitzian structure, depending as it does on an utter idealization of the structure of the sign, occurs at a significant cost. Out of the romantic and organicizing formalism of its axiological assumptions, the affinity of structuralism with the old New Criticism comes as naturally as leaves to either Keats's or Yeats's tree, and so too does the same fetishization of irony as a poetic feature. "The supremacy of poetic function over referential function does not obliterate the reference but makes it ambiguous."[28] What this typically unbending aphorism means is that, in a structuralist poem, every signifier will be simultaneously metaphor and metonymy. Jakobson's example is the girl in the Russian folk tale who comes to be symbolized by the willow under which she walks: ever after in the poem, girl and tree are metaphors, each of the other, by virtue of their metonymic intersection, just as the sequential movement of the poem is conditioned by their metaphoric equivalence.[29] In classical rhetoric, we would call this a synecdoche: the girl is represented by the tree or it by she, in that one daemonically possesses the other. In Jakobson's terms, however, what we have is a metaphoric metonymy and a metonymic metaphor, and the result, not surprisingly, is allegory:

> Similarity superimposed on contiguity imparts to poetry its thoroughgoing symbolic, multiplex, polysemantic essence which is beautifully suggested by Goethe's *"Alles Vergängliche ist nur ein Gleichnis"* (Anything transient is but a likeness). Said more technically, anything sequent is a simile. In poetry where similarity is superinduced upon contiguity, any metonymy is slightly metaphorical and any metaphor has a metonymic tint.[30]

Undoubtedly, poems, and allegories in particular, work this way:

think of Spenser's forests that metaphorize his heroes while they wander through them, or the play of light imagery in *The Faerie Queene*. The question is, How can structuralism work this way? What does it mean for a metonymy to be slightly metaphorical, and what is this "tint" that makes a metaphor a little metonymic? If structuralism is the diacritical science because it begins with the difference around which binary oppositions assemble, what happens to its scientific status when its own most fundamental opposites, metaphor and metonymy, are from the very beginning already implicated one in the other, the difference between them collapsed for the sake of hierarchicized, structured, "symbolic, mulitplex," allegorical meaning? If these seem merely abstract and theoretical issues, we can reformulate them again in terms of our original literary problem: How does time get into structure and structure into time, how does allegory begin and why does it continue?

For reasons that will become clearer later, I want to illustrate the problem with the opening of *The Canterbury Tales*, which is an instance of the poetical whose structurality has never yet been questioned, and where the allegorical relationship of space and time is a straightforwardly thematic as well as a formal issue. This is the case in several ways, but, for our purposes, most importantly so with regard to the opening description of the months and seasons, which is the stylized convention by means of which the Prologue places itself squarely in a tradition of allegorical beginning. In part, of course, such a description is a convention of courtly romance, one that Chaucer employs several times elsewhere (*The Legend of Good Women, The Book of the Duchess, Troilus and Criseyde*), and whose force he would know from the *Roman de la Rose*, which he had already translated, and where the description of May is preface to the allegorical dream-vision itself. But so too, and equally allegorical, the description of months and seasons is a long established convention immediately evocative of, and convenient to, cosmological and metaphysical invention, a way of alluding through allegorical structure to the mysterious order of the cosmos and the position of God as unmoved mover within it; here the Prologue can rely on a tradition that goes back to Lucretius, Ovid, and Vergilian eclogue, and that is thoroughly alive and popular throughout the Middle Ages, whether in manuscript decoration, cathedral ornament, or various scientifically and philosophically inclined compendia. The details and history of this convention, which have been magisterially summarized for us by Rosemond Tuve,[31] need not concern us now, save to the extent that they allow us to refer with some certainty to the explicitly allegorical intentions of *The Canterbury Tales* and to remark that here, as with any deployment of a convention within a literary tradition, we have precisely the joining of paradigm and syntagm by means of which a literary text will position itself within the structurality of literature as a whole (with the text presenting itself as either like or unlike others in the conventional paradigm—for Jakobson this would be the literary code, a structure of generic oppositions—at the same time as it actualizes the paradigm in the temporality of literary history, thc ugh whether Chaucer's *parole* is here intended ironically remains an open question).

In any event, it is with reference to this complex tradition of allegorical literature and to the burden of cosmological, theological, and scientific speculation that it carries, that we enter the poem. And it is also within this context that we discover in the Prologue's first two lines, with the piercing of March by April, the metaphoric metonymy that for Jakobson constitutes the specifically poetic effect. That is, when April with its sweet showers pierces the drought of March, we have the code of the months, or, more precisely, the system of oppositions which makes up the code, translated directly into consecutive sequence, such that the binary oppositions between the months—rainy April versus dry March, but, of course, within the tradition there are other oppositions at stake besides the merely meteorological—are projected systematically onto the continuous progress of the months through the year—after March, then April—in a progression that completes and corroborates itself only when the entirety of the monthly paradigm unfolds itself through the temporal totality, or what properly we should here call the syntagm, of the year. Inevitably—and for the author of a treatise on the astrolabe, tautologically—this is picked up by the surrounding or encapsulating astrological references, which tell us again that we are in the first

month, April, because the Ram has run through half his course and
therefore, as with April and March, that the paradigmatic zodiacal
opposition of Aries and Taurus is directly translatable onto or as the
sequence of metonymy unrolled by celestial rotation.

All this is a rather complicated way of saying what for a competent
reader should presumably go without saying, but, for the sake of
argument, let us assume that the initial structural disposition of these
first few images is then repeated with utter systematicity in the pattern of images which the poem develops throughout its opening few
lines, so that the series of oppositions, which we might summarize
as wet and dry, up and down, sky and earth, male and female,
fecundity and sterility, pagan as opposed to Christian divinities, inside and outside, near and far, health and illness—all function structurally in relation to each other and to themselves as kinds of mirror
images, indexes, of the first metaphorico-metonymic structuration
introduced by the intersection of March and April, each of them
graded as structure on sequence. Let us even assume that the same
thing happens metrically, so that the ictus on the unstressed position
that we get in April is structurally related to the stress on the stressed
position that we get with March, and that this in turn sets up a stress
structure of rhythmical and intonational patterning which the poem
will reserve for specifically metaphorico-metonymic emphasis; for
example, " . . . with his shóurĕs soote / Thĕ droúghte. . ." Let us also
assume, again only for the sake of argument and in pursuit of the
ideal structural analysis, that the themes introduced by our now
hypothetically structuralized Prologue imagery are in turn developed
in the tales themselves, and that this enlargement proceeds with the
same structural determinations that are sketched out in the first few
lines, so that the implicit hierarchy presumed in the order of months
is what finally lies behind the social hierarchy into which the pilgrims
fit, from the Knight on down to the Miller (as well as the dictional
hierarchy that governs the manner in which each tale is decorously
related), and that the primacy of male April to female March is the
structural source not only of the patriarchal orientation of the
marriage tales, but also of presumptively analogous arrangements of
cosmological and literary order which the tales regularly, allegorically

ally with this—as, say, in The Wife of Bath's prologue and tale, where familial, sexual, theological, and literary "authorities" are all developed in terms of the hierarchicized sexuality already built into the piercing of March by the potent, engendering liquidity of April. Finally, so as to complete this imaginary, exhaustively structural analysis, let us assume that the relation of April to March, developed as structure superinduced on sequence, also describes the most general literary features of *The Canterbury Tales* as a whole, so that, in the same way that Jakobson's metaphorized metonymies point both to themselves as signifiers and to the structure of signifiers from which they derive, so too do we have in little with April-March a prototypical enactment of the procedure by means of which Chaucer characteristically manages to distance his text from its own textuality—whether in the way the tales comment upon each other by reference to their common frame, or the way they point to themselves by stepping out of themselves, as with the Pardoner's claims for his own rhetoric, or, in that culminating instance of self-reflection so dear to dialectical Chaucerians, the way the narrator's tale of Sir Thopas lapses into the allegorical prose of the *Tale of Melibee,* accomplishing thereby an instance of mirroring self-mockery surpassed only by the absolute duplicity of the Retraction itself, where Chaucer either turns Pardoner or steps out of literature altogether, but in either case piously and conventionally defers to the only moral imperatives that his allegorical system allows him in the first place.

Having now assumed so much—and I realize that to suggest either the possibility or the shape of a completely successful, all-encompassing structural analysis of *The Canterbury Tales* is to assume a great deal—we are now entitled to ask in what way this structure accounts for the poeticality of the text. In what sense can our hypothesised structure explain either the pleasure or the meaning taken from, or generated by, a text organized by the projection of metaphoric equivalence onto metonymic succession. The poem tells us that when the sweet showers of April pierce the drought of March to the root, when Zephyrus inspires the crops in every woodland with his sweet breath, when small birds begin to make melody, "*thanne* longen folk to goon on pilgrimages." How does the structurality of the first few

lines which we have now assumed manage to generate this longing, or
to justify it, or to explain it? How does such structurality entice a
reader further into the poem, leading him on through and into its
sequentiality? How is structure extended, "longed," into time?

We might conceivably answer by referring ourselves directly to
the immediate referents of the text. Here it would be a simple positivist matter of fact that when spring comes, and the Ram runs
through half his course, and small birds begin to sing, *then,* by nature, people desire to go on pilgrimages, with professional pilgrims
rushing off to foreign shrines, while ordinary folk who happen to live
in England instead typically wend their way to Canterbury. This
would be an unsatisfying solution, I take it, not only because we can
assume other urges to be commonly operative in the spring but also
because such a realist's account ignores the spectrum of allegorical
reference which we respond to in the text, at the same time as it
fails to recognize the specifically literary, conventional dimension of
the opening. Alternatively, then, we might forgo the natural referents
of the text entirely and answer the question formally rather than
realistically by saying instead that the text presents us with a self-
contained structure of relations, in which elements are manipulated
as in a game, and that therefore there is neither need nor reason to
adduce any extraliterary explanation or justification at all for the
particular arrangements that the structurality of the text allows us
to observe. The most that we might hazard as explanation for the
pleasure that we take in such a text as we continue through it would
be the kind of vibratory sympathy between its organization and the
structure of our thought which Lévi-Strauss suggests in the overture
to *The Raw and the Cooked,* where he takes up the issue of the an-
thropologist's response to the phenomena with which he is engaged.[32]
I take it that this too is also unsatisfying, not only because it rather
sentimentalizes the reading experience, but, again, more importantly,
because it too ignores the manifestly allegorical intention of a text
that explicitly directs its structure, such as it is or as we have idealized
it, to correspond to other structures of experience—psychological,
physical, metaphysical, and literary—from which the text derives its
own authority and indeed much of its literary interest. How then, if

neither philistine realism nor naïve structuralism—what we have been taught sternly to call "mere formalism"—is adequate, might we account for the "longing" of *The Canterbury Tales*? If the piercing of March by April is the primal structural scene to which the text repeatedly recurs, how does that first image, with its astrological, calendaric eroticism, control the structural unfolding of so massive and perfected an allegory as *The Canterbury Tales* is generally pleasurably and meaningfully taken to be. In the terms of my title, how does the structure of the poem yield its allegorical desire?

For an answer, I turn to another famous essay by Jakobson in which he applies the procedures of structural analysis to phonemic patterning, and where he develops the theory of distinctive phonetic features which remains the greatest achievement of structural linguistics, recognized as such even by linguists with entirely different theoretical perspectives.[33] I should say in advance that it is because of Jakobson's theoretical success with the conceptualization of phonemes, which reduces the infinity of humanly producible sounds to a few significant phonological oppositions, that structural linguistics has become the prestigious model for disciplines that are only marginally, or at least not obviously, related to language per se. All of them readily pay the price of analogizing their subject matter to language in exchange for the rigorous structurality that Jakobson's method provides.

In principle, then—and my account will be perfunctory paraphrase—Jakobson begins with Saussurean diacriticality, the thesis that we perceive positivities as systems of differences rather than as simple existents whose being immediately imposes itself upon our senses. We hear the structured differences between phonemes rather than the phonemes themselves, as we know from the fact that what is a significant sound to a speaker of one langauge may not even be heard by the speaker of another. For each language, then, Jakobson proposes that a system of binary phonological oppositions may be constructed whose systematicity can account for all the potentially significant sounds producible within the language. This will be the phonological code of the *langue* which is actualized in metonymic *parole*. These systems naturally vary from language to language, depending on the phonological structure of each, but what concerns us now are features that, because of the structure of the human mouth, are universal phonological facts. Here, then, like a Ramist proposing his initial dichotomization, Jakobson applies structuralist methodology and searches out what would be the maximum binary opposition of which the mouth is capable, which he discovers in the first syllable, contrast of consonant and vowel, transcribed as /pa/. The constituents of this utterance, vocalic /a/ and the voiceless labial stop /p/, represent absolute phonological difference in the mouth: namely, with /p/ the buccal tract is closed at the front, whereas in /a/ the tract is opened at the end as wide as possible. As a labial stop, /p/ exists for but a moment and requires a minimum of energy for its articulation; in contrast, /a/ is a continual voicing of sound and requires maximum energy. Whereas /p/ is the stopping of sound, /a/ is pure vocality. For all these diacritical reasons, /pa/ is plausibly identified as the largest binary opposition the mouth can articulate and, as such, from a structuralist perspective, is conceptually the first syllable. This theoretical claim is, in turn, supported by studies in language acquisition and aphasia which report that /pa/ is both the first utterance children learn and the last that aphasics lose, striking empirical corroboration of Jakobson's structuralist claim that language begins and ends with the combination of vocalic /a/ with voiceless labial stop /p/ in the primal utterance, /pa/.

The hypothesis is clearly ingenious, and if we assimilate voiceless /p/ to its twin labial stop, voiced /b/, sound and sense begin in Jakobson's sense structurally to cohere, as, for example, when we call the infant incapable of speech a *baby,* or when the Greeks call foreigners whose speech is strange *barbaroi* because they *babble,* as at the Tower of *Babel,* or when we begin our alpha-bets by joining *A* to *B*.[34] But /pa/ is only the beginning of a system. In order to build a structure, at least two sets of oppositions are required so as to construct a series of proportions and *logoi* that can be actualized in speech. Thus Jakobson and the infant must identify a second binary opposition, structurally opposable to the first, so as to specify a paradigmatic code, and this they do by introducing the nasal consonant /m/. With the acquisition of /m/, the pure differentiality that was first presented by /pa/ is, as it were, plugged up, recuperated. As a nasal consonant, a continuant sound, /m/ combines the vocality of /a/ with the positionality of /p/ at the front of the mouth. As a little of one and a little of the other, /m/ is a kind of average or collapse or juncture of the original opposition, just as metaphor and metonymy seemed to collapse in Jakobson's theory. At this point, once /m/ is articulated as a distinctive feature in its own right, we have the diacritical material with which to establish a structure of phonological sound: /p/ and /m/ being both opposed to /a/, whereas /p/ and /m/ are also opposed to each other. As Jakobson puts it: "Before there appeared the consonantal opposition nasal/oral, consonant was distinguished from vowel as closed tract from open tract. Once the nasal consonant has been opposed to the oral as presence to absence of the open tract, the contrast consonant/vowel is revalued as presence vs. absence of a closed tract."[35]

Again, there is striking cross-cultural empirical support for Jakobson's claim. In nearly every natural language that has been observed, some variation of "Papa" and "Mama," or their reversal, as in "Abba" and "Ema," are the familiar terms for father and mother.[36] What I am concerned with right now, however, quite apart from whatever empirical power Jakobson's insight might possess, is how the first two terms of this series, /pa/ and /ma/, develop themselves as a structure. We remember that it is only with the introduction of the second opposition adduced by /ma/ that we can say we have a system. At that point, each term in the series can be seen as diacritically significant with respect to its opposition to another term in the structure. Until then, however, /pa/, insofar as it signifies anything, signifies only the sheer diacriticality through which the system as a whole is thought. But this original differential determination is thereupon lost, retroactively effaced, when the introduction of /ma/ "revalues" the first *valueless* contrast consonant/vowel, or silence/sound, that is, /pa/, as "presence vs. absence of a closed tract." In other words, /pa/ loses its original status as mark of pure diacriticality when it is promoted to the level of significant signifier within the system as a whole. This new significant /pa/ is utterly unrelated to the first simply diacritical /pa/ that it replaces, or, as Derrida would say, that it places under erasure. And it is precisely this occultation of the original /pa/, now structurally unspeakable because revalued as something else entirely, which allows the system to function as a structure in the first place. In short, the structure of significant sounds must erase the original marking of diacriticality upon which it depends, and from which it emerges, in order to signify anything at all. In a formulation whose resonance with contemporary literary criticism will be embarrassingly obvious, there is buried in the structurality of any structure the ghostly origin of that structure, because the origin will be structurally determined as a ghost, a palpably absent origin, by virtue of the very structurality it fathers. Every structure must begin with such an effacing, retroactive revaluation of its beginning, with such a murder of its diacritical source, just as Freud said when he identified the origin of human culture in the murder of the father, the primal /pa/, who lives on only in and as the guilty memory responsible for the structure of society.[37]

Turning back to the opening of *The Canterbury Tales*—which it will now be clear was selected precisely because there in the intersection of *A*pril and *M*arch we have also the juncture of /pa/ and /ma/— we can answer the question of how an allegory begins and why it continues. What we can say is that with its poeticality defined as structure superinduced upon metonymy, allegory initiates and continually revivifies its own desire, a desire born of its own structurality. Every metaphor is always a little metonymic because in order to have a metaphor there must be a structure, and where there is a structure there is already piety and nostalgia for the lost origin through which the structure is thought. Every metaphor is a metonymy of its own origin, its structure thrust into time by its very structurality. With the piercing of March by April, then, the allegorical structure thus enunciated has already lost its center and thereby discovered a project: to re-cover the loss dis-covered by the structure of language and of literature. In thematic terms, this journey back to a foreclosed origin writes itself out as a pilgrimage to the sacred founding shrine, made such by murder, that is the motive of its movement.[38] In terms of literary response, the structurality of the text holds out the promise of a meaning that it will also perpetually defer, an image of hermeneutic totality martyred and sacralized by and as the poetical. This is the formal destiny of every alleogry insofar as allegory is definable as continued metaphor. Distanced at the beginning from its source, allegory will set out on an increasingly futile search for a signifier with which to recuperate the fracture of and at its source, and with each successive signifier the fracture and the search begin again: a structure of continual yearning, the insatiable desire of allegory.[39]

Perhaps this is one reason why, as Angus Fletcher has remarked, allegory seems by its nature to be incompletable, never quite fulfilling its grand design.[40] So too, this explains the formal affinity of allegory with obsessional neurosis, which, as Freud develops it in the case of the Wolfman, derives precisely from such a search for lost origins, epitomized in the consequences of the primal scene, which answers the child's question of where he came from with a diacritical solution that he cannot accept and that his neurosis thereupon represses and denies. But this would in turn suggest the affinity of psychoanalysis not only with obsessionality, but also with allegory.[41] For the theoretical concern of the Wolfman case, argued out in the context of a polemic with Jung, is precisely to determine whether the scene of parental intercourse, the piercing of /ma/ by /pa/, observed by the Wolfman was indeed a primal scene or instead a primal fantasy. And when Freud, relying on a hypothesis of universal, cross-cultural phylogenetic inheritance, tells us that it is a matter of indifference whether we choose to regard it as either, we may well wonder whether the theory of the primal scene, which is in some sense at the center of every psychoanalysis, is not itself the theoretical primal fantasy of psychoanalysis, a theoretical origin that the theoretical structure of Freud's thought obliged him to displace to the recesses of mythic history.[42] The question becomes perhaps more urgent when we recall the theoretical status of what for Freudian metapsychology is its own maximum binary opposition, namely, the instinct theory, with its dualism of Eros and Death. For to the extent that these two instincts are different, it is only insofar as the recuperative, unifying impulses of Eros are provoked as response to the differentiating impulses of death, a /ma/ to the thanatotic /pa/. And even before this, death is already conceived by Freud as itself such a dualism, already extended into time as the compulsive, obsessive repetition of its own diacriticality, that is, the repetition compulsion, which is the vicious Freudian metonym of the metaphoricity of death. Is it any wonder, then, that for evidence of all of this Freud can but point in *Beyond the Pleasure Principle* to another piece of allegorical literature, to Plato's story of Aristophanes' story of divinely diacriticalized hermaphrodites, yet another case where desire originates in and as the loss of structure.[43] And it is by no means accidental that Freud develops these same Aristophanic themes elsewhere, as in the allegory of his gender theory, with its unending quest by both hetero-sexes for the castrated phallus, powerful only in the division it teaches in its loss.[44] And so too with psychoanalytic interpretation, which completes itself only when it points mutely to that

> passage in even the most thoroughly interpreted dream which has to be left obscure . . . a tangle of dream-thoughts which cannot be unravelled and which moreover adds nothing to our knowledge of the content of the dream. This is the dream's navel, the spot where it reaches down into the unknown. The dream-thoughts to which we are led by interpretation cannot from the nature of things, have any definite endings; they are bound to branch out in every direction into the intricate network of our world of thought. It is at some point where this meshwork is particularly close that the dream-wish grows up, like a mushroom out of its mycelium.[45]

Does this mean, then, that psychoanalysis as a science is "mere" allegory? Does the fact that the exposition of Freud's theory of the psyche acts out its own theorization mean that psychoanalysis is but a symptomatic instance of its own thwarted desire to know: a neurotic epistemophilia at the end of a bankrupt tradition of philosophy? It is thanks to the genius of Lacan that we can see in this theoretical self-reflection of psychoanalysis, mirror of Freud's original analysis of himself, both the historical necessity and the scientific validity of psychoanalytic allegoricization. For when Lacan makes the subject an effect of the signifier, when he defines the unconscious as the "discourse of the Other" (let us note, a direct translation of the etymology of allegory: ἄλλος, other; ἀγορεύω, to speak), he establishes psychoanalysis as precisely that science whose concern is the split in the subject occasioned by the subject's accession to language. If psychoanalysis has discovered anything, it is precisely this loss of the self to the self which we vaguely refer to when we speak of the function of the unconscious. And what Lacan has taught us, in a series of blindingly lucid formulations still defensively resisted by the psychoanalytic establishment, is that in the same way that *The Canterbury Tales* is divided and directed when it enters language, so too is the psyche when it learns to speak.[46] This famous Lacanian barring of the subject—the loss of being that comes from re-presenting oneself in language as a meaning, correlative with the formation of the unconscious and the onset of desire, the Oedipeanization of the subject, and the acquisition of a place in the cultural order through the recognition of the Name of the Father—is what makes the psyche a critical allegory of itself and is what justifies psychoanalysis as the allegory of that allegory. For it is in search of the meaning of this division of the subject through the dialectics of desire, brought on by the structurality of the logos, that psychoanalysis finds its own epistemological project and its own initiatory desire.

If, then, the structure of Freud's thought, as it develops, becomes immanent as theme, if Freud's theory repeatedly valorizes those very images of loss which make his conceptual representations possible in the first place, this is to say no more than that Freud's hermeneutics are at one with the object of their inquiry. This is not the internalist fallacy; rather, it is the way psychoanalysis realizes itself as practice—by determining its object under a concept (Hegel's definition of science). For psychoanalysis is no empty theory, but is instead the operative science of the unconscious, and the unconscious is precisely that part of the self lost to the self by its articulation, just as Freud's theory embodies itself only through its endless, questing theoretical self-deconstruction; or so the heroic, allegorical example of Freud and the rigorously figurative style of Lacan persuasively suggest.

This is to see in psychoanalytic structure and in psychoanalytic structuralism the conclusion of a search for wisdom that has motivated Western philosophy from the very beginning. In the declension

of theoretical speculation about the order of order that begins as
ontology, cosmology, theology, and that, starting with the Renaissance, is internalized in the sciences of man as anthropology, sociol-
ogy, psychology, there occurs a completing or a breaking of the
hermeneutic circle when psychology, defining the psyche as an effect
of the logos, is itself transformed, in Kenneth Burke's phrase, into
logology.[47] This is the Heideggerean theme straightforwardly developed in Lacan's thought. And, of course, it is against just this appeal
to the order of order and the meaning of meaning that Derrida has
directed his critique of Lacan, seeing in such a psychoanalysis nothing
but the inherited after-effects of Western logocentric metaphysics,
where the phallus is the castrating, fascistic, transcendental signified
that condemns man's desire to a forever unsatisfying nostalgia for the
lost origin of a chimerical Golden Age.[48] As an alternative, as we
now all know, Derrida proposes instead a metaphysics and a psychoanalysis of difference itself, *"La différance"* of both structure and
time, to be comprehended by a philosophy *avant la lettre,* before
structure, before logos; in short, a philosophy of the effacing and
trace of prelinguistic, diacritical /pa/.

But as Derrida is well aware, and as he repeatedly reminds the
most enthusiastic *Derridistes,* this return to structuralist first principles can occur only *after* the structural fact, for it is only *in* structure
that the origin and its loss emerges. The sign is always thought through
difference, but it is always eventually thought out to the signifying
conclusion that erases the difference upon which it depends, which is
why "difference cannot be thought without the trace."[49] Thus, if
Lacan is logocentric, as Derrida says, it is because Lacan characterizes
the first logocentric lapse through which *"différance"* itself will be
thematized and conceived, so that any criticism of Lacan, including
Derrida's, will already have committed the Lacanian lapse. This accounts for the positivist illusion that there are things before differences, but it also explains the intrinsic belatedness of every
deconstruction.[50]

For this reason, too, we cannot accept any of the so-called post-
structuralist critiques of structuralism, again including Derrida's, as
being themselves anything more than the aftereffects of structuralism.

They are already defined, by the criticism implicit in their "post" and in their hyphen, as the allegorical response to a metaphor of structure and a structure of metaphor in which they are already implicated and by which they are already implied. Whether the origin is perpetually displaced by Derridean *"différance,"* or whether it is historically located and crystallized by the Girardian catastrophe of "no-difference" whatsoever, the thematic valorization of origin as loss survives.[51] And post-structuralism therefore gains its prestige only insofar as it thus pro-longs itself as the critical metonymy of the structuralist metaphor.[52]

But this is also why we must stress again in what sense the scientific thematization of structure which we find in psychoanalysis spells an end to the tradition of literary allegory as we have known it since first century Alexandria. For when psychoanalysis itself turns into allegory, criticism for the first time in our tradition must admit to the irrecuperable distance between itself and its object. Having consciously formulated the allegory of its own desire, criticism must wake up from its dream of interpretation to a daylight where desire is but the memory of the night's desire. We have laid it down as a law of literary form that the diacriticality effaced by literary structure emerges as theme in the register of loss. Our example has been the way pilgrimage is thematized in *The Canterbury Tales,* but we might have illustrated the point with any of a wide variety of texts. We may lay it down as a second law that profoundly self-conscious texts eventually realize their responsibility for the loss upon which their literariness depends, and that, when this happens, this responsibility is itself thematized as sin. From silence, to difference, to loss, to sin— and sometimes, in texts whose literary integrity is absolute, through sin back to silence once again, as in the Retraction with which *The Canterbury Tales* concludes, where the allegory, as Derrida again would say, re-marks what is its most distinctive mark, re-tracts its constituting trait. These laws of literary form apply also to the structure of literary history, whether we consider the development of an individual author or the evolution of a literary genre.

But this leaves open a way for poetry and for the history of poetry to remain literary even in their silence, whereas criticism ceases to be criticism when it turns mute. Because the things of poetry are words, poetry can, in a way that criticism cannot, conclude itself when it cannot continue. When poetry can find no new words with which to maintain the meaning of its longing, it can lapse into significant literary silence, thereby pro-longing its desire ad infinitum, as when *The Shepheardes Calender* concludes by promising yet more poetry beyond its end, or the way *The Faerie Queene* concludes by breaking off before its end with the vision of Colin Clout making melody to the Muses and the image of his own desire.[53] But criticism, whose things are not words but the meanings of words, meanings forever foreclosed by words, will find in silence only the impetus for further speech and further longing, which it will thereupon thematize as its own responsibility for the loss of meaning. Whereas a poem can be closed poetically even by a gesture of self-abandon, criticism, discovering the futility of its pro-ject, can only go on and on, frustratingly repeating its own frustration, increasingly obsessed with its own sense of sin—unless, of course, in the psychoanalytic sense, it projects its own critical unhappiness onto literature whose self-deconstructions would then be understood as criticism.[54]

Thus it is that when the tradition of English pastoral which begins with Chaucer's Prologue finds its own conclusion, it remains literary even in its self-disgust. And Eliot, drawing the thematic structure of the genre to its absurdly melancholic, ultimate reduction, can still articulate a meaning pre-dicative of yet more poetic desire:

> April is the cruelest month, breeding
> Lilacs out of the dead land, mixing
> Memory and desire, stirring
> Dull roots with spring rain.

With his habit of making a beginning out of ends, Eliot can imagine that the gap in landscape poetry, which his poem proleptically prepares, will become a significant silence in a perpetually meaningful literary tradition that will forever feed meaning back into his *Waste Land*. In contrast, Freud, whose Judaic thematizations of guilt and sin, as in *Civilization and its Discontents,* are at least as forceful and serious as any of Eliot's Anglican regrets, can do no more than continue to repeat his themes with increasingly phlegmatic and precisely nuanced resignation, as in the fragment with which his corpus movingly concludes, prophetically and self-reflectively entitled "The Splitting of the Ego in the Process of Defence."[55] This is the insight into self-division and sin which psychoanalysis—*interminable* analysis—leaves as legacy to contemporary critical thought, which continues to repeat Freud's themes, though perhaps without the rigor of Freud's resignation. Here I refer to that note of eschatological salvation which sounds so strangely in current literary discourse, as when Girard looks forwards to a revivification of difference through sacralizing violence, or when Derrida, telling us it is not a question of choosing, includes himself amongst those who "turn their eyes away in the face of the as yet unnameable which is proclaiming itself and which can do so, as is necessary whenever a birth is in the offing, only under the species of the non-species, in the formless, mute, infant, and terrifying form of monstrosity."[56] It would seem, by the rules of the endgame Beckett wrote in *Waiting for Godot,* that contemporary thought here turns pastoral nostalgia for a golden age into the brute expectations of a sentimental apocalypticism. But we will wait forever for the rough beast to slouch its way to Bethlehem; so too, for a philosophy or a literary criticism of what the thunder said: DA.[57]

NOTES

1. Sigmund Freud, *The Interpretation of Dreams* (*1900*; 1959) in *The Standard Edition of the Complete Psychological Works of Sigmund Freud* (hereafter cited as SE), ed. James Strachey et al., 24 vols. (London: Hogarth Press, 1953-74), 4, chap. 2, "The Method of Interpreting Dreams: An Analysis of a Specimen Dream," pp. 105-21. The date in italic is the original publication date; the date in roman is that of publication in the SE.

2. Northrop Frye, *Anatomy of Criticism: Four Essays* (Princeton: Princeton University Press, 1971), p. 89.

3. Ibid., p. 90.

4. See Jean Pépin, *Mythe et allégorie: Les origines Grecques et les contestations Judéo-Chrétiennes* (Paris: Aubier, 1958), pp. 87-88. Plutarch is ambivalent about such figurative readings. On the one hand, "by forcibly distorting these (Homeric) stories through what used to be termed 'deeper meanings' (ὑπονοίας), but are nowadays called 'allegorical interpretations' (ἀλληγορίαις) some people say that the Sun is represented as giving information

about Aphrodite in the arms of Ares, because the conjunction of the planet Mars with Venus portends births conceived in adultery, and when the Sun returns in his course and discovers these, they cannot be kept secret" ("How the Young Man Should Study Poetry," *Moralia,* 19E, The Loeb Classical Library, vol. 1 [Cambridge: Harvard University Press, 1949], pp. 100–101). On the other hand, "Such, then, are the possible interpretations which these facts suggest. But now let us begin over again, and consider first the most perspicuous of those who have a reputation for expounding matters more philosophically. These men are like the Greeks who say that Cronus is but a figurative name for Chronus (time) . . . (ὥσπερ Ἕλληνες Κρόνον ἀλληγοροῦσι τὸν χρόνον . . .)" ("Isis and Osiris," *Moralia,* 363D, vol. 5, pp. 76–77).

5. See John D. Cooke, "Euhemerism: A Medieval Interpretation of Classical Paganism," *Speculum* 2, no. 4 (1927): 396–410. Cooke's survey of the medieval tradition concludes by noting that "Chaucer nowhere subscribes to the euhemeristic interpretation" (p. 409). For the Patristics, euhemerism is a strategy of anti-pagan polemic, but one can also argue, like Cicero, that certain heroes did indeed become gods, just as the myths detailing divine transmogrification report. Euhemerism is allied with etymologization, the search for the truth in and of words; see, for a famous example, Plato, in the *Cratylus.* As such, it is the beginning of a tradition that treats words as substantialized philosophical essences, a tradition that leads directly to Heidegger.

6. Edwin Honig, *Dark Conceit: The Making of Allegory* (Evanston, Ill.: Northwestern University Press, 1959).

7. Harold Bloom, *The Anxiety of Influence: A Theory of Poetry* (New York: Oxford University Press, 1973).

8. On Philo and the unknowability of God, see Harry Wolfson, *Philo: Foundations of Religious Philosophy in Judaism, Christianity, and Islam* (Cambridge: Harvard University Press, 1962), 2, chap. 11, esp. pp. 110–14. Wolfson says that nowhere in Greek philosophy before Philo is there "a conception of God as a being unknowable in essence and unnamable and ineffable" (2:115). Philo is not the first allegorizer, not even the first allegoricizing Alexandrian Jew; see R. M. Grant, *The Letter and the Spirit* (London: Butler & Tanner, 1957), pp. 31–33. What is important is that, drawing on Stoic and Jewish predecessors, Philo formulates the theological necessity for philosophical, allegorical exegesis in the face of divine ineffability; see Wolfson, *Philo,* 2:128–30. On Philo's exegetical method, see Wolfson, *Philo,* 1:87–138; also see Jean Daniélou, *Philon d'Alexandrie* (Paris: Arthème Fayard, 1957), chap. 4.

9. On the historical uncertainty of the literal history of Genesis and the allegorical consequences thereof for Philo's reading of scripture, see H. A. Wolfson, "The Veracity of Scripture from Philo to Spinoza," in *Religious Philosophy: A Group of Essays,* ed. H. A. Wolfson (Cambridge: Harvard University Press, 1961); see also Wolfson, *Philo,* 1:120–22. As for Philo's distance from his text, it is by no means clear that Philo knew Hebrew, but in any event he would have been working in a tradition that understood the *Septuagint* translation as authoritative because divinely inspired (Wolfson, *Philo,* 1:88). Philo assumes that prophecy, translation, and his own exegetical insights are secured by divine inspiration (Grant, *Letter and Spirit,* p. 34; Wolfson, *Philo,* 2:54).

10. Sir Alan Gardiner, *Egyptian Grammar; Being an Introduction to the Study of Hieroglyphs,* 3rd ed. (London: Oxford University Press, 1957), pp. 10–11. Along with bestiaries and the tradition of dream symbolism that goes back to Artemidorus, the Renaissance rediscovery of the Horapollo manuscript sparks the vogue for emblems (Ficino, Alciaṭi, Ripa); see George Boas's introduction to his translation of *The Hieroglyphics of Horapollo* (New York: Bollingen Foundation, Pantheon Books, 1950); Rosemary Freeman, *English Emblem Books* (New York: Octagon Books, 1970). Ong connects this to the transition from a

writing to a print culture, along with the rise of Ramist logic: Walter J. Ong, "From Allegory to Diagram in the Renaisance Mind: A Study in the Significance of the Allegorical Tableau," *The Journal of Aesthetics and Art Criticism* 17, no. 4 (June 1959): 423-40. The hieroglyph remains a topos for allegorical speculation up through Pound's and Fenellosa's sense of the ideogram, of which Derrida speaks approvingly when he takes up the hieroglyph as an instance of "irreducibly graphic poetics," Jacques Derrida, *Of Grammatology*, trans. Gayatri Chakravorty Spivak (Baltimore: Johns Hopkins University Press, 1974), pp. 92-93, 334-335. The metaphorics of picture *versus* word, sensible *versus* intelligible, are picked up by Freud when he distinguishes conscious word-representations (*Wortvorstellungen*) from unconscious thing-representations (*Sachvorstellungen*); "The Unconscious" (*1915*; 1957), SE, 14:201-4; see also appendix C, pp. 209-15, for relevant portions of Freud's 1891 monograph *On Aphasia*. Similarly, as has lately been more and more stressed, Freud is regularly biased against the pictorial female (body) as opposed to the legible male (soul); so too, psychoanalytic therapeutics consists of translating a traumatic visible "scene" into intelligible words—"the talking cure." On the relation between Freudian madness and Freudian misogyny, see Shoshana Felman's excellent "Women and Madness: The Critical Phallacy," *Diacritics* 5, no. 4 (Winter 1975): 2-10. There is, however, a tension in all of Freud's developments of these issues, so that psychoanalysis in effect repeats within itself the Inigo Jones–Ben Jonson argument about *ut pictura poesis* and emblematic theatrical representation. See D. J. Gordon, "Poet and Architect: The Intellectual Setting of the Quarrel between Ben Jonson and Inigo Jones," *Journal of the Warburg and Courtauld Institutes* 12 (1949): 152-78. This is the same tension we can note in the Mosaic Freud's ambivalent obsession with things Egyptian—"Moses an Egyptian." Freud refers directly to Artemidorus's *Oneirocriticon* at the beginning of *The Interpretation of Dreams*; and bases his analysis of Leonardo on a reference to Horapollo, "Leonardo Da Vinci and a Memory of His Childhood," (*1910*; 1955), SE, 11:88-89. The argument about picture *versus* words is repeated once again, in the controversy between Lacan and Laplanche, as to whether the unconscious is the condition of language (Laplanche) or language is the condition of the unconsicous (Lacan): see Jean Laplanche and Serge Leclaire, "The Unconscious: A Psychoanalytic Study," *French Freud: Structural Studies in Psychoanalysis,* Yale French Studies, no. 48 (1972):118-78; originally in *L'Inconscient*, VIe Colloque de Bonneval (Paris: Desclée de Brouwer, 1966); see Lacan's introduction to Anika Lemaire, *Jaques Lacan,* trans. David Macey (London: Routledge & Kegan Paul, 1977). This argument will lead to two kinds of psychoanalytic aesthetics: compare and contrast with Lacan's theory of the gaze, the philosophical Kleinianism of Richard Wollheim, *On Art and the Mind* (Cambridge: Harvard University Press, 1974), esp. "The Mind and the Mind's Image of Itself," pp. 31-51. Wolheim's would be the strongest alternative to a Lacanian hermeneutics.

11. Grant, *Letter and Spirit,* esp. pp. 62-63; for a summary of the development of orthodox exegesis, see R. P. C. Hanson, *Allegory and Event: A Study of the Sources and Significance of Origen's Interpretation of Scripture* (London: SCM Press, 1959). For the orthodox horror of Gnostic infinite exegesis, see Irenaeus *Adversus Haereses* 2.19.1; see also J. Fineman, "Gnosis and the Piety of Metaphor: The Gospel of Truth," *The Rediscovery of Gnosticism: Studies in the History of Religion,* ed. B. Layton (Leiden: Brill, 1980). Not all Gnostics are docetic, including the Valentinians; see E. Pagels, "Gnostic and Orthodox Views of Christ's Passion: Paradigms for the Christian's Response to Persecution?", also in *The Rediscovery of Gnosticism.*

12. Erich Auerbach, "Figura," in *Scenes from the Drama of European Literature,* trans. R. Manheim (New York: Meridian, 1959), pp. 11-76 (originally published in *Neue Dantestudien* [Istanbul, 1944], pp. 11-71).

13. Quintilian *Institutio Oratoria* 8.6.14-15; cf. Cicero: *Orator* 94; *De Orat.* 3.166.

14. Thomas Wilson, *The Arte of Rhetorique* (1553) (Gainesville, Fla.: Scholars' Facsimiles & Reprints, 1962) p. 198.

15. "But the greatest thing by far is to be a master of metaphor. It is the one thing that cannot be learned from others; and it is also a sign of genius, since a good metaphor implies an intuitive perception of the similarity in dissimilars," *Poetics,* 1459A 5-6, in *The Basic Works of Aristotle,* ed. R. McKeon (New York: Random House, 1941), p. 1479. For Aristotle on metaphor and proportional analogy, see *Poetics,* 1457B 6-33.

16. Abraham Fraunce, *The Arcadian Rhetorike* (1588), ed. Ethel Seaton (Oxford: Basil Blackwell, 1950), pp. 3-4.

17. Roman Jakobson, "Linguistics and Poetics," in *The Structuralists: From Marx to Lévi-Strauss,* ed. R. and F. DeGeorge (New York: Anchor, 1972), p. 95. Hereafter cited as LP. Originally published in *Style and Language,* ed. Thomas A. Sebeok (Cambridge: M.I.T. Press, 1960). Talaeus, *Rhetorica* (1548), cited in Lee A. Sonnino, *A Handbook to Sixteenth Century Rhetoric* (New York: Barnes & Noble, 1968), p. 121.

18. Roman Jakobson and Morris Halle, eds., "The Metaphoric and Metonymic Poles," in *Fundamentals of Language* (The Hague: Mouton, 1971), pp. 90-96. Angus Fletcher, *Allegory: The Theory of a Symbolic Mode* (Ithaca: Cornell University Press, 1964), pp. 1-23; see also Graham Hough, *A Preface to the "Faerie Queene"* (London: Gerald Duckworth, 1962), p. 106ff.

19. LP. p. 95.

20. George Puttenham, *The Arte of English Poesie* (1589), facsimile reproduction (Kent, Ohio: Kent State University Press, 1970), p. 196.

21. Fletcher, *Allegory,* pp. 279-303.

22. LP, p. 109.

23. LP, p. 96.

24. LP, pp. 89-95.

25. LP; see also Roman Jakobson, "Quest for the Essence of Language," *Diogenes,* 5, no. 51 (1965): 21-37.

26. Jurii Tynianov and Roman Jakobson, "Problems in the Study of Language and Literature," in DeGeorge and DeGeorge, *The Structuralists,* p. 82.

27. Similarly, because messages about the code are selected from the code, Lacan denies the possibility of a radical concept of metalanguage: "There is the relation here of the system to its own constitution as a signifier, which would seem to be relevant to the question of metalanguage and which, in my opinion, will demonstrate the impropriety of that notion if it is intended to define differentiated elements in language." Jacques Lacan, "On a Question Preliminary to any Possible Treatment of Psychosis," in *Ecrits,* trans. Alan Sheridan (New York: W. W. Norton, 1977), p. 185.

28. LP. p. 112.

29. LP. p. 111.

30. LP, p. 111.

31. Rosemond Tuve, *Seasons and Months: Studies in a Tradition of Middle English Poetry* (Paris: Librairie Universitaire, 1933).

32. Claude Lévi-Strauss, *The Raw and the Cooked: Introduction to a Science of Mythology,* trans. John and Doreen Weightman (New York: Harper & Row, 1970). Originally published as *Le Cru et le cuit* (Paris: Librairie Plon, 1964).

33. Roman Jakobson, "Phonemic Patterning," in Jacobson and Halle, eds., *Fundamentals of Language,* pp. 50-66.

34. We are justified in thus assimilating /p/ with /b/ because at this stage the distinction between voiced and voiceless has not yet been made. "As the distinction voiced/voiceless has not yet been made, the first consonant may be shifting and sometimes indistinct,

varying between types of /b/ and types of /p/, but still within a distinct "family of sounds." R. M. Jones, *System in Child Language* (Cardiff: University of Wales Press, 1970), 2:85. Our alphabet reflects this "family" orthographically, writing "p" as upside-down "b."

35. Jakobson, "Phonemic Patterning," p. 51.

36. Roman Jakobson, "Why 'Mama' and 'Papa,'" *Selected Writings* (The Hague: Mouton, 1962), 1:538-45.

37. Freud, *Totem and Taboo,* SE, 13, 1-161, esp. 141-46.

38. Thus *The Canterbury Tales* begins with a beginning already past the beginning, with the Ram already having run half his course. In liturgical iconography, this is the *first* period of "erring, or wandering from the way": "The whole of this fugitive life is divided into four periods: the period of erring, or wandering from the way; the period of renewal, or returning to the right way; the period of reconciliation; and the period of pilgrimage. The period of erring began with Adam and lasted until Moses, for it was Adam who first turned from God's way. And this first period is represented, in the Church, by the part of the year which runs from Setuagesima to Easter. During this part of the year the Book of Genesis is recited, this being the book which contains the account of the sin of our first parents." Jacobus de Voraigne, *The Golden Legend,* trans. Granger Ryan and Helmut Ripperger (New York: Longmans, Green, 1941), pp. 1-2; cited in Robert P. Miller, *Chaucer: Sources and Backgrounds* (New York: Oxford University Press, 1977), p. 14. Adam's fall (which brings death into this world) is an affective projection of this origin-displaced-from-itself—a decisive example in our tradition of the way literature thematizes its own enabling displacement as sin. Woman, namely Eve, is the characteristic occasion of this disjunction, which is why in literature she is /ma/, not /pa/. From this Lacan develops a theory of desire.

39. I am concerned here with the way literary structures are thought and so feel no obligation to restrict my argument to cases that explicitly instance Jakobson's phonological thesis; nevertheless, in the course of writing this essay, I have enjoyed collecting concrete examples, as in the first line of the *Iliad* from which I take my epigraph, where the wrathful *Mῆ* is joined to the stress on *Πη* in the first syllable of Lacan's and Achilles' Name of the Father. With regard to the pastoral tradition that I focus on in the essay, from Chaucer's Prologue through Spenser to Eliot, we should think of Marvell's "The Garden," which opens with another Pa–Ma:

> How vainly men themselves amaze
> To win the palm, the oak, or bays.

and tells another story of Eden lost through diacriticality:

> Two paradises 'twere in one
> To live in paradise alone.

There are also examples from the novel; for example, *Mansfield Park* or *The Charterhouse of Parma* (Parme), or "Stately plump *Bu*ck *Mu*lligan," or, my favorite, because its three syllables sum up Lacan's theory of the acquisition of language through the castration of the paternal metaphor: *Moby Dick* (the female version of which, of course, is *Madame Bovary*).

40. Fletcher, *Allegory,* pp. 174-80.

41. The issue of Freud's and psychoanalysis' obsessionality is a subject for another essay. It takes the hermeneutic form of attempting to plug up what are thematized as gaps. The culminating moment of Freud's analysis of the obsessional Ratman comes, for example, when Freud's interpretation *participates* in the Ratman's deepest homosexual fantasies:

> Was he perhaps thinking of impalement? "No, not that; . . . the criminal was tied up . . ."
> —he expressed himself so indistinctly that I could not immediately guess in what

position— " . . . a pot was turned upside down on his buttocks . . . some rats were put into it . . . and they . . ."—he had again got up, and was showing every sign of horror and resistance—"bored their way in . . . "—Into his anus, I helped him out.

"Notes upon a Case of Obsessional Neurosis" (*1909*; 1955), SE, 10:166. Murray Schwartz suggested this reading of the Ratman to me. I would say that we can follow out the same language and desire, not only in Freud's biography, but in psychoanalytic theory and meta-theory—a hermeneutic sodomy. This anal thematic also follows from the structure of "Pa/Ma." I develop this point briefly in terms of the difference between a philosophical and a literary name in "The Significance of Literature: *The Importance of Being Earnest*," in *October* 15 (1981).

42. "From the History of an Infantile Neurosis" (*1914*; 1955), SE, 17. "I should myself be glad to know whether the primal scene in my present patient's case was a phantasy or a real experience; but taking other similar cases into account, I must admit that the answer to this question is not in fact a matter of very great importance," p. 97.

43. "Beyond the Pleasure Principle" (*1920*; 1955), SE, 18.

44. SE, 19; 1961. "The Dissolution of the Oedipus Complex (*1924*; 1961); "The Infantile Genital Organization" (*1923*; 1961); "Some Psychical Consequences of the Anatomical Distinction between the Sexes" (*1925*; 1961). Freud's psychoanalytic theory develops as a whole in exact imitation of the little boy whose sexual development the gender theory describes, with the theory itself passing through oral, anal, and phallic stages as it strives to develop a grown-up theory of desire. In the course of this canonical development, a moment of castration disavowal occurs in the essay "On Narcissism" (*1915*; 1961), in which Freud denies the importance of castration. The bad faith of this theoretical disavowal effects Freud's subsequent rethinking of psychoanalytic metapsychology, which is why his theory never fully resolves its Oediups Complex and therefore never fully justifies, or even attains, the coherent theoretical genitality to which it aspires.

45. "Interpretation of Dreams" (*1900*; 1953), SE, 5:525; see also SE, 4:111n.

46. These themes run through all of Lacan's work. In *Ecrits,* see "The Mirror Stage as Formative of the Function of the I," "The Function and Field of Speech and Language in Psychoanalysis," "On a Question Preliminary to any Possible Treatment of Psychosis," "The Signification of the Phallus," and "The Subversion of the Subject and the Dialectic of Desire in the Freudian Unconscious." With regard to the subjective occultation induced by metaphor, see especially Lacan's formulas for metaphor and metonymy in "The Agency of the Letter in the Unconscious or Reason since Freud." See also J. Fineman, "Gnosis and the Piety of Metaphor."

47. Kenneth Burke, *The Rhetoric of Religion: Studies in Logology* (Berkeley and Los Angeles: University of California Press, 1961); idem, "Terministic Screens," in *Language as Symbolic Action* (Berkeley and Los Angeles: University of California Press, 1966), p. 47.

48. The "Pa/Ma" model phonologically instantiates what Heidegger describes more generally in terms of the history of metaphysics: "In the service of thought we are trying precisely to penetrate the source from which the essence of thinking is determined, namely *alētheia* and *physis,* being as unconcealment, the very thing that has been lost by 'logic.'" *An Introduction to Metaphysics,* trans. R. Manheim (New York: Anchor Books, 1961), p. 102. For Derrida's criticism of Lacan, see "Le Facteur de la vérité," in *La Carte postale: de Socrate à Freud et au-delà* (Paris: Flammarion, 1980); an early version of this in *Poétique/* 21 (1975); and a version of this in *Graphesis: Perspectives in Literature and Philosophy,* Yale French Studies, no. 52 (1975). For Derrida's criticism of Heidegger, which proceeds by applying Heidegger's critique of Western metaphysics to itself, see "'ὀυσία and γραμμή': A Note to a Footnote in *Being and Time,*" in *Phenomenology in Perspective,* ed. F. J. Smith

(The Hague: Martinus Nijhoff, 1970); "The Ends of Man" in *Philosophy and Phenomeno-logical Research* 30, no. 1 (1969); and *Marges de la philosophie* (Paris: Minuit, 1970).

49. Derrida, *Of Grammatology*, p. 57.

50. For this reason, I think it is a mistake to assimilate Derrida and Lacan each to the other, and to see in the critical practice of both an equivalent response to textuality, e.g., Gayatri Spivak, "The Letter as Cutting Edge," *Literature and Psychoanalysis,* Yale French Studies 55/56:208–26; Barbara Johnson, "The Frame of Reference: Poe, Lacan, Derrida," in ibid.:457–505. This is to reduce the historical importance that their confrontation repre-sents both for psychoanalysis and for philosophy. Derrida is very much son to Lacan's father, which is why he attempts the critical parricide of "Le facteur de la vérité" or *Posi-tions.* In this sense, Derrida is quite right to characterize the Lacanian enterprise in terms of a passé Hegelian project. On the other hand, in accord with the Freudian paradigm, Derri-da's philosophical success only makes the mortified Lacan that much more authoritative.

51. René Girard, *Violence and the Sacred* (Baltimore: Johns Hopkins University Press, 1977); originally published as *La Violence et le sacré* (Paris: Editions Bernard Grasset, 1972).

52. Thus *Of Grammatology* positions itself with an attack on structural linguistics, dia-criticalizing difference itself, pt. 1, chap. 2, pp. 27–73.

53. Spenser self-consciously expands Chaucer's description of months and seasons into allegorical eclogue when both he and Colin Clout, poet-hero of *The Shepheardes Calendar,* look directly back to Tityrus-Chaucer, "the loadestarre of our language" (EK, quoting Lydgate in the preface), as to an inspiring origin and poetic source that now is lost forever: "The God of shepheards *Tityrus* is dead" (June, 81). In accord with a familiar Renaissance theory of poetic imitation, Spenser dramatizes the situation of the poet whose poetic desire grows out of his foredoomed effort to match an original model, which he lags after, from which he is distanced, and which he therefore adores:

> Goe lyttle Calender, thou hast a free passeporte,
> Goe but a lowly gate emongste the meaner sorte.
> Dare not to match thy pipe with Tityrus his style,
> Nor with the Pilgrim that the Ploughman playde a whyle:
> But followe them farre off, and their high steppes adore.

(Envoy to December)

Out of the death of Tityrus, then, or the death of Chaucer (the reference to the pilgrim-ploughman is to pseudo-Chaucer, which Spenser would have taken as authentic; see Alice S. Miskimin, *The Renaissance Chaucer* [New Haven: Yale University Press, 1975], p. 93) comes *The Shepheardes Calender*'s allegory of poetic vocation, which concludes only when Colin himself becomes an eclogue ("he proportioneth his life to the foure seasons of the year," Argument, December) and, in the December-winter of his years, forswears poetry the better to look forward to his death. There is play here, surely, as there always is in the poetry of silence, but the play is real-ized very seriously by Spenser when he omits the emblem at the end of December, thereby marking the conclusion of his poem with the very silence about which Colin merely speaks. This missing emblem at the end (corresponding to Chaucer's absent origin at the beginning of the Prologue) is the promise of yet more poetry, a way of concluding, without betraying, the impulse to indefinite extension which is the essence of allegory. This is the only appropriate conclusion to an eclogue, which, according to the hierarchy of genres, is but the poetical beginning of a poet's career—as EK reminds us in the preface to the poem. When Spenser gives up his Shepheardes weeds and Oaten reeds for the sterner trumpets of epic, he concludes the allegory of his own poetic vocation; at the same time, Colin Clout comes home once again, this time to see the image of his desire disappear (*FQ,* VI, 10; all Spenser citations are from *The Poetical Works of Edmund Spenser,* ed. J. C. Smith and E. de Selincourt (Oxford: Oxford University Press, 1912).

For the infinite intentions of allegory, its intention to enclose its own infinities, see Bunyan's "Apology" for *The Pilgrim's Progress:*

> And thus it was: I, writing of the way
> And race of saints in this our gospel day,
> Fell suddenly into an allegory
> About their journey and the way to glory,
> In more than twenty things, which I set down;
> This done, I twenty more had in my crown,
> And they again began to multiply,
> Like sparks that from the coals of fire do fly.
> Nay then, thought I, if that you breed so fast,
> I'll put you by yourselves, lest you at last
> Should prove *ad infinitum,* and eat out
> The book that I already am about.

54. See, for example, Gayatri Spivak: "Je voudrais suggérer la possibilité d'envisager la poésie dans une perspective exactement contraire [contrary to a common understanding that would see poetic language as that in which sign and sense are identical, as in music], comme ce qui tend à maintenir la distance entre le signe et le sens sémantique. J'aurai recours, pour étayer mon argumentation, à le notion de'allégorie. "Allégorie et histoire de la poésie: Hypothèse de travail," *Poétique* 8 (1971):427–41, 427.

In effect, I am suggesting that we are still entitled to retain the idea of the book, the poem, the artifact, as opposed to the infinite, indefinite, unbounded extension of what is currently called textuality. Thus I also maintain the critical force of the distinction between literature and its criticism, though, in accord with my argument above, this distinction only becomes speakable or operative relatively recently with the conclusion of psychoanalytic hermeneutics. What distinguishes the literary from its criticism is that the logocentric book or poem can effect the closure of representation precisely because it can structure silence, as silence, into its discourse, just as language does with the combination of consonant and vowel. The result is a polysemic, structured literary universe. If contemporary literary criticism can do this, it chooses not to and thus pronounces itself the ongoing voice of the inconclusive textuality it attributes to literature.

I realize that Derrida would characterize the distinction between structure and time which structuralism thus proposes as dependent upon, in Heidegger's phrase, a "vulgar concept of time" (see *Of Grammatology,* p. 72). My concern is, however, with how these concepts have functioned and continue to function as decisively powerful metaphors in the Western literary critical tradition, regardless of how philosophically untenable they may have been for thousands of years, for they have had their historical effect even as phantasms. More precisely, I am assuming here, and drawing the conclusion that follows from, the *necessary* and perennial "recuperation," if that is what it should be called, of *différance* by logocentrism. This is a decisive, repeated, and historical metaphysical occurrence, with its own directionality, one that determines the contours and the contents of both our literary and our philosophical traditions. Thus we will even agree that all literary texts share the same indeterminate meaning, for they can make even their own silence echo itself. But we conclude, therefore, for just this reason, that this predetermined indeterminacy of meaning in turn determines a specific literary significance. Only sentimentally can one deny the necessity or the specificity of this significance, which inexorably generates the (meaningless but significant, phantasmatic but nevertheless effective) distinction between the literary and the philosophico-critical. At the level of generality with which we deal here, this literary significance is, generically, the significance of literature, but, in principle, there is no reason why we cannot characterize this significance more precisely in local cases so as to speak to the thematic particularities of a given text's literariness. For example, if we were presently engaged upon a close literary reading of the opening lines of the Prologue to *The Canterbury Tales*—and it should be clear that we are not now so engaged—we would necessarily take up the way the lines erotically regret the allegorical Pa/Ma structure that they nevertheless refresh. Thus there is something immediately and noticeably disturbing about the way a traditionally female April is made to fecundate a traditionally male March, and this is the case not simply because conventional sexual agency is in this way instantly reversed. By tradition, woman is receptively but not ejaculatively moist, so it is doubly peculiar to introduce April in terms of "his shoures soote." The same thing is true in reverse for "The Droughte of March" (Mars), though in our literature the male is only rarely thematized as actively damp. Similarly, the image of veins, the conduit of liquid, themselves bathed by a liquidity in which they are immersed—"And bathed every veyne in swich licour"—establishes an antistructure of invaginated categoriality whose insides and outsides, contents and forms, introvertedly coalesce. Again, we have preparation in these first few lines for larger thematizations in *The Canterbury Tales* as a whole; for example, the stipulated reversal of sex roles and of the norms of specifically literary, bookish, patriarchal "Auctoritee" in the Prologue and the story of the Wife of Bath. Yet these and other imagined alternatives to the structure of allegorical desire all serve to reinscribe the initial literary authority of Pa/Ma. Thus the riddle of the Wife of Bath, "What thyng is it that wommen moost desiren" (line 905), has as its answer the desire of women to be men:

> Wommen desiren to have sovereynetee
> As wel over hir housbond as hir love,
> And for to been in maistrie hym above.

(lines 1038-40)

All Chaucer citations are from F. N. Robinson, ed., *The Works of Geoffrey Chaucer* (Boston: Houghton Mifflin, 1957). The enigmatic power of the question of desire, which is the question that constitutes desire, thus survives even its answer, as was the case with Freud: "The great question that has never been answered and which I have not yet been able to answer, despite my thirty years of research into the feminine soul, is 'What does a woman want? (Was will das Weib?).'" Reported by Ernest Jones, *The Life and Work of Sigmund Freud*, ed. L. Trilling, S. Marcus (New York: Basic Books, 1961), p. 377. This is why Lacan, characteristically faithful to the literary tradition out of which psychoanalysis derives, says: "il n'y a pas de dames." *Le Séminaire de Jacques Lacan: Encore* (Paris, Éditions du Seuil, 1975), p. 54.

55. "The Splitting of the Ego in the Process of Defence" (*1940*) SE, 23:275-78. The essay takes up the "rift in the ego which never heals but which increases as time goes on," p. 276. Freud's illustrative example is castration disavowal.

56. Girard, *Violence and the Sacred*. See also Jacques Derrida, "Structure Sign, and Play in The Discourse of the Human Sciences," in *The Languages of Criticism and the Sciences of Man*, ed. R. Macksey and E. Donato (Baltimore: Johns Hopkins Press, 1970), pp. 247-65; also published in Derrida's *L'écriture et la différence* (Paris: Editions du Seuil, 1967). If Girard is the theoretician of an unthinkable sacred Origin, and Derrida the philosopher of an indefinitely deferred Origin, then Foucault, with his inexplicable transitions between epistemic *frames,* is, despite his disclaimers, the post-structuralist of missing middles. And

Foucault shares post-structuralist millenarianism: "In attempting to uncover the deepest strata of Western culture, I am restoring to our silent and apparently immobile soil its rifts, its instability, its flaws; and it is the same ground that is once more stirring under our feet." Michel Foucault, *The Order of Things* (New York: Vintage Books, 1970), p. xxiv; originally published as *Les Mots et les choses* (Paris: Editions Gallimard, 1966).

57. See Lacan, *Ecrits,* the end of "Function and Field of Speech and Language," esp. pp. 106-7.

Robert M. Durling

Deceit and Digestion in the Belly of Hell

I

My title is meant to suggest that the portion of Dante's *Inferno* devoted to the sins of fraud corresponds to the human belly and that both in the punishments he imagined for the fraudulent and in his conception of the sin itself Dante drew upon the idea of the preparation and digestion of foods. My discussion here forms part of a series of essays on the structure of Dante's Hell as parallel to the human body—the circles of incontinence to the head (for that is what the incontinent sinner loses), the circle of violence to the breast (where the two natures, human and bestial, are joined), the circles of fraud to the abdomen.[1] This giant projection of the human body draws upon the traditional notion of the Body of Satan as the infernal counterpart of the Body of Christ, the Church.[2] It is Babylon, Babel, or confusion; among the persistent motifs of the *Inferno* is the association of sin with perverted or distorted bodily functions. The body-parallel is also of fundamental importance in the other *cantiche* of the *Commedia* as well, though I will not be able to discuss them in detail here.[3]

The belly of Hell is the appropriate place for the punishment of fraud because, traditionally, knowledge or truth is like food; it nourishes the soul. This association of food and knowledge is ancient and, I suppose, ubiquitous; it all began, after all, when Adam and Eve ate the apple. For Christians, the Truth—Christ—was the Bread of Life both as Eucharist and as the Logos.[4] St. Paul develops the analogy between food and truth at some length in 1 Corinthians 3: the new Christian is a babe in the spirit and must be nourished with milk—easier doctrine—until he is ready for meat.[5]

The term *digestion* itself is one of the interfaces between ideas of bodily and mental process. Latin *digero* meant properly to force apart, to separate, hence to distribute. Any multiple can be categorized and arranged: digested. Lewis and Short cite instances of digesting (arranging) the hair, asparagus beds, a library.[6] Applied to mental activity, *digero* meant especially to set in order. Cicero[7] says that subject matter must be distributed among the different parts of a speech: one digests it. Quintilian[8] says questions must be digested, or set in order.

For any expression to take place, a prior digesting must take place. The classic statement of this analogy is in Seneca's Epistle 84, a text that echoes down the tradition in writers as diverse as Macrobius, Bacon, and Swift, not to mention Dante:

> We must imitate the bees, and whatever we have heaped together in our various readings we must separate (for things are preserved better when separated from each other) and then, apply the energy and faculty of our own wit, combine these various juices into one flavor. . . . What in our own bodies we see Nature do without any conscious effort of ours (for the foods that we take in are a burden as long as they keep their own qualities and swim solid in the stomach, but once they have been changed from what they were, then they go over into strength and blood), we must perform on those things that nourish the mind, so that whatever we swallow we do not permit to remain unchanged, lest it be foreign. Let us digest it (*concocquamus illa*); otherwise it goes into the memory, not into the wit. Let us faithfully give books our assent and make them our own, that we may put together one thing out of many.[9]

Dante continually draws on this passage, and I shall repeatedly return to it (and to parts of it I have not yet quoted). Already in the *Convivio* (*Banquet*), we find him entitling a long, ambitious work and giving a lengthy introduction to its contents in terms of the parallel between food and philosophical knowledge, which he terms the Bread of the Angels.[10] It ought not to occasion surprise, then, when we find the analogy is of basic importance in the *Commedia*. Indeed, it is one of the most important strands in Dante's metaphorics, and an examination of it leads us close to some of the fundamental issues of his poetics. The Bread of the Angels as philosophical—that is, scientific—knowledge is one of the most frequently invoked metaphors of the *Commedia*. For instance, at the beginning of *Paradiso* 10, Dante devotes a long passage to the marvelous art that produced the precise angle (23½°) between the celestial equator and the ecliptic; it is one of the chief instances of the precision of God's art, for the conditions of life on earth would be drastically altered were the angle changed in the slightest.[11] Dante then writes:

Or ti riman, lettor, sovra 'l tuo banco,
dietro pensando a ciò che si preliba,
s'esser vuoi lieto assai prima che stanco.
    Messo t'ho innanzi: omai per te ti ciba.

Paradiso 10.22–25

[Now stay, reader, on your bench, thinking back over what you have had a foretaste of, if you want to be joyful long before you tire. I have served you: now feed yourself.][12]

The words of the poem, then, are the dish in which the doctrine of the poem has been served up to the reader; if he has read 10.1–21, he has already eaten a sample, he has "prelibato," and can begin to appreciate the happiness that Dante claims for those who are nourished by this Bread.

The importance of the food metaphor is already implied when Dante asks Ciacco, in the circle of the gluttons, "whether Heaven sweetens or Hell poisons" the prominent Florentines of the previous century, "se 'l ciel li addolcia o lo 'nferno li attosca" (6.84). The analogy is given great prominence in one of the climaxes of the poem, Dante's meeting with his ancester Cacciaguida in the sphere of Mars. In *Paradiso* 15–18, Cacciaguida foretells, "in plain terms," "senza ambage," without periphrasis, Dante's future exile; he imposes on him the calling of poet of the *Commedia* and metaphorically knights him for his "milizia." The episode is the culmination of the elaborate series of partial and veiled prophecies about Dante's exile, a series that began with Ciacco; it is the fullest and the definitive parallel in the poem with its classical model, Aeneas's meeting with Anchises in *Aeneid* 6. It cannot be too strongly stressed that it occurs at the point of the *Paradiso* that corresponds to the transition to the Malebolge, the circle of the abdomen of the Body of Satan.

"Giù per lo mondo sanza fine amaro,
e per lo monte del cui bel cacume

li occhi de la mia donna mi levaro,
    e poscia per lo ciel, di lume in lume,
ho io appreso quel che s'io ridico,
a molti fia sapor di forte agrume;
    e s'io al vero son timido amico,
temo di perder vita tra coloro
che questo tempo chiameranno antico."
    La luce in che rideva il mio tesoro
ch'io trovai lì, si fé prima corusca,
quale a raggio di sole specchio d'oro;
    indi rispuose: "Coscienza fusca
o de la propria o de l'altrui vergogna
pur sentirà la tua parola brusca.
    Ma nondimen, rigmossa ogne menzogna,
tutta la tua vision fa manifesta;
e lascia pur grattar dov'è la rogna.
    Ché se la voce tua sarà molesta
nel primo gusto, vital nodrimento
lascerà poi, quando sarà digesta. . . ."

Paradiso 17.112–32

["I see well, father, how time is spurring, toward me to give me the kind of blow that is heaviest for one who is least prepared; therefore it is well that I arm myself with foresight so that, if the dearest place is taken from me, I may not lose the others because of my songs.

"Down through the endlessly bitter world and up along the mountain from whose lovely summit my lady's eyes have lifted me, and then through Heaven from light to light, I have learned things which, if I retell them, will taste very bitter to many people; but if I am a timid friend to the truth, I fear I will lose life among those who will call this time ancient."

The light where my treasure was laughing, that I found there, first flashed like a gold mirror in the sun, then replied: "A conscience dark with its own or another's shame will find your words harsh. But nonetheless, rejecting every falsehood, make manifest all your vision, and let them scratch where they itch. For if your voice is painful at the first taste, later it will leave vital nourishment, when it is digested. . . ."]

As this passage may suggest, the problematic of deception is closely connected with the central concerns of Dante's poetics. To establish and clearly maintain a sharp distinction between poetry and fraud is essential to it. Here the antithesis is defined as that between food and poison: the devices of the fraudulent may taste sweet at first, but later they turn to bitterness;[13] Dante's poetry may at first taste bitter but will later "leave vital nourishment." The phrase conflates the functions of food and of medicine, thus complicating the antithesis as derived from Boethius's *Consolatio Philosophiae*,[14] where if the Muses of Comedy are "meretriculae" who nourish the sick man's disease with their "dulcibus . . . venenis" (the self-pity they encourage is based on delusion), Philosophia brings medicines that though bitter to the taste become sweet in the stomach: "quae restant ut degustata quidem mordeant, interius autem recepta dulcescant" (3.P.1)[15] However, some very large problems are involved here. For one thing, although Dante expresses his gratitude to Cacciaguida for predicting his exile in literal terms, the poem itself is, of course, no simple literal statement. For another, if truth (or the testimony of personal insight) is food, it must be served up in language and in writing. Language inherently involves us in the problematic of the duality between container and thing contained—in the classic terms of medieval rhetoric, integument and nucleus—a duality that is basic to Dante's conception of fraud. Dante's poetics—no doubt any poetics—is inextricably bound up with the problem of deception; what is interesting in Dante's case is the thorough awareness of the problem he shows and the complexity of his treatment.

The belly is a container of major importance, and a special association of fraud with the belly is the basis of the entire Malebolge. As the belly of Hell, the Malebolge are of course dysfunctional; they do not nourish, they poison the body of which they are a part, and they represent perhaps the most gigantic case of constipation on record. References to food, to cooking, to the various parts of the digestive tract, to excretion and excrement, are legion, along with allusion to some dozen diseases that were in Dante's time thought of as resulting from malfunction of the digestive system. Several of the Malebolge are filled with fluids, and such punishments as those of the barrators, who are boiled in pitch (*Inferno* 21–22); the thieves, who undergo changes and exchanges of form, incineration, agglutination (*Inferno* 24–25); the simoniacs, who are burned by oily flames (*Inferno* 19); and the flatterers, who are immersed in shit (*Inferno* 18) involve sharply focussed parodies of cooking and digestion. There is probably an allusion to the range of meanings of "digero" in such passages as:

> O somma sapienza, quanta è l'arte
> che mostri in cielo, in terra e nel mal mondo,
> e quanto giusto tua virtù comparte!

Inferno 19.10-12

> [Oh highest wisdom, how great is the art that you show in the heavens, on earth, and in the evil world, and how justly your power subdivides!]

It is surely significant that the rivers of Hell do not, like the river of blood in a human body,[16] originate within the Body of Satan itself, but from outside, from the tears of the Old Man of Crete; they move inward, to be ultimately frozen and impacted in Cocito[17]: If it was the envy of the Devil that first let loose insatiability on the world, as Virgil says of the she-wolf in *Inferno* 1.111, his punishment is that his devices return upon him. This pattern, too, is basic to Dante's treatment of fraud, and he combines it with the motif of the container filled to overflowing ("già trabocca il sacco," *Inferno* 6.50) or to bursting.[18]

In all the Malebolge there is no more striking instance of the connection between fraud and the swollen belly than Master Adam, the counterfeiter of florins, whom we meet in *Inferno* 30, the last of the Malebolgia cantos, in the last *bolgia*. He is strategically placed to be emblematic of all of the Malebolge; we might call him the very belly of the belly of Hell, for his dropsy has swollen his belly out of all proportion:

> Io vidi un, fatto a guisa di leuto,
> pur ch'elli avesse avuta l'anguinaia
> tronca da l'altro che l'uomo ha forcuto.
>   La grave idropesì, che sì dispaia
> le membra con l'omor che mal converte
> che 'l viso non risponde a la ventraia,
>   faceva lui tener le labbra aperte
> come l'etico fa, che per la sete
> l'un verso 'l mento e l'altro in su rinverte.

Inferno 30.49-56

[I saw one shaped like a lute, if only he had been cut short at the groin, from the part where a man is forked. The heavy dropsy which dis-pairs the members by ill disposal of the humors, so that the face does not answer to the belly, made him hold his lips apart, like the hectic who, for thirst, curls one lip toward his chin and the other upward.]

The commentators have noticed that Dante's description of this case of dropsy fits, in a number of respects, the clinical description that was current in his day, which is similar in both Avicenna's and Averroes' medical encyclopedias.[19] Gianfranco Contini established that certain of Master Adam's symptoms are those of the variety of dropsy known as "tympanite,"[20] characterized by swelling of the belly, which becomes filled with wind and drumlike, while the rest of the body is emaciated.[21] Dante's "l'umor che mal converte" is, as we shall see, a reference to the physiology of dropsy. Before turning to physiology, however, I would like to raise the question of the appropriateness of this punishment to Master Adam's sin. The generally accepted explanation is that first offered by Alfred Basserman, who cited the description of Avarice in Alain of Lille's *De planctu Naturae*:

Iam dives, divitiarum naufragus in profundo, hydropicae sitis incendiis sitit opes, in medio ipsarum positus tantalizat.[22]

[The rich man, shipwrecked in the deep sea of riches, with burning hydroptic thirst thirsts for wealth, placed in the midst of it he is like Tantalus.]

This is, of course, a valid enough explanation, as far as it goes.[23] There can be no doubt that Dante, who knew the *De planctu Naturae* well and often referred to it, does indeed have it in mind here, as well as, perhaps, the passages in Pliny and Gregory the Great[24] on which Alain is drawing. Furthermore, in the Malebolge fraud is as often as not shown to be motivated by greed as well as by malice. But is the explanation likely to be so generic? May we not expect Dante's conception to involve a more precise contrappasso, to be more directly related to fraud as such, even to the particular species of fraud of which Master Adam is guilty?

The contrappasso is indeed quite precise, and it provides a principle according to which all the motifs in the episode are interrelated, as well as the Malebolge as a whole. Master Adam coined florins of 21 carats instead of the regulation 24 carats. He introduces, as he says, "tre carati di mondiglia." In other words, he introduced impurities into the melted gold when preparing it for minting. Thus his punishment involves a corresponding impurity and excess of the watery humor in his own body, "l'acqua marcia."[25] The implications are rich. First, the punishment depends on a parallel between the coining of florins and the process of digestion.

Although there were some points of divergence in the theory of digestion,[26] its main lines were agreed upon.[27] After food has been softened and partly liquefied in the mouth (no digestion, properly speaking, taking place there), the stomach performs the so-called first digestion, reducing the food to chyle, a fluid from which the usable portion is extracted by the intestines. The intestines then send the chyle via the mesenteric veins to the liver, where the so-called second digestion takes place, the conversion of the chyle to blood. There was also thought to be a third digestion, in which the heart further refined a portion of the blood and combined it with spirit, carried in the arteries; and a fourth digestion, whereby a small portion of heart's blood was further refined into semen.

All of these "four digestions" were imagined on the model of the cooking of food: the natural vital heat "concocted" the food, breaking down its outward form and making its essential qualities available for assimilation, which both Aristotle and Galen thought of as a kind of agglutination of blood to the organ.[28] Master Adam's dropsy is, then, a disorder of the digestive process, and specifically of the "second digestion": his liver (imagining that he has one!) is not adequately converting the chyle into blood; "l'omor che mal converte" becomes, instead, stagnant watery humor ("acqua marcia") that cannot be assimilated by the body, but distends and distorts it.

Now the analogy between digestion and coining is close. Like food, the gold must be cooked; its outward form in the raw state must be broken down; the gold must be separated from the dross; and the purified gold, cast in the shape of spheres of the appropriate size, is placed in a matrix on an anvil, where a blow of the hammer produces the flat disk of the imprinted coin.[29] To make florins with three carats of alloy, Master Adam had to disorder the concoction of the ore by adding a quantity of base metal to the refined gold. This moment, interestingly, does correspond to the "second digestion" in the liver.[30] In this view, then, Master Adam's dropsy internalizes in his body what he did to the florin.

An important part of Master Adam's punishment is, of course, his thirst, and perhaps the most famous lines in the canto refer to it:

> "Li ruscelletti che d'i verdi colli
> del Casentin discendon giuso in Arno,
> facendo i lor canali freddi e molli,
>
> sempre mi stanno innanzi, e non indarno,
> ché l'imagine lor vie più m'asciuga
> che 'l mal ond'io nel volto mi discarno.
>
> La rigida giustizia che mi fruga
> tragge cagion del loco ov' io peccai
> a metter più li miei sospir in fuga.
>
> Ivi è Romena, là dov'io falsai
> la lega suggellata del Battista. . . ."[31]

Inferno 30.64–74

["The little streams that from the green hills of the Casentino flow down to the Arno, making their channels cool and moist, are always before me, and not in vain, for their image parches me far more than the disease that wastes my features. The rigid justice that probes me takes occasion from the place where I sinned to make my sighs come faster: there is Romena, where I falsified the currency stamped with the Baptist. . . ."]

These lines reveal a further dimension of the contrappaso, for not only does the image of the streams poignantly increase Master Adam's thirst, the steams themselves are emblematic at several levels. They prefigure the clear stream of the Earthly Paradise (*Purgatorio* 18.25–33) and the river of light in *Paradiso* 30.61 ff. They are a figure of baptism, of course, and it is "the league (alloy) signed by the Baptist" that Master Adam has falsified. God's justice, then, takes occasion from the place of Master Adam's sin because, when faced with the streams he should have seen in them the emblem of baptism, should have made the place of his sin the occasion of his conversion.

Implicit throughout the passage is the analogy between the earth and the human body. As Seneca wrote: "It is pleasing that the earth is ruled by Nature according to the example of the human body, in which there are veins and arteries, the receptacles respectively of blood and spirit. In the earth, too, there are separate passageways for water and for wind, which Nature has fashioned so similar to those in our own bodies that our ancestors named the passageways for water 'veins.'"[32] Just as the earth also has its humors and distempers, so the streams of the Casentino are signs of its health.

In terms of the larger projections of the human body, Master Adam's punishment is particularly interesting. For in falsifying the florin he has introduced impurities into one of the vital fluids of the body politic: he has inflated the currency, and his distended belly is itself a figure of a distempered economy. Here it is possible to observe with particular clarity the process of Dante's adaptation of traditional materials, perhaps even the nucleus of his original conception. Behind Dante's Master Adam lies a particular variant of the fable of Menenius Agrippa, familiar to English readers in Shakespeare's *Coriolanus* and Sidney's *Apology for Poetry*.[33] Dante no doubt knew it in his beloved Livy's version (*Ab urbe condita* 2.32–33), but the fable had by his time already had a rich progeny, especially from the twelfth century onward.[34] Livy's fable of the rebellion of the members of the body against the greedy belly was a particular favorite of John of Salisbury's, and John's various adaptations of the analogy between the body politic and the human body have an interesting difference from Livy's: John introduces the idea of the malfunction of the various organs of the body, including the stomach.[35]

In the long discussion of this analogy in books 5 and 6 of the *Policraticus,* developing the Platonic notion that the health of the body politic depends on the harmonious functioning of its various classes, John argues that none must grow excessively, none must become a burden to the rest. In John's system of detailed correspondences we find, I think, the germ of Dante's treatment of Master Adam, as well, perhaps, of his entire treatment of the Body of Satan.

For John, the head of the body politic is the king; the heart is the Senate (the repository of wisdom); the stomach and intestines are the tax-gatherers and treasurers, rather than the ruling class, as in Livy's version.[36] Here is already implicit the notion of money, portable wealth, as parallel to bodily humor, especially to blood, the digested food. John's point is that accumulation of excessive wealth on the part of these officers of the crown is a kind of failure of the digestive process: "If they eat too greedily and do not sufficiently digest (i.e., distribute), they generate diseases either incurable or difficult. For it is impossible for anyone to follow both justice and money" (5.9).[37]

The analogy between digested wealth—money—and digested food—blood—is left implicit by John, but it is quite close to the surface. It becomes fully explicit in such a text as Nicholas of Oresme's *De moneta*, written ca. 1373, long after Dante's death, of course, but, like the *Commedia*, based in many respects on the *Policraticus*. Except for the fact that Nicholas does not here specify the swollen part, he might be describing Master Adam: "Just as a body is ill disposed when its humors flow excessively to one member, so that it is swollen by them and becomes too large, while the rest become dry and attenuated, and the necessary proportion is lost, and such a body cannot long survive; so conformably is the case in a kingdom when riches are attracted immoderately by anyone of its parts."[38]

Both John and Nicholas speak of wealth in the traditional terms of something whose nature is to be accumulated. Although money is termed "currency" in this period, the notion of the circulation of money is foreign to the conception, which is rather that of the current or river of blood that carries food to the members where it is, precisely, accumulated. The notion of wealth as inherently parallel to the circulation of the blood was to have to wait until after Servetus's and Harvey's great discoveries. Nicholas calls Master Adam's crime—debasing the currency—the worst of the three disorders of currency (the others are banking and usury). He identifies it as a modern problem. As Dante knew, Master Adam was no isolated phenomenon, particularly in his being in the employ of feudal rulers.[39]

II

Master Adam's punishment, then, represents counterfeiting as a disease, a distemper of the digestive system of the body politic; the state of Master Adam's body mirrors the state of his soul, the technology of his crime, and the effects of his crime on society. All of the forms of fraud punished in the Malebolge violate in some way "lo vinco d'amor che fa natura" (*Inferno* 11.56); this means that they sin against the body politic. The barrators, for instance, are boiled in pitch, a figure for their secret profiteering: the pitch that caulks the ship of state (cf. the simile of the Venetian *arzanà* in *Inferno* 21.7–18) is precisely "lo vinco d'amor," which is the foundation of society, parallel to the charity that bonds the Church, compared by Augustine to the pitch used to caulk Noah's Ark.[40] In other words, the pitch that conceals the barrators is a figure for the public trust they abused. Dante makes a similar point about the simoniacs, for, in being driven further and further into the chinks in the rock they are like caulking.

To hazard a preliminary formulation, Dante's allegorical method as seen here may be described as a way of focusing and combining a wide range of abstract considerations—religious, metaphysical, cosmic, social, moral—in representations of the human body. Master Adam's belly is an extreme case of a basic allegorical principle: the individual's actions and their significance are inscribed in his body and become legible there. This includes, in Hell, his status as member of the Body of Satan. The fraudulent are punished for the effect they have on society, and the remarkable fantasies of destruction and disease which begin Cantos 28 and 29 represent ills of the body politic.

Another aspect of the relation of fraud to the belly requires comment. One of the focuses of the idea of violence and hardness in *Inferno* 30 involves the idea of coining money by hammering.

> E l'un di lor, che si recò a noia
> forse d'esser nomato sì oscuro,
> col pugno li percosse l'epa croia.

Quella sonò come fosse un tamburo;
e mastro Adamo li percosse il volto
col braccio suo, che non parve men duro,

    dicendo a lui: "Ancor che mi sia tolto
lo muover per le membra che son gravi,
ho io il braccio a tal mestiere sciolto."

    Ond' ei rispuose: "Quando tu andavi
al fuoco, non l'avei tu così presto;
ma sì e più l'avei quando coniavi."

Inferno 30.100–111

[And one of them, who perhaps took it ill to be named so darkly, with his fist struck the swollen liver. That resounded as if it were a drum; and Master Adam struck his face with his arm, that seemed no less hard, saying to him: "Although motion is taken from me by my members, which are heavy, I have my arm free for such a need." And he replied: "When you were going to the fire, you did not have it so ready; but so, and more, when you were coining."]

The exchange of taunts goes on, fascinating Dante and making him subject to Virgil's rebuke. Part of the point is the vulgarity and painfulness of what Master Adam and Sinon say to each other: they no longer engage in deception; in fact, they tell the truth, but Hell "li attosca," since the only truths they can tell poison and sicken them, there is no true gold in their exchange. When Virgil rebukes Dante, however, the parallel shows Dante able to learn, to progress, and to be forgiven.[41]

Part of the point is to stress the parallelism among the various strands of Dante's metaphorics: coining, counterfeiting, and exchange; speech, especially fraudulent; disease, especially fever and dropsy; the body and the body politic and the Body of Satan. Coining is being referred to also in the very exchange of blows;[42] it is, of course, an important instance of the imposition of form on matter, that fundamental Aristotelian category, and as such it had a number of traditional metaphoric meanings, including the sexual: offspring resemble the father, as the coin bears the image of the ruler; the act of generation stamps the form derived from the father on the matter provided by the mother.[43] The sexual connotations of the idea of

coining are referred to in the very first of the Malebolge, where Vene-
dico Caccianemico's confession that he induced his sister to sleep
with Obizzo da Este is interrupted by a blow from the demon's whip
and the taunt, "Via/ruffian! qui non son femine da conio" (*Inferno*
18.66). Here, instead of blood in the womb being generatively
stamped, the entire woman is being coined into money. This sin is
the first we meet in the Malebolge, and it directly follows one of
which it is a kind of inversion: usury, punished in the last circle of
violence (*Inferno* 17). The usurers sin against natural fertility not
only because human industry should imitate Nature's but also because of the traditional view, deriving from Aristotle, that it was un-
natural for coin, made of "sterile" metal, to "beget" interest.[44] The
usurers pander to coin, the panders coin women.

Usurers and panders both have their parallels with Master Adam,
for the production of semen is part of the digestive process, and the
belly as locus of digestion is closely related to the belly as locus of
generation. Master Adam's distempered belly is also a womb preg-
nant with social disaster, like the Trojan Horse, which is referred to
so frequently in the Malebolge cantos as to be, along with the counterfeit coin, one of Dante's main symbols for fraud. Outwardly fair,
supposedly an offering to the goddess of wisdom, the Horse is called
a *womb* by Virgil—his words are *alvum* and *uterus*. A conspicuous
reference to it occurs in the last passage quoted: "Ricorditi, spergi-
uro, del cavallo" says Master Adam (line 118). There is also an important implicit allusion, for Sinon's resounding blow to Master
Adam's belly is a grotesque parallel to the incident in *Aeneid* 2
where Laocoon, seeking to penetrate the secret of the Horse, hurls
his spear against its side and makes its hollow womb resound.[45] Both
counterfeit coin and Trojan Horse are bellies, versions of the container.

Now, poetry, too is brought forth in a process analogous to giving
birth or begetting, just as it depends on a kind of ingestion and digestion. Seneca makes the point in the passage quoted earlier:

> Let our mind do this: let it hide everything that has helped it, show forth
> what it has fashioned. Even if a certain similarity should appear which your

admiration has deeply fixed in you, I want the resemblance to be like that of a son, not that of a statue: a statue is a dead thing. "What then? will it not be understood whose writing you are imitating? whose argumentation? whose wise sayings?" I think that sometimes it is not understood, if a man of great ability has stamped his own form on what he has taken from whatever exemplars he wished, so that all has been fused into unity.[46]

Here, at first, the model of the imitation is analogous to the father, the admiring mind to a conceiving womb; the process is reversed when the writer "stamps his own form on what he has taken," for he is now thought of as the father, the active partner in the process of generation, and, because of his creative power, his work can in turn fertilize other minds. Dante uses this metaphorics in many passages, for instance, in the following, which describes his reaction to learning the identity of Guido Guinizelli:

> . . . io odo nomar se stesso il padre
> mio e de li altri miei miglior che mai
> rime d'amor usar dolci e leggiadri,[47]

Purgatorio 26.97–99

> [. . . when I hear my father name himself, my father
> and that of all others, my betters, who ever used
> sweet and graceful rhymes of love.]

This metaphorics also appears in the interview with Bonagiunta da Lucca, which will require more extended discussion. Before leaving Seneca, however, we must note the curious phrase with which the last passage quoted begins: the writer hides, he says, all that has helped him. In these terms, the writer does his best to commit a kind of fraud; he leads the reader to think what he owes to others is original. It is true that Seneca then goes on to describe the ideal case as one in which the debts are discernible, but transcended in the imaginative unity achieved out of many; nonetheless, the issue is a serious one.

Leaving for later the parallel between poetry and generation, and keeping in mind Seneca's use of the term *impressit* ("stamped"), for both writing and paternity, we may turn briefly to another important instance of the coin metaphor, placed by Dante to be conspicuously

parallel to the Malebolge; it occurs in his examination on faith by
St. Peter in *Paradiso* 24. After quoting and interpreting Heb. 10:1,
Dante is asked if he has faith in his purse:

> "Assai bene è trascorsa
> d'esta moneta già la lega e 'l peso;
>   ma dimmi se tu l'hai ne la tua borsa."
> Ond' io: Sì ho, sì lucida e sì tonda,
> che del suo conio nulla mi s'inforsa."

Paradiso 24.82–87

["The alloy and the weight of this money has flowed past very well; but
tell me if you have it in your purse." And I: "Yes I have, so bright and so
round that nothing brings its coinage into doubt."]

After Dante explains the basis of his Christian faith (the "large
rain" of the Holy Spirit on the Bible, the miracles, the conversion of
the world to Christianity), he is asked to confess "what he believes":

> "O santo padre, e spirito che vedi
> ciò che credesti sì, che tu vincesti
>   ver' lo sepulcro più giovani piedi,"
>   comincia' io, "tuo vuo' ch'io manifesti
> la forma qui del pronto creder mio,
> e anche la cagion di lui chiedesti. . . ."

Paradiso 24.124–29

["O holy father, spirit that see what you believed with such faith that you
surpassed younger feet to the tomb," I began, "you wish me to manifest here
the form of my belief, and you have also asked its cause. . . ."]

He then recites an expanded version of the first phrases of the Apos-
tle's Creed, concluding:

> "De la profonda condizion divina
> ch'io tocco mo, la menta mi sigilla
>   più volte l'evangelica dottrina.
>   Quest' è 'l principio, quest' è la favilla
> che si dilata in fiamma poi vivace,
> e come stella in cielo in me scintilla."

Paradiso 24.141–47

["About the *deep* condition of the divine on which I now touch, the teachings of the Gospels repeatedly seal my mind. This is the beginning, this is the spark that then dilates itself in livelier flame and scintillates in me like a star in the sky."]

The coinage metaphor permeates this entire passage, and there are many parallels with the terminology of fraud, as well as a number of allusions to Master Adam.[48] Faith is the coin of the realm, the toll for the passage to the Kingdom of Heaven. Dante cannot produce his faith directly, however, he can only produce statements about it. These are important, of course, insofar as for him the problem of faith is definable in terms of orthodoxy, the correct "form" of faith. The examination establishes that Dante can speak acceptably about his faith; St. Peter and the other blessed souls see the quality of Dante's faith in God as part of their vision of God: we must take their word for it.

So in a sense must Dante, for what is perhaps most striking about the coinage metaphor in this passage is that it represents Dante as estimating his own faith by what in the coin are externals: his coin of faith is "so bright and round that nothing brings its coinage into doubt" (or, "none brings its coinage into doubt")—it has the color of true gold and the full roundness of new minting. But as the reference to counterfeits, to doubtful coinage, serves to remind us, neither color nor imprint is a perfectly reliable criterion. The point is partly that Dante himself cannot be the one to guarantee what is by definition a gift of grace: only God can know it fully. There is a level on which Dante himself must take it on faith that he has faith. He lays claim to it, but it must be guaranteed by God.

I mentioned earlier that the streams of the Casentino which haunt Master Adam are infernal parallels to the clear stream of the Earthly Paradise and to the river of light of *Paradiso* 30. Dante refers to his confession here with another parallel:

> . . . mi volsi a Beatrice, ed essa pronte
> sembianze femmi perch' io spandessi
> l'acqua di fuor del mio interno fonte.

Paradiso 24.55-57

[I turned to Beatrice and she made prompt signs that I should pour forth the water of my internal fountain.]

The image of the fountain is parallel to the coin imagery also, for both express the sense of an inner boundary, from the other side of which the water wells up. The soul's experience of its own ground is necessarily mediated;[49] ultimately, Dante's inner fountain derives from the fountain of living waters under God's throne (Apoc. 22.1) and looks forward to the river of light in Canto 30.[50] God is both beyond and what is most internal to the soul: Paradise is both outside the world, beyond the *primo mobile,* and within it, as is made clear in Dante's vision of the nine orders of angels circling the point of infinite intension in *Paradiso* 28.[51]

III

In Nicholas of Oresme's explanation of the two aspects of a coin, imprint and material, there is no mention of a *valor impositus,* an "imposed value," conventional or legal. The true value of a coin is that of the material, and the function of the imprint is to vouch for the nature of the metal: "A figure is stamped on coins which, known to all, may signify the quality of the material of the coin and the truth of its weight, so that, all suspicion removed, the value of the coin may be known without trouble."[52] Coins bear the name of God or a saint, as well as the sign of the Cross, says Nicholas, in order to *testify,* "in testimonium veritatis monete in materia et pondere."[53] Aquinas speaks of the proper relation between signs and their meanings in almost identical terms. Truth is a relation of conformity either between things and the understanding or between *signa* and *signata.*[54] The problem of the essential arbitrariness of signs[55] is, in this view, less important than the problem of their misuse. For signs come into being, arbitrary or not, because of man's desire to express a meaning. Lying is wrong, then, because it violates the *natural relation* of signs to meaning, as well as the natural relation of trust among men, on which society is based.[56]

The idea of truth as a natural relation between signs and meaning is part and parcel of a conception of justice as analogous to the natural health of the human body. The metaphorics of the Malebolge appeal to these conceptions constantly. The poem also shows clearly that it is not possible to restore any simple or straightforward relation between *signa* and *signata*, or among men. Once death comes into the world, even the natural health of the body is only temporary and eventually gives way to mortality. This is true at every level. In the political realm, there is no possibility of Florence or any of the other communes being restored to right proportion; Florence is hydroptically swollen with "la gente nuova e i súbiti guadagni" (*Inferno* 16.73).[57] The Holy Roman Empire is a disastrous failure; Europe is drifting toward dynastic anarchy. Whatever is to save or reform the body politic will have to be something more than the body analogy enables one to imagine. The last *bolge* before the descent to the utter immobility of Cocito present the body politic as diseased and dismembered. In the Earthly Paradise, the just relation between flesh and spirit is no sooner reached than it is invaded and transcended before the political question can be asked. It is Beatrice who predicts the political future, and she does so in terms that are deliberately incomprehensible, where allegory has moved toward the extreme case of enigma.[58]

This is the limit case of the fact that the relation between signs and meanings in the *Commedia* is extremely complex and shifting, rather than simple and natural. The more complex it becomes, the more urgent becomes the question of the relation of Dante's poetry to the sin of fraud. Arachne, the Trojan Horse, Phalerus's bull, Master Adam's belly and his coining—these are all distorted versions of Dante's own enterprise. He represents them apotropaically, to encompass them and ward them off, to teach the reader to penetrate the colors and webs of fraudulent rhetoric, to read Dante's allegory, and to see (or at least to grant) the difference.

It is striking that Seneca says that in order to digest books we must give them our faithful assent, we must swallow them. Here again we find the metaphorics of knowledge closely associated with those of deception. The trickster cooks up his scheme, the victim swallows his story, and once the victim has swallowed the story, he is caught in it. The deceiver seeks to make the victim swallow what will then swallow the victim. This tropic reversal of container and thing contained pervades Dante's treatment of fraud, providing the retributive pattern: the spinner is caught in his own web, which turns out to be part of the larger web spun by the greater spider, Satan.[59]

How does the poet avoid the analogous danger? Poetry, too, has an integument and a nucleus; the poet, too, is a weaver of webs. The fundamental fictional assumption of the poem—that it represents God's judgments—is dangerously close to a lie.

At one level, Dante's answer would seem to be quite simple: the poet writes out of love, not out of malice; he actively seeks to provide nourishment, not poison. At this level, the problem is identical with that of the moral purification and straightening of the will. In the part of the *Purgatorio* which corresponds to the Malebolge— Cantos 19–27—we find the purification of avarice, gluttony, and lust. These vices must be overcome at the literal level, where they refer to literal riches, food, and sexuality. There is also a more figurative level, where they refer to spiritual wealth, food, and creativeness, and where distortion is equally possible. For the cantos develop the parallelism between the physical body and the soul's other modes of expression, especially poetry, and they contain Dante's most direct statements on his poetics.

There are countless parallels with the Malebolge. For instance, the avaricious, bound hand and foot, are immobile like the counterfeiters; Statius, who was readied for Christianity by the power of Virgil's poetry, is suddenly freed to walk about the circle, in direct contrast to Master Adam, who dreams vengefully of dragging himself an inch in a hundred years (*Inferno* 30.83). It is Statius who explains to Dante the metamorphoses of the human foetus in Canto 25.[60] While Virgil, Statius, and Dante are moving from the circle of gluttony to that of lust, Dante asks how it is possible for disembodied souls to grow thin:

> "Como si può far magro
> là dove uopo di nodrir non tocca?"

Purgatorio 25.20–21

["How can they become thin, where need of nourishment does not touch them?"]

Statius's reply takes us back to first principles, to the development of the foetus as governed by the formative power of the soul, to God's joining to the animal soul the rational. The point is the superiority of soul to body as principle of causality. That it is Statius and not Virgil who replies and that *Aeneid* 6.733 is echoed in lines 103–5, emphasizes that Dante is having Statius correct the Platonic-Stoic view that the body is the source of the perturbations of the soul;[61] rather, it is the soul itself whose affects are mirrored in the body and which must be purified. Statius then explains how the disembodied soul makes itself a body of air:

> "Tosto che loco lì la circunscrive,
> la virtù formativa raggia intorno
> così e quanto ne le membra vive.
>
>   E come l'aere, quand' è ben piorno,
> per l'altrui raggi che 'n sé si riflette,
> di diversi color diventa addorno;
>
>   così l'aere vicino si mette
> e in quella forma ch'è in lui suggella
> virtualmenta l'alma che ristette;
>
>   e simigliante poi a la fiammella
> che segue il foco là 'vunque si muta,
> segue lo spirto sua forma novella.
>
>   Però che quindi ha poscia sua paruta,
> è chiamata ombra; e quindi organa poi
> ciascun sentire infino a la veduta.
>
>   Quindi parliamo noi e quindi ridiam noi;
> quindi facciam le lagrime e ' sospiri
> che per lo monte aver sentiti puoi.
>
>   Secondo che ci affliggono i disiri
> e li altri affetti, l'ombra si figura;
> e quest' è la cagion di che tu miri."

Puragatorio 25.88–108

["As soon as place circumscribes it there, the formative power radiates in the same way and to the same degree as when in living members. And as the air, when it is very moist, is adorned with various colors by another's rays that it reflects in itself; so the soul puts on the air that is near it and by its own powers seals it with the form that is within it; and then, like the flame that follows the burning wherever it goes, so its new shape follows the spirit.

"Because it takes its appearance thence (from the soul), it is called a shade; thence it makes organs for every sense as far as sight. Thence we speak and thence we laugh; thence we make the tears and the sighs that you may have heard around the mountain. According as desires and other affects afflict us, the shade shapes itself; this is the cause about which you wonder."]

The discussion of embryology is, of course, relevant to the purification of lust, which we are now approaching; after he has passed the wall of flame, Dante will be ready to enter the Garden, which figures the reconciliation of spirit and flesh. But what for our purposes is particularly interesting about this passage is that the idea of the soul clothing itself ("si mette") with an airy body is a kind of transposition to the visible realm of speech, in which the soul imposes the form of words on the air by means of physical vibrations that cause radiating soundwaves.[62]

It would seem that for the disembodied, the transparent air offers no opacity to the expression of the soul, there seems to be no resistance inherent in the medium, as there is in the case both of the natural body and of actual speech. Deception is out of the question for these souls: their affects are directly mirrored. For the embodied, the situation is much more complex. The opacity of the body and of sounds makes possible deception both of oneself and of others: the pen may fail to follow the dictator:

"Ma dì s'i' veggio qui colui che fore
trasse le nove rime, cominciando
Donne che avete intelletto d'amore.'"
   E io a lui: "I' mi son un che, quando
Amor mi spira, noto, e a quel modo
ch'e' ditta dentro vo significando."
   "O frate, issa vegg' io," diss' elli, "il nodo
che 'l Notaro e Guittone e me ritenne
di qua dal dolce stil novo ch'i' odo!

Io veggio ben come le vostre penne
di retro al dittator sen vanno strette,
che de le nostre certo non avvenne;

    e qual più a gradir oltre si mette,
non vede più da l'uno a l'altro stilo";
e, quasi contentato, si tacette.

Purgatorio 25.49-63

["But tell me if I see here him who brought forth the new rhymes, beginning, *'Ladies who have understanding of love.'*"

And I to him: "I am in myself one who, when Love breathes in me, take
note, and in that manner that he dictates within I go signifying."

"Oh, brother, from here I see," he said, "the knot that held back the
Notary and Guittone and me from this side of the sweet new style that I
hear! I see well how your pens follow closely after the dictator, which certainly did not happen with ours; and whoever most tries to go beyond will
not see any other difference between the two styles"; and, as if contented, he
fell silent.]

As Dante represents the problematic of poetic inspiration here, it
has two phases, each involving the boundary between inner and outer,
each with its troubling similarity with deception. On the one hand,
there is the striving to receive, to hear the dictation of Love ("quan-
do/Amor mi spira, noto"). How is the poet to know that it is Love?
If this inspiration comes from beyond, it will always come veiled.
The poet will have to recognize it through its veils, as he recognizes
Beatrice in the Earthly Paradise, "sanza di li occhi aver più cono-
scenza" (*Purgatorio* 30.37). As we have already seen, for Dante the soul
inhabits the body as its container; in relation to the ground of its
existence, the soul is itself a kind of container [63] into which the
waters rise or the spirit breathes. The soul is always seeking to penetrate the veil of the external world or to penetrate further inward.
The collocation of this passage with the purification of gluttony indicates that the harkening after the dictation of Love must be a constant discipline: it must be Love that is heard, not some other motive.

The other phase is that of outward expression, the making of
signs, which must follow the internal melody ("e a quel modo/
ch'e' ditta dentro vo significando").[64] Here again the reversal of

inner and outer takes place, perhaps in a more obvious way. The poet must calculatingly and knowingly fashion the poetic sign from above and from outside; yet at the same time he must breathe life into from within, for the process is parallel to nature's art in the foetus and to God's breathing into it the living spirit (*Purgatorio* 24.70–74). The poet must speak through the poem as an extension of his own body.

Dante's central metaphors for poetry, as for fraud, derive from the two chief vital functions of the body, nutrition and generation, because for him man is a sign-making animal by the same token that he is an embodied spirit. The problematic of the sign is for him inseparable from that of the body; in fact, it is contained within it. Body metaphors are involved in all levels of spiritual activity. Nourishment and generation are also, of course, two chief modes of exchange between the inside of the body and the outer world, and Hell and Purgatory are differentiated by being associated with what is returned to the outer world in the two functions: Hell is the belly that produces shit; Purgatory, the belly that produces new life.[65] Furthermore, the various models of the larger unity of humanity— the body of Satan, the body politic, the Body of Christ—are all patterns in which individuals are contained as organs in larger structures they only partly know. In these larger structures, as Dante saw, we are each allegorized beyond our knowledge and perhaps against our wills, contained by our limitations and by our devices. Nowhere is this more evident than in the activity of interpretation: the meta-allegorical is a further allegory; the interpreter must always make a choice; and his interpretation is itself an allegory of his motives,[66] visible to those who can read.

If Dante's allegory insists on the continuity of the verbal sign with the body, if it consists very largely in articulating ways in which the bodies of others are inscribed with their relation to the whole, the converse is that it is necessary for him to engage in the poem, as fully as possible, his relation to his own body. This is the case in many ways, some perhaps rather obvious and, at first glance, not very different in Dante from other poets. If the poem represents Dante's relation to his language, we must take account of his insistence on the bodily aspect of language. He never tires of speaking of poetry as representing the poet's *voice*. The gift of poetry is rooted in physical expressiveness.

Dante must engage his own body in the poem in another, quite literal way. The poem has a physical existence; it must be physically written down, and it is long. The process of composition (digestion and gestation) takes Dante's best efforts for many years; it is physically exhausting.

Furthermore, Dante speaks in the first person in the poem, and he thus acknowledges a responsibility to account for his bodily existence within the poem.[67] His practical circumstances are therefore clearly identified.[68] So, too, in general terms, is the state of his body. In one of the most important expressions of his yearning to return to Florence, Dante hopes that the poem will win over the cruelty that excludes him. The poem, he remarks, has been making him thin for many years, "m'ha fatto per molti anni macro" (*Paradiso* 25.3). This is in part a penitential thinness, like that of Forese and the others purging gluttony (*Purgatorio* 23–24); it guarantees that the poet is not a Master Adam. It is still possible, however, that the writing of the poem is exhausting Dante in a fuller and more dangerous sense. While it is true that Dante's conception of his poetic inspiration shows him, like Augustine, yearning for God as what is most deeply internal to himself, there is also the sense in which God remains for Dante, terrifyingly, the radically Other. The body is mortal, and death approaches. Short of the grave, one is never done with the baffling difficulty of dealing with the body. Resurrection is a cardinal tenet of the faith, but in the meantime Dante must deal with harsher experiences.

One of the most moving and revealing occurrences of the idea of eating in the *Commedia* occurs early in Dante's interview with Cacciaguida, when his ancestor predicts his exile:

> "Tu lascerai ogne cosa diletta
> più caramente; e questo è quello strale
> che l'arco de lo essilio pria saetta.
>
> Tu proverai sì come sa di sale
> lo pane altrui, e come è duro calle

lo scendere e 'l salir per l'altrui scale. . . ."

Paradiso 17.55–60

["You will leave everything you love most dearly; and this is the arrow which the bow of exile shoots first. You will experience how salty the bread of another tastes and what a harsh path it is to go down and go up another's stairway. . . ."]

This is part of the supposedly literal passage for which Dante expresses his gratitude to Cacciaguida, but it is striking that we find here some of the fundamental metaphors of the poem: arrow, stairway, bread. These motifs underlie all three *cantiche:* they account for principles of motion, for hierarchical stepwise arrangement, for the possibility of direction, for value, for the value of poetry. Exile, the state of being outside the native container, will, says Cacciaguida, embitter all these literal aspects of life. If the literal stairways leading to the presence of the powerful are harsh, if the literal bread they give is salty with tears, there is no longer any simple up and down or any simple, merely natural relation to food. The same is true at the figurative level: Dante has no direct and simple relation to his poem or to its major symbols. The hierarchical universe and the Bread of the Angels remain at some important level the stairway of the Other and the bread of the Other.

There can be no simple compensatory reversal of the outward bitterness of life into inner sweetness for Dante. The disasters, public and private, are so intense that Dante can only live by attempting to digest them into the poem; there is no being done with them. The inner boundary, too, remains; life in the body is lived on the frontier between ultimate inner reality and the outer world. Dante dare not allow the poem to become a mere self-indulgence, a saving only of himself, his own private honeycomb. He must adopt the amazing and arrogant role of prophet and attempt to change the world. He must give his genius its full scope, make all his genius manifest, pretend to speak for God, risk egomania.

The more serious and ambitious the poem becomes, then, as Dante's effort to understand the nature of his historical moment, to digest the experience of his own life and his own time, the more agonizingly ambiguous and difficult becomes the problem of the relation between allegory and deceit. Within the poem, everything that is said to lie beyond the two boundaries of the world, the outer and the inner, is made up, is a fiction. Has the faith become a fiction? One ultimate difference Dante clearly hopes exists between his poetic enterprise and that of the deceivers of Malebolge is that, whereas the deceiver is mystified in supposing he can escape implication in his own act, can remain manipulatively external to his web, Dante sees and accepts the impossibility of this. He sees and represents the difficult ambiguity of the relation between his poem and the infernal deceits; he points out the critical difficulty of knowing when he writes from love and when from other motives; he understands the necessity for the weaver always to be on guard against being trapped in his own web. Ultimately, that is what must occur; Dante must knowingly abandon himself to the poem, pour his energies into it, allow himself to be contained and defined by it. He must accept the duality of bodily existence and entrust to the poem— and to those who were to come after—both his claim to be writing out of love and his death.

NOTES

1. See my "'Io son venuto': Seneca, Plato, and the Microcosm," *Dante Studies* 93 (1975): 95–129, and "Farinata and the Body of Christ," *Stanford Italian Review* (forthcoming). C. Fumagalli, "Poesia addominale di Malebolge," *Annali dell'Istituto di studi danteschi* 1 (1967): 359–72, perceptively discusses the frequent references to the belly in the Malebolge, but apparently does not see their rationale.

2. For this traditional notion, see Augustine's *De genesi ad litteram* 11.24.31–25.32 (*P.L.* 34, 457–58); cf. *Enarr. in Ps.* 139.7 (in vss. 5–6), 13 (in vs. 10). On Augustine's doctrine of the Church as the body of Christ, see his *Commentaire de la première épître de S. Jean,* ed. Paul Agaesse (Paris: Les Editions du Cerf, 1961), pp. 87–95.

3. As a general description, one could say that Purgatory renews, straightens out God's image in the body as well as in the soul, and that Paradise is conceived as a kind of growing up into the Head of the Mystical Body.

4. Perhaps the fullest discussion of the idea is in Augustine's commentary on John 6 (*P.L.* 33, 1958–96).

5. "Et ego, fratres, non potui vobis loqui quasi spiritualibus, sed quasi carnalibus. Tanquam parvulis in Christo, lac vobis potum dedi, non escam: nondum enim poteratis." (vss. 1–2). The idea is also a commonplace in the medieval *artes poeticae*; see below, notes 13 and 22. Bernard of Clairvaux begins his series of sermons on the Song of Songs by quoting this

passage and developing the parallel between breaking bread (an allusion to the words of consecration in the Mass, "Et accepto pane gratias egit, et fregit, et dedit eis, dicens: Hoc est corpus meum, quod pro vobis datur: hoc facite in meam commemorationem," Luke 22:19) and "opening," that is, interpreting, a text. I leave largely out of consideration that other food of the soul, justice: "Beati qui esuriunt et sitiunt justitiam: quoniam ipsi saturabuntur" (Matt. 5:6), which also figures largely in the *Commedia.*

6. The examples are, respectively, from Ovid, Cato, and Suetonius. C. T. Lewis and C. Short, *A Latin Dictionary* (1879; reprint ed., Oxford: Clarendon Press, 1969), pp. 576–77.

7. *De inv.* 1.30.49.

8. *Inst. Orat.* 1.2.37.

9. Unless otherwise identified, all translations are my own.

". . . nos quoque has apes debemus imitari et quaecumque ex diversa lectione congessimus separare (melius enim distincta servantur), deinde adhibita ingenii nostra cura et facultate in unum saporem varia illa libamenta confundere. . . . Quod in corpore nostro videmus sine ullo opere nostro facere naturam (alimenta quae accepimus, quamdiu in sua qualitate perdurant et solida innatant stomacho, onera sunt; at cum ex eo quod erant mutata sunt, tunc demum in vires et sanguinem transeunt), idem in his quibus aluntur ingenia praestemus, ut quaecumque hausimus non patiamur integra esse, ne aliena sit. Concocquamus illa; alioqui in memoriam ibunt, non in ingenium. Adsentiamur illis fideliter ac nostra faciamus, ut unum quiddam fiat ex multis." (*Ad Lucilium epistolae morales,* ed. L. D. Reynolds [Oxford: Oxford University Press, 1965], p. 286). Seneca is, of course, drawing on the famous passages in *Aeneid* 1 and *Georgics* 4 where the bees are represented as an ideal commonwealth. For the continuation of the passage, see below, note 46.

10. *Convivio* 1.1.

11. The point is a traditional one, from Aristotle's *De gen. et corrupt.* onward.

12. I quote from Petrocchi's critical text, as reprinted in *La Divina Commedia,* ed. C. H. Grandgent, rev. C. S. Singleton (Cambridge: Harvard University Press, 1972).

13. This is a familiar topos, for instance in the medieval *artes poeticae:* Evrard l'Allemand writes in the *Laborintus* (ed. E. Faral, *Les arts poétiques du xie et xiie siècle,* fasc. 238 [1924; reprint ed., Paris: Bibliothèque de l'École des hautes études, 1958], p. 341): "Florent palpones, quorum sub melle venenum Lingua parit, miseros proditione premit" (lines 115 f.); cf. lines 891 ff.: "Decipiunt multi natura vulpis iniquae. In ficta fabricant simplicitate dolos. Angelicum vultum praetendunt daemonis artem Occultant, fraudis ebrietate fluunt. Limum sub gemma, sub melle tegunt aconita, Spinam sub flore, sub speculoque lutum."

14. I cite the *Philosophiae Consolatio,* ed. Ludwig Bieler, C. C. 94 (Turnhold: Brepols, 1957).

15. The terms of Dante's antithesis are significantly different from the pair *poison-drug* investigated with brilliant results in Plato's *Phaedrus* by Jacques Derrida ("La pharmacie de Platon," in *La dissémination* [Paris: Editions du Seuil, (1972)], as the rest of this essay will attempt to show.

16. See Aristotle, *De part. anim.* 2.1 (647a), trans. as *Parts of Animals* by A. L. Peck (Cambridge: Harvard University Press, 1968), pp. 115–17: "The faculties of sensation and of motion and of nutrition are situated in one and the same part of the body. . . . In blooded animals this part is the heart. . . . [The viscera] are all composed of the same material . . . and this is because they are situated upon the channels of the blood-vessels and on the points of ramification. All these viscera (excluding the heart) may be compared to the mud which a running stream deposits; they are as it were deposits left by the current of blood in the blood-vessels. As for the heart itself, since it is the starting-point of the blood-vessels and contains the substance (*dynamis*) by which the blood is first fashioned, it is only to be expected that it will itself be composed out of that form of nutriment which it originates."

17. Since the Malebolge are the belly of Hell, one would expect references to the river system of Hell, particularly since in the circle of violence there are so many clear references to the bloodstream and to the physiology of the heart, conceived along Aristotelian lines.

18. The notion of fraud as particularly liable to be caught in its own engines is also a commonplace; Geoffroi of Vinsauf writes in the *Poetria nova,* for instance (ed. Faral, *Les arts poétique du xie et xiie siècle,* p. 202): "qui damnum Intulit in simili damno stetit. Ultio digna Fraudis in auctorem simili pede fraude reversa" (lines 170-72).

19. Avicenna, *Liber Canonis,* Reprographischer Nachdruck der Ausgabe Venedig 1507 (Hildesheim: Georg Olms, 1964), ff.300r-305v; Averroes, *Liber Colliget,* in *Opera Aristotelis cum Averrois Commentariis,* Venetiis apud Junctas, 1562-74 (Frankfurt: Minerva, 1962), *Supplementum* 1, ff. 1-174.

20. Gianfranco Contini, "Sul xxx dell'*Inferno,*" *Paragone* (August 1953); now in *Varianti e altra linguistica* (Turin: Einandi, 1970), pp. 447-57.

21. Contini writes: "Bartolomeo Anglico, nel vii del *De proprietatibus rerum,* premesso che nell'idropisia *"virtus digestiva degneratur in epate"* (e il vocabolo e ripetuto assai spesso), individua una variante, la timpanite, così chiamata *"quod ad modum tympani sonat venter,"* nella quale *"extenditur venter et sonat sicut tympanum,"* *"collum et extrema efficiuntur gracilia,"* le sete si fa ardente. Il *"leppo,"* l' *"arsura,"* il "capo che ti duole" sono da loro parte, presso il medesimo trattatista, sintomi della *"febris putrida"* (distinta dall *"effimera"* e dall' *"ethica"*): *"dolor capitis, malicia anhelitus, sitis et similia"* (Ibid., p. 455).

22. Alfred Bassermann, in *Deutches Dantejahrbuch* n. F., 5, 179 ff.: cited by Contini, "Sul xxx dell'*Inferno,*" p. 451 n. 1, and p. 455. See also E. R. Curtius, *European Literature and the Latin Middle Ages,* trans. Willard Trask (New York, 1953), pp. 134 ff., 280 f. The passage from Alanus is in T. Wright, *The Anglo-Latin Poets* (London, 1872), 2: 489.

23. It is mentioned by the *Chiose anonime*; see G. Biagi et al., *La Divina Commedia nella figurazione artistica e nel secolare commento* (Turin: UTET, 1933), 1: 714.

24. Gregory the Great, *Moralia in Job* (*P.L.* 75, 441, 478; cf. Rhabanus Maurus, *P.L.* 112, 953, 1088; Bernard of Clairvaux, *P.L.* 183, 106).

25. So Iacopo della Lana: "Questo pone l'Autore per alegoria, che sì come lo soperchio di xxj carrati fino a la fineza del zusto fiorino è metallo infermo e male digesto, cussì in parte di quisti appar umore mal digesto e infermo . . ." (Biagi, *La Divina Commedia*).

26. The dogmatic Aristotelians, such as Averroes, and European adapters of Averroes, such as Albertus Magnus, attacked Galen's theories whenever they departed from Aristotle's, as when Galen sided with Plato in locating the power of nutrition in the liver or the rational soul in the brain.

27. In what follows, I draw mainly on Aristotle's *De partibus animalium,* with occasional reference to Galen's *De usu partium* and *De naturalibus facultatibus*; see Charles Singer, *A Short History of Anatomy and Physiology from the Greeks to Harvey* (New York: Dover, 1957); C. Singer and E. Underwood, *A Short History of Medicine,* 2nd ed. (New York: Oxford University Press, 1962); R. E. Siegel, *Galen's System of Physiology and Medecine* (New York: Karner, 1968). Dante seems to have depended mainly on the works of Aristotle and of such popularizers as Albertus Magnus. I have not found any evidence that Dante had any interest in Galen, whose work was available in translations by Gerard of Cremona and William of Moerbecke.

28. See *De part. anim.,* 2.646a-650b; Galen, *On the Usefulness of Parts of the Body,* trans. Margaret T. May (Ithaca: Cornell University Press, 1968), 2: 204-77.

29. For the practice of minting in Dante's day, see M. Bernocchi, *Le monete della repubblica fiorentina* 4 vols. (Florence: Olschki, 1974-76); see also R. Bogaert, "Geld (Geldwirtschaft)," *Reallexikon für Antike und Christentum* (Stuttgart: Hiersemann, 1950-); A. E. Monroe, *Monetary Theory before Adam Smith* (Boston: Houghton Mifflin, 1923); J. Gil-

christ, *The Church and Economic Activity in the Middle Ages* (London: St. Martin's Press, 1969).

30. Thus the phrase "l'epa croia" (line 102) would be technically precise. See Francesco da Buti's gloss: " . . . converte il fegato in nutrimento delle membra, imperò che parte dell'umore va al fegato e quivi si converte in sangue, e di sangue in carne; ma nell'idropico non si fa siffatta conversione, ma si converte in acqua" (Biagi, *La Divina Commedia,* 1.714).

31. Contini ("Sul xxx dell'*Inferno*," p. 452) cites the parallel with the parable of Dives and Lazarus (Luke 16:24), noted by Cian and Cesari, as well as with Virgil's *Eclogue* 10.42. In a paper written as a graduate student, Ronald L. Martinez pointed out the important relation between the *acqua marcia* of Master Adam's belly and the living waters of John 7: 37-38: "Si quis sitit, veniat ad me et bibat. Qui credit in me, sicut dicit Scriptura, flumina de ventre eius fluent aquae vivae" (see H. Rahner, "Flumina de ventre eius: Die patristische Auslegung von Joh. 7, 37-38," *Biblica* 22 [1941]: 269-302, 367-403).

32. *De naturalibus quaestionibus* 3.5 (ed. P. Oltramare, 2nd. ed., 2 vols [Paris: Les belles lettres, 1961]: "Placet natura regi terram, et quidem ad nostrorum corporum exemplar, in quibus et venae sunt et arteriae, illae sanguinis, hae spiritus receptacula. In terra quoque sunt alia itinera per quae aqua, alia per quae spiritus currit; ideoque ad similitudinem illa humanorum corporum natura formavit ut maiores nostri aquarum appellaverint venas." For Dante's interest in the *Natural Questions,* see Durling, " 'Io son venuto': Seneca, Plato, and the Microcosm."

33. Heinrich Gambel, *Die Fabel "Vom Magen und den Gliedern" in der Weltliteratur, (Zeitschrift für romanische Philologie,* Beiheft 80 [1934]); Wilhelm Nestle, "Die Fabel des Memenius Agrippa," *Klio* 21 (1927): 350-56; R. M. Ogilvie, *A Commentary on Livy. Books 1-5* (Oxford: Oxford University Press, 1965), pp. 312-59.

34. See Leonard Barkan's *Nature's Work of Art. The Human Body as Image of the Cosmos* (New Haven: Yale University Press, 1975), pp. 69-75.

35. Even in his poetic version of the fable (*P.L.* 199, 1005), which follows Livy closely in other respects, John of Salisbury inserts a sermon against gluttony. The members are rebelling against a swollen and excessively heavy belly—it is "turgidus." In a long speech, the tongue not only complains of the belly's insatiability, asserting that man should live for reason rather than for food, but also lists the many crimes committed for the sake of the belly, its own being sedition and fraud.

36. "Est autem res publica, sicut Plutarcho placet, corpus quoddam, quod divini muneris beneficio animatur et summae aequitatis agitur nutu et regitur quodam moderamine rationis. Ea uero quae cultum religionis in nobis instituunt et informant, et Dei (ne secundum Plutarchum deorum dicam) cerimonias tradunt, vicem animae in corpore rei publicae obtinent. . , . Princeps uero capitis in re publica obtinet locum uni subjectus Deo et his qui vices illius agunt in terris, quoniam et in humano corpore, ab anima uegetatur caput et regitur. . . . Cordis locum senatus optinet, a quo bonorum operum et malorum procedunt initia. . . . Oculorum aurium et linguae offici sibi uindicant judices et presides prouinciarum. . . . Quaestores et commentarienses (non illos dico qui carceribus praesunt, sed comites rerum privatarum) ad uentris et intestinorum refert imaginem. Quae, si immensa auiditate congesserint et congesta tenacius reseruauerint, innumerabiles et incurabiles generant morbos, ut uitio eorum totius corporis ruina immineat. . . . Pedibus uero solo iugiter inhaerentibus agricolae coaptantur." *Policraticus* 5.2, ed. C. Webb (Oxford: Oxford University Press, 1909), 1: 540-41.

37. "Si enim reficiantur avidius et minus digerant, generant morbos aut incurabiles aut difficiles. Impossibile siquidem est quemquam justitiam et pecuniam sequi." *Policraticus,* ed. Webb, 1: 562. See also H. Liebeschutz, *Medieval Humanism in the Life and Writings of John of Salisbury,* Warburg Studies 17 (London: Warburg Institute, 1950), pp. 23-26,

43-44; Liebeschutz considers John's entire treatment to be based on Robertus Pullus's lectures in Paris.

38. "Sicut enim corpus male disponitur, quando humores excessive fluunt ad unum eius membrum, ita quod illud membrum sepe ex hoc inflammatur et nimium ingrossatur, reliquis exsiccatis et nimis attenuatis, tolliturque debita proporcio, neque tale corpus potest diu vivere; ita conformiter est de communitate vel regno, quando diviciae ab una ipsius parte attrahuntur ultra modum," _The De moneta of Nicholas Oresme and English Mint Documents,_ trans. Charles Johnson (London: Nelson, 1956), p. 43. Nicholas goes on to compare an excessively rich prince to a gigantically swollen head. Nicholas is repeating well-established precepts; see essentially the points made by Aquinas in his _De regimine principum_ (1266), which of course draws heavily on John of Salisbury. See _Divi Thomae Aquinatis Opuscula philosophica,_ ed. R. M. Spiazzi (Turin: Marietti, 1954), pp. 283-84, 900-902.

39. Nicholas explains that when the alloy of a currency is debased (and 21 carats for 24 was historically the prevalent mode), the heavier coins tend to be hoarded or taken out of the realm; they were often melted down and sold as gold, their face value now being less than their weight value (Johnson, _The De moneta of Nicholas Oresme,_ pp. 25-32). Aquinas condemns devaluation in similar terms (_De regime principum,_ p. 902). For a suggestive discussion of the notion of inflation of currency in relation to Chaucer's poetry, see Eugene Vance, "Chaucer's _House of Fame_ and the Poetics of Inflation," _Boundary_ 2, 6 (1979).

40. _De unitate Ecclesiae,_ 5.9.

41. The quarrel between Master Adam and Sinon is also parallel to Beatrice's confrontation of Dante with his past disloyalties in _Purgatorio_ 31. At the end of this section I shall discuss the parallels with Dante's examination on faith in _Paradiso_ 24.

42. In having the blows directed to face and belly, Dante is referring to the structure of the counterfeit coin (a just face imprinted on distempered gold—parallel to the spatialization of the process of fraud in the figure of Geryon), as well as to the Trojan Horse, on which see below. When he says, "'l viso non risponde a la ventraia" (line 54), Dante could almost be quoting such classic definitions of fraud as Aquinas, for example, _Summa theol._ 2a 2ae, Q. 111, art. 2: "Mala ergo intentio in hypocrisi consideratur sicut signatum, quod non respondet signo." See below, notes 54 and 56.

43. This is the view developed in Statius' account of human reproduction in _Purgatorio_ 25. 37-48.

44. _Politics_ 1.10, 1258a-b.

45. "'Equo ne credite, Teucri./quidquid id est, timeo Danaos et dona ferentis./sic fatus validis ingentem viribus hastam/in latus inque feri curvam compagibus alvum/contorsit. stetit illa tremens, uteroque recusso/insonuere cavae gemitumque dedere cavernae" (_Aen._ 2.49-53).

46. "Hoc faciat animus noster: omnia quibus est adiutus abscondat, ipsum tantum ostendat quod effecit. Etiam si cuius in te comparabit similitudo quem admiratio tibi altius fixerit, similem esse te volo quomodo filium, non quomodo imaginem: imago res mortua est. 'Quid ergo? non intellegetur cuius imiteris orationem? cuius argumentationem? cuius sententias?' Puto aliquando ne intellegi quidem posse, si magni vir ingenii omnibus quae ex quo voluit exemplari traxit formam suam impressit, ut in unitatem illa conpetant" (_Ep. moral._ 84.7-8, pp. 286-87).

47. Guinizelli's reply to Dante is closely related: "Ed elli a me: 'Tu lasci tal vestigio,/per quel ch'i' odo, in me, e tanto chiaro,/che Lete nol può torre né far bigio' " _Purgatorio_ 26.106-8). The notion of the memory as a belly figures prominently in Augustine's discussion in book 10 of the _Confessions,_ for instance 10.8.13, "ineffabiles sinus eius" (ed. G. Cappello [Milan: Marietti, 1948], p. 344); cf. "Ibi sunt omnia distincte generatimque servata quae adita _ingesta_ sunt" (ibid.); "Nec ea tamen videndo _absorbui_" (10.8.15: 346); and

esp. 10.14.21: "Nimirum ergo memoria, quasi venter est animi; laetitia vero atque tristi-tia quasi cibus dulcis et amarus, quando memoriae commendantur, quasi traeiecta in ven-trem recondi illic possunt, sapere non possunt" (pp. 352-53). Augustine's other metaphors for the memory include fields, palace, cave, treasure house.

48. Line 85 echoes the terminology of *Inferno* 11.54 ("quel che fidanza non imborsa"); *Inferno* 11.49 and 11.89 refer to God's justice as like the act of coining: it "seals with its sign" (*suggella/del segno suo*) and "hammers" (*martella*). Master Adam is alluded to, espe-cially in the terms *lega* and *peso* in line 84 (for *peso*, cf. *Inferno* 30.83-84) and in the ref-erence to doubt of the minting in line 87. *Hammering* on an anvil is mentioned again in line 102, *enclosing* in line 98, *sealing* in line 143.

49. This is also the Augustinian theme of "Nescio unde venerim huc," *Conf.* 1.6.7; see be-low, note 51.

50. As it looks back to Master Adam's *standing water* and the streams of the Earthly Paradise; see above, note 31.

51. Dante is sharply aware of the Augustinian meditation on containers and contained: "Et quomodo invocabo Deum meum. . . ? Quoniam utique in me ipsum eum invocabo, cum invocabo eum. Et quis locus est in me, quo veniat in me Deus meus, quo Deus veniat in me, *Deus qui fecit coelum et terram*? Itane, Domine Deus meus, est quicquam in me, quod capiat te? An vero coelum et terra, quae fecisti et in quibus me fecisti, capiunt te?

"An quia sine te non esset quidquid est, fit ut quidquid est capiat te? Quoniam itaque et ego sum, quid peto ut venias in me, qui non essem, nisi esses in me? Non enim ego iam in inferis et tamen etiam ibi es; nam si et si *descendero in infernum, ades*. Non ergo essem, non omnino essem, Deus meus, nisi esses in me. An potius non essem, nisi essem in te, *ex quo omnia, per quem omnia, in quo omnia*? Etiam sic, Domine, etiam sic. Quo te invoco, cum in te sim, aut unde venias in me? Quo enim recedam extra coelum et terram, ut inde in me veniat Deus meus, qui dixit: *Coelum et terram ego impleo*?

"Capiunt ergo te coelum et terra, quoniam tu imples ea? An imples et restat, quoniam non te capiunt? Et quo refundis quidquid, impleto coelo et terra, restat ex te? An non opus habes ut a quoquam continearis, qui contines omnia, quoniam quae imples, continendo imples? Non enim vasa, quae te plena sunt, stabilem te faciunt, quia etsi frangantur, non effunderis et cum effunderis super nos, non tu iaces, sed erigis nos nec tu dissiparis, sed colligis nos" (*Conf.* 1.2-3).

52. " . . . in eis imprimeretur figura que cunctis notoria significat qualitatem materie numismatis et ponderis veritatem, ut amota suspicione posset valor monete sine labore cognosci" (Johnson, *The De moneta of Nicholas Oresme*, p. 10). The point is from Aris-totle *Politics* 1.9.1256b.

53. Johnson, *The De moneta of Nicholas Oresme*, p. 22. Nicholas (p. 14) explicitly recog-nizes that counterfeit coins can have the same color and imprint as genuine ones.

54. "Veritas . . . est . . . aequalitas quaedam intellectus vel signi ad rem intellectam et sig-nificatam . . . ille qui dicit verum profert aliqua signa conformia rebus" (*Summa theol.* 2a 2ae, Q. 109, art. 1). "Mendacio autem est malum ex genere: Est enim actus cadens super in-debitam materiam: cum enim voces sunt signa naturaliter intellectuum, innaturale est et in-debitum quod aliquis voce significat id quod non habet in mente" (Q. 110, art. 3).

55. In *Paradiso* 26, Adam acknowledges the essential arbitrariness of verbal signs: "Opera naturale è ch'uom favella;/ma così o così, natura lascia/poi fare a voi secondo che v'abbel-la" (lines 130-32).

56. "Dicendum quod quia homo est animal sociale, naturaliter unus homo debet alteri id sine quo societas humana conservari non posset. Non enim possent homines ad invicem con-vivere nisi sibi invicem crederent, tanquam sibi invicem veritatem manifestantibus" (*Summa theol.* 2a 2ae, Q. 109, art. 3).

57. Cacciaguida's account of the gradual decadence of Florence as resulting from its exceeding its early narrow bounds provides a parallel not only with *Inferno* 16, but also with Master Adam himself (*Paradiso* 16.34–154; see esp. lines 67–69: "Sempre la confusion de le persone / principio fu del mal de la cittade, / come del vostro il cibo che s'appone." *Confusione* is literally *melting together.*)

58. For *aenigma* as the extreme form of allegory, see Quintilian *Inst. Orat.* 8,6,14.

59. Seen from above, the plan of the Malebolge resembles a great spider web, as well as the intestines. Dante refers to Arachne in *Inferno* 17.18; she was, of course, a well established figure for the Devil: "Araigne note le dyable, Qui ne cesse de ses las tendre Pour les gens engignier et prendre, Si com l'iraigne ses las tent" (*Ovide moralisé*, 6.917–21). Along with the antithesis between food and poison in the *Commedia* is that between spider and bee.

60. My former student Ronald Martinez is preparing a detailed analysis of the parallels between Statius's account of the foetus and the metamorphoses of *Inferno* 24–25.

61. "Hinc metuunt cupiuntque, dolentque gaudentque, neque auras / dispiciunt clausae tenebris et carcere caeco" (*Aen.* 6.733–34) was quoted prominently in *Inferno* 10.58–59. See P. Courcelle, "Interprétations néo-platonisantes du livre vi de l'*Enéide*," *Entretiens sur l'Antiquité classique. Recherches sur la tradition platonicienne* 3 (1955): 93–136, esp. 111–15; cf. *De civ. Dei* 14.3.

62. There is thus an important parallel with the struggle of the souls of the false counselors to master the tongues of flame with which they must speak: *Inferno* 26.85–90, 27.7–18.

63. See above, note 51.

64. Latin *modus* means both measure and melody; the ambiguity is surely intended and looks forward to the melody that precedes the procession of *Purgatorio* 29.

65. Hence the parallelism between the passageways in the rock of the Mountain of Purgatory and the troughs of the Malebolge.

66. In the *Inferno,* the theme of interpretation—and misinterpretation—is especially prominent in the cantos of Paolo and Francesca (5), Cavalcante and Farinata (10), Ugolino (32), all of whom misuse and misinterpret texts, ranging from a book (5), to Dante's "ebbe," (10), to a prophetic dream and the promise of salvation; in these and other cases (such as Master Adam's disregarded streams), we watch the character failing to grasp the allegory offered him and therefore doomed to act out the allegory of his own negative intention.

67. In the first book of the *Convivio,* as part of his explanation for writing the *Convivio* in the vernacular, Dante speaks of his gratitude to his native language, for it was through it his parents were joined together and he was begotten (1.13).

68. Cf. Giuseppe Mazzotta, *Dante, Poet of the Desert* (Princeton: Princeton University Press, 1979). "The prophet, for Dante, is one who is engaged in *reading* the signs of the times and who, sustained by faith, bears witness to his own words with the reality of his life" (p. 299); "If Christ is the Word made flesh, Francis, stripped of clothes and wounded in the flesh, makes his own body into a word, a text in which the signs, literally inscribed on the flesh, *are* their own unambiguous allegorical meaning and reenact Christ's life" (p. 301). Dante must die into the poem, in this view, in imitation of Christ.

Michael Fried

Representing Representation:
On the Central Group in Courbet's *Studio*

In the space of just a few months in the winter of 1854/55, the most gifted and controversial French painter of his generation, Gustave Courbet, made an enormous picture that ranks with Velásquez's *Maids of Honor* and Vermeer's *Artist in His Studio* as one of the three supreme representations of representation in Western art. Courbet called his picture *The Painter's Studio, real allegory, summing up a phase of seven years in my artistic life* (fig. 1).[1] He hoped to exhibit it, along with a number of other works, in the Exposition Universelle des Beaux-Arts to be held in Paris later in 1855, but the official jury rejected the *Studio* along with another very large painting, the *Burial at Ornans,* which he considered central to his achievement; and rather than submit tamely to what seemed to him a brutal affront, he resolved to hold a counter-exhibition devoted solely to his art in a temporary structure built, at his expense, as near to the Exposition Universelle as he could get. Characteristically, Courbet expected to draw vast crowds and, at twenty sous a head, to make a financial killing while embarrassing the government. In these expectations he was of course disappointed: by all accounts attendance at his Pavillon du Réalisme was sparse, so that far from coming out flush he ended up taking a loss.

Although the painting at the heart of these events was actually done in a makeshift studio in Courbet's native town of Ornans, the studio it depicts is the one he occupied on the rue Hautefeuille in Paris from the late 1840s until 1871. The composition comprises roughly thirty figures divided, to a casual glance, into three more or less distinct groups: on the left, an assortment of figures who traditionally have been seen as representing various general types rather than specific individuals, for example, a Jew, a *curé,* a veteran of 1793, a huntsman, an undertaker's mute, a destitute Irishwoman nursing an infant, and so on; on the right, a number of persons who for the most part are identifiable as friends and supporters of the artist, in-

Figure 1. Courbet, *The Painter's Studio,* 1854–55. Paris, Louvre. Photo Musées nationaux.

cluding Baudelaire (seated reading at the far right), Proudhon, Champfleury, Max Buchon, and Alfred Bruyas (Courbet's chief patron); and, in the middle of the canvas, Courbet himself seated painting a landscape before the attentive gazes of a naked woman and a peasant boy.

The full title of the *Studio* and especially the provocative oxymoron, "real allegory," have led numerous scholars to try to expound its iconographic program. In these attempts they have relied heavily on a long, undated letter from Courbet to Champfleury, his friend and critical champion, in which the painting is described in some detail. Indeed we owe to that letter and a few others much of the understanding we have of the general significance of the figures on the left; and certain broad distinctions the letter sketches, most importantly between "all the shareholders, that is, friends, workers, and art lovers" (*tous les actionnaires, c'est-à-dire les amis, les travailleurs, les amateurs du monde de l'art*) on the right, and "the other world of ordinary life" (*l'autre monde de la vie triviale*) on the left, have been fundamental to most interpretations of the composition as a whole.[2] Not that the existence of written documents has produced consensus —far from it. Thus the *Studio* has been interpreted by Nochlin as a Fourierist allegory; by Bowness as "the modern artist's declaration of independence, of absolute freedom to create what he wants to create"; by Hofmann as a dense layering of fundamental themes such as the ages of man, the social tensions of the mid-nineteenth century, the metamorphosis of womanhood, the conflict between the claims of higher truth and fidelity to objective fact, etc.; by Toussaint as a possibly subversive political statement charged with Masonic symbolism; while most recently Rubin has connected the *Studio* with aspects of Proudhon's political thought.[3]

Let me say at once that I have no wish either to adjudicate between these and other interpretations or to put forward an interpretation of my own if by that one means a reading of the entire composition in terms of a system of symbolic equivalences, whether invented by Courbet, derived by him from outside sources, or both. Instead I propose to limit my remarks to a consideration of just one portion of the remarkable painting now before us—the central group organized around the self-portrait of Courbet at his easel (fig. 2)—in an attempt to analyze more finely, or at any rate more concentratedly, than has hitherto been done Courbet's representation of the act, the immediate context, and the emerging artifact of representation. I take the central group to comprise the following elements:

—The figure of the painter, seated on a high-backed wooden chair (more precisely, on a cushion on the chair), holding in his left hand a rectangular palette, several brushes, and a palette knife and, in his right hand, a long, rather fine-tipped brush with which he is adding a stroke to the almost completed picture on the easel before him.

—The figure of a naked woman, said by Courbet in his letter to Champfleury to be a model watching him paint and described by an early interviewer as a personification of truth.[4] She stands directly behind the painter's chair and with her left hand holds against her upper body a sheet of white cloth which, however, fails to cover her breast and flank. Almost lost in shadow, the woman's right forearm and hand are raised to her head. On the floor alongside her, in the

Figure 2. Courbet, *The Painter's Studio,* detail of central group. Photo Giraudon.

near foreground and partly obscuring a low wicker stool, the clothes she was previously wearing lie crumpled in a heap.

—The figure of a small boy in simple peasant dress who stands as nearly as possible in front of the painter and seems to be gazing up at the latter's extended right arm and hand. Because he has been depicted largely from the rear, we see almost nothing of his face.

—The unfinished picture itself, a large squarish canvas placed low on an upright easel and angled slightly back into space, on which the painter has represented a river landscape reminiscent of the countryside around Ornans, with cliffs, trees, and, in the immediate foreground, what appears to be a waterfall. There is also a small house on the riverbank to the left, and it may be that which the painter is in the process of brushing in.

Other items that should at least be mentioned are the white cat playing with a ball at the painter's feet and two figures on the margin of the central group proper, the Irishwoman seated on the floor to the left of the easel, and, above and behind her, the plaster mannequin whose awkward pose recalls images of martyred saints. In this connection it should be noted that Courbet in his letter to Champfleury describes the *Studio* as divided into two rather than three parts and associates the image of himself and the naked model with the gathering of *actionnaires* on the right—a perfectly logical association from a thematic point of view. But there is in Courbet's art another sort of logic that cuts across the grain of many seemingly plausible thematizations, and in the articulation of the central group as a pictorial entity in its own right, as well as in the shadowy annexation to the central group of the Irishwoman and the mannequin, we catch an early glimpse of that second logic at work.

My procedure in this essay will be as follows. I shall begin by comparing the figure of the painter at his easel with one of the best-known of Courbet's numerous self-portraits of the 1840s; the point of the comparison will be to offer a preliminary reading of features of Courbet's depiction of himself in the *Studio* that either have never been remarked or, if remarked, have never been taken seriously. It will then be necessary to place that reading in historical context by summarizing what I see as the evolution of a principal tradition within French painting from the middle of the eighteenth century to the advent of Courbet. Next I propose to look briefly at two major figure paintings that preceded and, I shall suggest, led up to the *Studio*; once again a comparison between those works and the central group will prove helpful in making sense of the latter. Finally, I shall zero in on the central group itself, with particular emphasis on the relationship between the painting on the easel and the figures of the painter, the model, and the peasant boy. The basic assumption on which I shall be working throughout this essay is that by treating the central group as a distinct entity and by exploring some of the connections that can be drawn between that group and other works in Courbet's *oeuvre*, it will prove possible to bring the light and, what is more, to give precise significance to aspects of Courbet's realism (or "Realism") that previous attempts to construe the *Studio* in terms of a single syntagmatic structure have tended to make and keep invisible.

Students of Courbet's art have always been aware of his extraordinary predilection for the self-portrait as a genre, a predilection that was at its most intense, or at least its most explicit, during the 1840s (i.e., during the first decade of his career). And it should not have escaped anyone's notice that the *Studio* is in effect an expanded self-portrait, one of several works of the mid-1850s that suggest a personalization of the enterprise of painting comparable to that which produced the early self-portraits.[5] And yet no one has tried to approach Courbet's portrayal of himself in the *Studio* by way of a comparison with his early, or for that matter his later, self-portraits. This is what I mean to do in as brief a compass as can be managed, by relying on conclusions reached in an earlier essay on Courbet's self-portraits of the 1840s.[6] There I argued that whereas previous writers have seen in Courbet's frequent depictions of himself either glorifications of his good looks, studies of his emotional and psychological states, or records of significant phases in his life (or some combination of all three), what for Courbet was more profoundly at stake in the early self-portraits was a desire to represent pictorially a certain consciousness of being one with his body—to find pictorial means by which to evoke his intense absorption in his own live bodily being (his bodily liveness, phenomenologists would say).

Here, for example, is probably the most ambitious of the self-portraits of the 1840s, the *Man with the Leather Belt* (1845–46?; fig. 3). This painting is usually discussed in terms of its relation to Venetian, Spanish, and Dutch prototypes; but what seems to me to require commentary is not its rootedness in tradition—Courbet made no secret of his resolve to surpass the old masters on their own ground—but rather its peculiar modernity, by which I mean its quite prodigious strangeness as regards *mise-en-scène*, mood, action, and accessories. In the place of a systematic analysis, I offer the following summary observations:

Figure 3. Courbet, *Man with the Leather Belt,* 1845–46? Paris, Louvre. Photo Musées nationaux.

1. The image of the sitter has deliberately been pitched very near the surface of the picture—so near, in fact, that we are made to feel that the sitter's lower body, cut off by the bottom framing edge, thrusts beyond the plane of the picture surface into our space or "world." This impression of extreme physical proximity is given further point by the way in which the leather-bound portfolio (at once a metaphor and a metonymy for the sitter) juts beyond the edge of the table top on which it rests; and it is perhaps more subtly reaffirmed by a general overloading of the bottom portion of the painting, which has the effect of calling into question what might be termed the ontological impermeability of the bottom framing edge—its capacity to contain the representation, to keep it in its place, to

establish it at a fixed distance from both picture surface and beholder.

2. The curious, abstracted, almost somnolent mood indicated by
the sitter's facial expression, especially when contrasted with the
physical tension apparent in the actions of his hands and the posture
of his upper body, seems almost to solicit the type of interpretation—
phenomenological rather than psychological or autobiographical—
that I attributed to the early self-portraits as a group a moment ago.
In the *Man with the Leather Belt,* as in others among those paintings,
an implicit devalorizing of vision—I am thinking now not only of the
sitter's averted gaze but also of his deeply shadowed eyes—connotes
an emphasis on the body as experienced from within rather than as
perceived from without. (In the *Wounded Man* (fig. 12), another
fascinating self-portrait, the sitter's eyes appear to be closed, while
in the famous *Man with a Pipe* they are barely open.) Somnolence as
such, no more than suggested in the *Man with the Leather Belt,*
emerges in the self-portraits generally, as elsewhere in Courbet's art,
as a metaphor for the life of the body, the signifier of a "primordial"
or somatic order of vital activity located for the most part below
conscious awareness.

3. By far the most unsettling feature of the *Man with the Leather
Belt* is the prominence given to the sitter's hands, whose actions, I
wish to claim, become intelligible only when they are viewed in
terms of the painter's desire to make manifest within the painting
an intense conviction of his own embodiedness. Thus the sitter's left
hand gripping his belt with what appears to be an excessive expense
of physical effort may be seen as striving to experience not merely
the texture, thickness, resistance, etc. of the leather belt but also, by
virtue of that very excess, *its own* activity, its "being," as a grasping,
feeling, substantial living entity. Much the same may be said of the
sitter's right hand, whose state of tension, apparently devoid of any
practical rationale, evokes its possession from within even more
perspicuously than does the action of the hand gripping the belt.
In the essay previously alluded to, I show that hands play an analogous role throughout the early self-portraits.

4. Not only does Courbet seem to have wished to avoid all feeling

of confrontation between sitter and beholder; there is a further sense in which the sitter may be described as represented, although not literally from the rear, at any rate in a bodily attitude that in at least one salient particular is wholly congruent with what we know a priori to have been the painter's orientation as he stood or, more likely, sat before the canvas. I refer to the principal gesture of the sitter's right hand as it strains back into the picture to touch, but not quite to support, his cheek and jaw. The crucial feature of that gesture as I see it is that while only slightly straining verisimilitude, it contrives to accomplish something that one might have thought largely unattainable within the conventions of the self-portrait: to align the sitter's right hand with that of the painter or, to put this more strongly, to create a situation in which the two right hands can plausibly be imagined to coincide, to become *one*. Indeed it often appears that Courbet's ultimate object in the self-portraits involved nothing less than abrogating *both distance and difference* between himself and the representation of himself: as though what I have characterized as Courbet's desire to reconstitute pictorially his absorption in his live bodily being could be satisfied only to the extent that he was able *to translate himself bodily into the painting on which he was working,* as extravagant as this may sound and as unrealizable an ideal as we are likely to find it. Another accessory in the *Man with the Leather Belt* is worth remarking here—the cast of a sculpture then thought to be by Michelangelo, which stands on the table to the left of and just behind the sitter's right arm and shoulder. (The cast, viewed largely from the rear, represents a male figure with one arm raised and bent back behind his head.) By virtue of its posture, which has analogies with that of the sitter, and more importantly its orientation, which I take to be in agreement with that of the sitter's right hand, the cast invites being seen not only as an acknowledgment of the painter's preoccupation with his embodiedness but also as an index of the "translational" pressures at work in the picture as a whole.[7]

If we now compare the *Man with the Leather Belt* with Courbet's representation of himself in the central group of the *Studio* two general facts emerge. In the first place, the self-portrait in the central group is plainly distanced from and independent of its creator in ways that I have tried to show the earlier self-portrait is not: there is no question of the painter *of* the *Studio* coinciding with, or even closely approaching, the representation of the painter *in* the *Studio*. (In this regard, if in no other, the composition or *mise-en-scène* of the *Studio* may be described as conventional.) But it does not follow that our observations about the earlier picture are without relevance to the later one. If we turn our attention to the relationship between painting and painter that we find represented in the central group, and if we are prepared to bracket for the time being the fact that the painter is shown working there not on a self-portrait but on a landscape, it becomes clear that between that depicted relationship and the real (or perhaps I should say imaginary) one expounded in connection with the *Man with the Leather Belt* there exist significant features in common. For example, the figure of the painter in the *Studio* has been represented seated in such close proximity to the canvas on which he is working that he scarcely seems to have room for his legs. His right leg especially appears to have nowhere to go except into the canvas, and it comes as something of a shock to realize that his right lower leg and foot are angled back under his chair—an impossible arrangement, as anyone who tries it quickly discovers. The impression that results, of an obscure merging of the painter's lower body with the dark bottom portion of the picture on his easel, is not unrelated to the implied dissolution of the boundary between the "worlds" of painting and beholder that I called attention to in my comments on the bottom framing edge in the *Man with the Leather Belt.*

Or consider the fact that the relationship between the figure of the painter and the picture on the easel in the central group, far from being the natural (i.e., conventional) one of mutual facing, is conspicuously oblique, sidelong, averted. This is sometimes rationalized as an attempt by Courbet, whose vanity was legendary, to display his fine "Assyrian" profile at whatever cost to the verisimilitude of the scene. But explanations of this type have a limited usefulness. Beyond a certain point it becomes necessary to remark, first, that the *mise-en-scène* of the central group is such that very nearly the whole of the painter's body is projected against, and in an important sense comprehended by, the landscape that he is in the process of painting, exactly as if he were meant to be perceived leaning back against the cliffs and trees rising above the riverbank at the right (cf. the *Wounded Man,* among other works); and second, that the painter's posture relative to the canvas on which he is working is strikingly similar to the posture of the sitter in the *Man with the Leather Belt.* There also the figure of Courbet turns his right shoulder toward the canvas, tilts his head back and toward the side, and seems to slide forward in his chair, an impression enhanced by the unexpected congruence between the pillow on which the painter is seated in the central group and the forward thrust of the portfolio in the early self-portrait.

Probably the most telling affinity between the *Man with the Leather Belt* and the self-portrait in the central group involves the treatment of hands. In my discussion of the former I said that the sitter's bodily attitude enables us to imagine two right hands, the sitter's and the painter's, coinciding. Now I want to propose that the sense of extreme tension conveyed by the sitter's right hand and wrist may be seen as an expression of the physical effort involved *in the act of painting,* of wielding a brush or knife to apply paint to canvas, as that act was later represented by Courbet in the *Studio.* And this raises the further possibility that the sitter's left hand gripping his belt in the early self-portrait may be understood as condensing into a vivid image of strenuous activity the much less intense, though indefinitely protracted, effort involved in holding a palette and brushes in the manner of the painter in the central group. These observations can be generalized to suggest, first, that Courbet's self-portraits of the 1840s often contain within them more or less displaced representations of the painter's hands acting to produce those paintings, and second, that this came about not because Courbet sought, for modernist or other reasons, to allude to the process of painting, but because his determination to be "true" to the present-tense actuality of his embodiedness all but left him no choice.[8]

Other points of resemblance between the *Man with the Leather Belt* and the central group might be cited—for example, the somewhat marginal presence in each of a sculpture, and the draping of a piece of cloth over a corner of the portfolio in the one and a corner of the picture on the easel in the other—but rather than pause over these and other lesser affinities, let us move on to consider the wider implications of our findings so far.

This will require digressing from Courbet in order to provide the rudiments of a historical context. In essays published during the past several years, as well as in a recent book, I try to show that there emerged in the 1750s and 1760s in France (and only there) an intense and largely conscious preoccupation on the part of both painters and art critics with the representation of figures *wholly absorbed* in their actions, activities, and states of mind and, by virtue of that absorption, *entirely oblivious* to the presence before the canvas of the beholder. I go on to argue that it was above all else the desire to establish the supreme fiction of the beholder's nonexistence—the metaillusion that no one was really there, standing before the picture—that actuated the rise of a new, dramatic conception of painting, which found its first major avatar in Greuze and its paradigmatic expression in David's *Oath of the Horatii* (1784-85; fig. 4), *Death of Socrates* (1787), and *Lictors Returning to Brutus the Bodies of His Sons* (1789). I suggest further that a central tradition within French painting, not only in the late eighteenth century but also throughout much of the nineteenth, may largely be understood in terms of the efforts of successive generations of painters to respond in one way or another to the ever more perspicuous inability of the original Davidian paradigm and its subsequent revisions and transformations to negate or neutralize what might be thought of as the primordial convention that paintings are made to be beheld.[9]

Thus David himself came to regard the *Horatii* as theatrical in the pejorative sense of the word,[10] and in the *Sabines* (1796-99; fig. 5), his next major history painting after the *Brutus,* we find that the fervor, muscularity, compositional starkness, and dramatic lighting of the earlier canvases have been replaced by an expressive restraint, a suave, ostensibly "Greek" mode of linear abstraction, a dissemination of incident, and a cool, silvery atmosphere that together produce a very different effect. To some of David's students, the radical sect

Figure 4. David, *Oath of the Horatii*, 1784–85. Paris, Louvre. Photo Musées nationaux.

sometimes called the *Barbus,* the *Sabines* did not go far enough in the direction of abstraction and antidrama.[11] In Stendhal's art criticism of the 1820s, however, the *Sabines* is excoriated precisely for its emphasis on pose and self-display at the expense of action and expression, and a call goes out for a renovation of painting that would put an end to the frozen gestures and mannered posturing summed up in the phrase "the imitation of Talma"—a catchword that suggests just how pervasive a certain theatricality had come to seem.[12] By all odds the most profoundly conceived (if nonetheless foredoomed) attempt to detheatricalize the relationship between painting and beholder while cleaving to the values of pictorial drama was made by Géricault in the *Raft of the 'Medusa'* (1818–19; fig. 6), a work of colossal dimensions that depicts the last survivors of a shipwreck, after nearly two weeks of horror on the open sea, mounting a desperate collective effort to attract the attention of a brig so distant as to be barely visible on the horizon. One way of characterizing that collective effort might be to say that the figures on the raft are *striving to be beheld* by a potential source of vision located at the farthest limit of illusionistic space, a source that, if it could be activated, would rescue them *from being upheld by us*: as if our presence before the painting were the ultimate cause of their plight, or as if the presence of beholders threatened to make theatrical even their sufferings. The unworkableness of such a solution, the sheer hyperbole of the conceit on which it depends, is acknowledged by the tragic figure group in the left foreground, for whom, it seems clear, the possibility of rescue no longer exists. By 1824, the year Géricault died and Stendhal inveighed against the Davidians, most French painters of subjects involving the human figure appear to have accepted the theatricalization of action and expression as a condition of their

Figure 5. David, *Sabines,* 1796–99. Paris, Louvre. Photo Musées nationaux.

Figure 6. Géricault, *Raft of the 'Medusa'*, 1818–19. Paris, Louvre. Photo Musées nationaux.

art; while throughout the 1830s, in the work of Delaroche and other virtuosi of the so-called *juste milieu,* the theatrical was not simply tolerated but embraced.

Against the background of these developments, Courbet's attempt in the *Man with the Leather Belt* (and, I have claimed, in the early self-portraits generally) to reconstitute within the painting his absorption in his live bodily being can be seen as strongly antitheatrical in its implications. For not only was that effort of reconstitution as I have presented it guided less by the data of vision than by other ranges of feeling and sensation. Even more important for my argument is the recognition that Courbet, in seeking to revoke both distance and difference between himself and the representation of himself, was in effect striving to annul, if not his own identity as beholder, at any rate something fundamental to that identity, that is, his presence outside, in front of, the painting before him.

This antitheatrical animus, implicit in the self-portraits, comes powerfully to the fore in Courbet's great "Realist" or, as I shall call them because of their significance in his development, *breakthrough* pictures of 1848–50—the *After Dinner at Ornans* (1848–49; fig. 7), the *Stonebreakers* (1849), the *Burial at Ornans* (1849–50; fig. 8), and the *Peasants of Flagey Returning from the Fair* (original version 1850). Both the originality of the breakthrough pictures in this regard, and their relation to previous attempts to come to grips with the problem of the beholder, may be brought out via a comparison with Géricault. Put succinctly, whereas Géricault in the bulk of his work, including the *Raft,* remained faithful to a dramatic conception of painting stemming ultimately from David's *Horatii,* Courbet, whose career began roughly twenty years after Géricault's closed, seems intuitively to have recognized that the dramatic as such had become irremediably theatrical—that the conventions that once had

Figure 7. Courbet, *After Dinner at Ornans,* 1848–49. Lille, Musée des Beaux-Arts. Photo Musées nationaux.

Figure 8. Courbet, *Burial at Ornans,* 1849–50. Paris, Louvre. Photo Musées nationaux.

served to promote the fiction that the beholder did not exist now only called attention to his presence—and that therefore no attempt to detheatricalize the relationship between painting and beholder could succeed that did not break with the conventions of pictorial drama wherever they were found. The implications of this rejection of the dramatic extended to all aspects of Courbet's mature pictorial practice, including his preference for subjects involving figures absorbed not in action or passion but in what may be described, not quite tautologically, as absorptive states and activities of an almost mechanical or somnambulistic sort; his avoidance of decisive or otherwise "fecund" narrative moments in favor of scenes of stasis, repetition, reverie, slow continuous movement, sustained but not particularly intense effort—in short, temporal dilation and protraction; his refusal to pursue pictorial unity through formal and expressive contrast even when, as a consequence of that refusal, his paintings were widely criticized for failing to hold together; and finally, most importantly for us, his elaboration of various compositional strategies, foreshadowed in the self-portraits, which broadened or generalized—made less narrowly personal—the determination that we divined at work in the *Man with the Leather Belt* to transform or dissolve the conventional relationship between painting and beholder.

Two such strategies in particular are crucial to the remainder of this essay. The first seeks to reduce to an absolute minimum all sense of distance and indeed of separateness between representation and beholder, as a step toward absorbing the beholder into the painting in an almost corporeal way. Thus in the *Burial at Ornans* the apparent extreme proximity, panoramic dimensions, and lifelike internal scale of the image, together with the placing of an open grave at the bottom center of the canvas (where it is truncated by the bottom framing edge), express what I interpret, only somewhat metaphorically, as a resolve to cut the ground out from under the feet of the beholder and by so doing leave him nowhere to stand outside the painting itself. An analogous distance-collapsing device in the *After Dinner at Ornans* makes use of the checked cap hanging from a moulding above the head of the second figure from the left: instead of seeming to be situated back in space where it belongs, the cap appears to coincide with, or at least to approach, the surface of the painting. The second compositional strategy, often used in combination with the first, involves depicting a prominent figure, almost always in the near foreground, to a greater or lesser extent from the rear. In compositions of this type—the *After Dinner at Ornans* is a case in point—the effect of the figure portrayed from the rear is not to close off the representation but rather the opposite: to remove all sense of confrontation between painting and beholder and thereby to facilitate the virtual merging of the latter into the former that we saw take place with regard to Courbet "himself" in the *Man with the Leather Belt.*

In these and other respects the paintings of Courbet's breakthrough and after at once go far beyond yet repeatedly hark back to the self-portraits of the 1840s. On the one hand, the later works, with their far wider range of subject matter, often vastly enlarged dimensions, more intense evocation of materiality, and pervasive concern with nature, may be characterized as the products of a constantly renewed attempt to abolish the *impersonal or "objective" conditions* constitutive of the very possibility of spectatordom. On the other hand, because the *first* beholder, not just chronologically but ontologically, was Courbet himself, such an attempt inevitably involved a struggle to revoke *his own* spectatordom, *his own* embodied presence before the canvas, with the result that a highly determinate but also highly protean personal element continued to play a major role in his art. (The notion of narcissism, sometimes invoked to cover Courbet's seeming infatuation with his own image, falls far short of being able to deal with such a problematic.) In this connection it is surely significant that the first of the "breakthrough" pictures, the *After Dinner at Ornans*, contains not only an outright self-portrait (the second figure from the left)[13] but also, in the personage of Courbet's friend Marlet seen from the rear lighting his pipe with a burning brand, a particularly close analogue to what by now we cannot help surmising was the painter's actual situation as he brought that painting into being. And although none of the figures in the *Burial at Ornans* appears to represent the painter, or painter-*beholder,* in either of these ways, I find it suggestive that there can be made out immediately to the left of the open grave and truncated by the bottom framing edge the blade of a shovel, the shaft of which is to be imagined extending toward the beholder's right hand, as if it were the handle of a painter's brush or knife.[14]

We are now in a position to look briefly at two ambitious paintings of the first half of the 1850s that seem to me to lead up to and in important respects to anticipate the central group in the *Studio*— the notorious *Bathers* (1853; fig. 9) and the less well-known but increasingly admired *Wheat Sifters* (1853–54; fig. 10). Our first impression, seeing the two works together, is of a comprehensive series of oppositions: outdoors versus indoors; naked versus clothed; leisure versus labor; a mannered, almost Rococo exchange of gestures versus simple actions absorbed wholly in themselves; vertical versus horizontal rectangular formats; relatively deep versus relatively shallow space; a color scheme keyed to the traditional contrast between dark green foliage and brilliant flesh tones versus one based on an unexpected juxtaposition of closely valued areas of warm, pale, radiant hues; and so on. But these and other differences are in the end probably outweighed by various affinities between the two paintings. For example, unlike the breakthrough pictures with their wholly or predominantly male casts of characters, the *Bathers* and the *Wheat*

Figure 9. Courbet, *Bathers,* 1853. Montpellier, Musée Fabre. Photo Bulloz.

Sifters are given over to the representation of women, though the latter also includes a young boy. This is a significant shift and I shall return to it shortly.[15] A further, more striking affinity concerns the treatment of the respective principal figures as regards bodily attitude and orientation relative to the beholder. In each picture, that figure has been depicted with hips thrust forward, head deeply bent, right arm outstretched, and left arm and hand mostly hidden from view but holding something, precisely as if the pose of the upper body of the kneeling sifter were adapted from that of the standing

Figure 10. Courbet, *Wheat Sifters,* 1853–54. Nantes, Musée des Beaux-Arts. Photo Studio Madec.

bather, or as if the poses of both were based on a prior model or schema. And of course the figures in question have been represented not only from the rear but also from the same angle of approach (cf. the figure of Marlet lighting his pipe in the *After Dinner*). Other similarities include the presence of subsidiary figures (and, in the left-hand portion of the *Bathers,* a large boulder) setting off the principals, an arrangement that goes against the more egalitarian-seeming compositional norm of the breakthrough pictures, and the strong suggestion, especially in the *Wheat Sifters,* that we are looking down at the scene as a whole. In short, the *Bathers* and the *Wheat Sifters* turn out to bear a surprisingly intimate relation to each other, and the question before us is what to make of that fact.

What I make of it is this. I see in the principal figure in each painting—the standing bather and the kneeling sifter—a synecdoche for the painting itself; and I see in the actions depicted in the two paintings, as well as in aspects of the *mise-en-scène* in both, a working out, almost an acting out, of some of the more extreme implications of Courbet's antitheatrical enterprise as I have described it so far. The shift of gender and compositional tactics between the breakthrough pictures of 1848–50 and the *Bathers* and the *Wheat Sifters* of 1853–54 thus becomes intelligible as part of a larger shift, call it a tendency toward self-representation, within Courbet's art. At any rate, the use of a predominant female figure to stand for the painting she inhabits may be viewed as asserting a fundamental, corporeal equivalence between painting and painter-beholder, and moreover as projecting the painting as an object of desire with which union of a sort is not only conceivable but "natural."

There is in addition a close and by now familiar connection between the poses and actions of the respective principal figures in the *Bathers* and especially the *Wheat Sifters* and the activity of painting as delineated in the *Studio,* but before analyzing that connection I want to comment on an aspect of the *Bathers* that has not yet been mentioned. I refer to the fact that it depicts a scene of beholding, one in which the standing bather is beheld from a side we cannot see —more or less from the front—by her seated companion. The "exchange of thoughts" that Delacroix was the first of many to find incomprehensible is to this extent readable: the companion's gesture expresses surprised admiration while that of the standing bather conveys a sense of modesty.[16] And if we take seriously my proposal that the principal figure be considered a synecdoche for the painting, it follows that the *Bathers* can be interpreted as representing a relationship between *itself,* imagined to be facing *away* from us, and a beholder who views it not from our side of the picture surface but from the *other* side, imagined to be the painting's *front.* It is not clear whether such a relationship denotes an attempt almost physically to remove the painting from the ambit of the beholder standing before the canvas; several features of the *Bathers*—notably the implied movement of the principal figure back into illusionistic space, the uncharacteristically distanced quality of the entire scene, and a certain airlessness owing to an unusually high degree of technical finish— encourage us to think along those lines. Be this as it may, a comparison

with the central group in the *Studio* suggests that the *Bathers* remains firmly tied to one particular "external" beholder: the *first*
beholder, or *painter*-beholder, the backward lean of whose upper
body and the position of whose arms as portrayed in the central
group are represented with only minor variations in the figure of
the standing bather. (The possible equivocation that my reading un-
covers, between a desire to sever relations with the beholder and a
compulsion to translate the painter-beholder into the painting, may
help explain the special discomfort that viewers have always felt in
the presence of the *Bathers*.)

Let me quickly add that the connection between the figures of the
standing bather and the painter at his easel is by no means the only
one that can be drawn between the *Bathers* and the central group.
The reader who has come this far will doubtless already have been
struck by the resemblance between the two monumental nudes, the
bather and the model. And there is a further, more tenuous but
nevertheless not insignificant link between the respective actions of
the seated companion, who looks up in admiration at the standing
bather, and of the peasant boy and the artist's model, both of whom
are shown gazing, from different points of view, at the painter and/or
his painting.

If in this context we turn our attention to the *Wheat Sifters,* we
recognize at once that it constitutes a middle term between the
Bathers and the central group in the *Studio.* To begin with, the figure
of the principal sifter, while unmistakably recalling that of the standing bather, is shown not gesturing toward someone else but, like the
figure of the painter at his easel, absorbed in a task requiring sustained physical effort. Then, too, the sifter's backward-swaying upper body and even her kneeling position seem distinctly closer than
the attitude of the standing bather to the pose of the painter leaning
back in his chair with his legs jammed uncomfortably beneath him.
There is also a progression of sorts as regards the treatment of the
motif of beholding in the three works. In the *Bathers,* as we have
remarked, the principal figure is directly beheld by her seated companion; in the *Wheat Sifters* the latter has been succeeded by a small
boy peering intently into a wooden cabinet in which sifted grain has

been stored (exactly where his attention is directed is less important than where it is *not*, i.e., toward the kneeling sifter); while in the central group the standing model herself looks on over the painter's shoulder, and a small boy who could be the brother of the one in the *Wheat Sifters* appears to gaze raptly up at the painter's right hand. One might also tentatively associate the young woman seated on the floor abstractedly picking bits of grain out of a dish in the *Wheat Sifters* with a personage on the fringe of the central group in the *Studio,* the Irishwoman nursing an infant in the shadow of the painting on the easel.[17]

To my mind, however, the most impressive of all connections that can be drawn between the *Wheat Sifters* and the central group involves seeing the fall of sifted wheat onto a ground cloth in the earlier work—an occurrence rendered by Courbet as a shower of flecks and granules of seemingly still sticky brownish ochre pigment onto a large rectangle of white canvaslike material—as an analogue to or transformation of the very process of painting, of transporting and affixing paint to canvas. The connection is underscored by the surprising resemblance between the pattern formed on the ground cloth by the fallen wheat and the treatment of foliage in the trees dominating the upper portion of the painting on the easel in the central group. It is further reinforced by the similarity between the loosely spread ground cloth with its creases and folds and the length of grayish fabric draped over the upper left corner of the painting on the easel. And the connection assumes a still more provocative significance when we recognize that the position of the kneeling sifter on top of and, in effect, encompassed by the ground cloth can be read as enacting the incorporation of the painter-beholder within the painting that I have said was a primary objective of Courbet's antitheatrical enterprise.

I realize that within a few pages I have associated the figure of the kneeling sifter with the painting itself, with the painter-beholder, with the process of applying paint to canvas, and now with the acting out of a particular relationship between painting and painter-beholder, but far from being embarrassed by this glut of meanings I contend that some such overdetermination of motifs and relationships is a hallmark of Courbet's art throughout his career. Let me make clear, however, that I do not wish to suggest that Courbet actually conceived of either the *Bathers* or the *Wheat Sifters* in the terms developed in this essay. My claim is rather that both paintings are structured by something like an expanded body-image of himself in the act and situation of painting, and that that expanded body-image is itself to be understood as a function of (as structured by) the problematic of painting and beholder that I have tried to show emerged as central to French painting roughly a century before.

It is time to start bringing matters to a close by redirecting attention to the central group and, in particular, to the painting on which the figure of the painter is shown working. Previous commentators on the *Studio* have been struck by the fact that it was only after 1855 that landscape as a genre came to play a major role in Courbet's art, so that by giving pride of place to the picture on the easel he was not so much reviewing a phase in his artistic life as looking forward to a phase to come. They have also found it deeply puzzling that Courbet the avowed "Realist," in an immense canvas seemingly intended as a manifesto, should have portrayed himself at work on a painting of a natural scene without having the original, the scene "itself," before his eyes. These are important cruxes, but rather than address them head-on I want to make a few observations concerning the relationships among the painting, the painter, and the model. I remarked earlier that the painter's lower body appears virtually to merge with the dark bottom portion of the painting on the easel. Now I want to suggest that the painting on the easel, representing as it does a river landscape issuing, in the immediate foreground, in a waterfall, is at least subliminally to be perceived as *flowing into* the figure of the painter: as if the implied movement of the painter's lower body *into* the painting is reciprocated, or anticipated, by a countermovement of the painting *out toward* the painter. What is more, the outward flow of water (or waterlike representations) does not stop when it reaches the painter; on the contrary, the falling, spreading folds of the white sheet that the standing model presses to her breast, as well as the seething pinkish whirlpool of her discarded dress, and, finally, the minor cascade of the white cat playing at the painter's feet, may be seen as visual metaphors for the outward flux, descent, and eddying of waters whose ostensible source is the very painting that the painter has been depicted bringing to completion.[18]

All this implies that the figure of the painter in the central group is as it were already immersed in the painting on which he is working *and* that the painting itself cannot be identified merely with the canvas rectangle on the easel. These implications in turn are given added force if, on the basis of our discussion of the *Bathers* and the *Wheat Sifters,* we consider the possibility that the figure of the artist's model may be regarded as a synecdoche for the painting toward which she faces: seen in that light, the fact that she stands directly *behind* the figure of the painter as much as asserts that the latter is physically subsumed, one might almost say enclosed, within the painting he is making, wherever the ultimate limits of that painting are taken to lie. Certain partial accords between the figures of painter and model—for example, between the contour of his left shoulder and that of her haunch, or even between his head and her naked breast—further hint at an overcoming of physical boundaries between both persons and things. And we are all but compelled to perceive the figure of the model as bearing an intimate relation to the painting on the easel, not only by the role she plays in connection with the waterlike representations of the white sheet and discarded dress but also by the exquisite series of parallels, unmistakable as soon as discerned, between, on the one hand, the angles at which the trees in the upper portion of the painting emerge from the hillside and spread their branches and, on the other, the characteristic forward tilt of the model's head as well as the precise curves of her neck and hairdo.[19] The image thus produced evokes an ideal of harmony or oneness between the human figure and the natural scene. But it must be emphasized that that ideal is here primarily a means of identifying the figure of the model, who is, I have argued, no mere personification of humankind (or of anything else), with the painting on the easel, which represents, as I have tried to demonstrate, something other than simply a view of nature. We see now why it is misleading to think of the painter in the central group as engaged in painting a landscape in the restricted definition of the term: it would be nearer the truth of our findings to say that he is shown representing the central group as such, wherever *its* ultimate limits are taken to lie. We also see why it is no less misleading to think of him as doing so in the absence of the scene "itself": there is an important sense in which a certain scene of representation, comprising at least the canvas on the easel and the painter seated before it, and grounded in what I have claimed was a decisive problematic within French painting from the mid-eighteenth century on, must be imagined to have been there all along.

Finally, it should be clear that one consequence of the identification of the naked model with the painting on the easel is that her status as an independent beholder of that painting is thoroughly neutralized. But what of the figure of the peasant boy standing in front of the painter? Recent x-rays of the *Studio* reveal that he was a late addition, and he is not mentioned in Courbet's letter to Champfleury. I suggest that we think of him as representing the painter-beholder *of,* as distinct from *in,* the *Studio*—more precisely, as acknowledging the distancedness and separateness of the painter-beholder *from* the *Studio* as a whole, which is, as I noted earlier, compositionally and scenographically conventional in ways that the other works by Courbet that we have examined, and a fortiori the central group considered as an image of relationship between painting and painter-beholder, are not. At the same time, that the boy appears to have his attention riveted not on the painting on the easel but rather on the painter's active, productive right hand may be taken as emblematic of an enterprise that called for the painter to follow that hand into the painting.[20]

POSTSCRIPT

The double movement into the painting and out toward the painter-beholder that I have argued characterizes the relationship between the figure of Courbet and the picture on his easel in the central group also characterizes many of Courbet's landscapes, most conspicuously views of certain favorite sites involving grottoes and flowing water. For example, in the fine depiction in the Baltimore Museum of Art of the covered stream known as *Le Puits noir* (ca. 1860–65; fig. 11), what appears at the left-most portion of the middle of the canvas to be the mouth of a cave not only attracts the eye but is felt to solicit the beholder's bodily presence within the painting[21]; while the shallow expanse of water that occupies almost the entire foreground is perceived as flowing, if not out from the cave, at any rate toward the picture surface and beyond. This basic structure—a cave or clearing or analogously beckoning motif in the middle distance juxtaposed with water flowing toward the beholder in the near foreground—occurs in numerous works by Courbet, in many of which the direction of the movement of water is more emphatic than in the Baltimore

Figure 11. Courbet, *Le Puits noir* (or *The Grotto*), ca. 1860–65. Baltimore, Museum of Art, the Cone Collection. Photo Museum.

picture.[22] Still another feature of that picture turns up often in Courbet's landscapes, and it too is best understood in terms of our analysis of the central group: the darkly brilliant reflection of the cave mouth and surrounding rock masses in the mirrorlike surface of the stream. I see in that reflection, as in similar reflections elsewhere in Courbet's art, an image of *nature's absorption in the act of representing itself*—one so authoritative, because seemingly so impersonal, that it is tempting to surmise that the figure of the painter at work in the central group amounts merely to an anthropomorphizing of a power or faculty that Courbet saw as belonging *essentially* to nature. But of course it would be far truer to our argument to conclude that the vision of the natural world as absorbed in self-representation, which shines forth from many of Courbet's most impressive landscapes, ultimately expresses a desire to achieve a nontheatrical relation to the painting before him—a desire that, as we have seen, led Courbet time and again to represent in one form or another his activity as a painter.[23]

NOTES

1. The title in French reads: *L'Atelier du peintre, allégorie réelle déterminant une phase de sept années de ma vie artistique.* The painting's dimensions are 359 cm. by 598 cm., or just under twelve feet by about nineteen and one-half feet. For a recent account of the circumstances surrounding the one-man exhibition, see Jack Lindsay, *Gustave Courbet: His Life and Art* (New York: Harper & Row, 1973), pp. 135–44.

2. For the text of the letter, see Hélène Toussaint, "Le dossier de 'L'Atelier' de Courbet," in the exhibition catalogue, *Gustave Courbet (1819–1877)* (Paris, Grand Palais, September 1977–January 1978; London, Royal Academy, January–March 1978), pp: 246–47. Toussaint believes that the letter was cooked up by Courbet to mislead the authorities should they happen to suspect the true meaning of his painting, which she takes to be at least implicitly critical of the government, and goes on to argue that the figures in the left-hand portion of the composition represent not merely general types, but specific individuals who themselves are representative of larger social groups, issues, or tendencies (pp. 247–65). Hereafter the catalogue will be referred to as Toussaint, *Courbet.*

3. Linda Nochlin, "The Invention of the Avant-Garde: France 1830–80," in *Avant-Garde Art,* ed. Thomas B. Hess and John Ashbery (New York: Macmillan, 1967, 1968), pp. 3–24; Alan Bowness, *Courbet's 'Atelier du peintre',* Fiftieth Charlton Lecture on Art (Newcastle upon Tyne: University of Newcastle upon Tyne, 1972), p. 30; Werner Hofmann, *The Earthly Paradise: Art in the Nineteenth Century,* trans. Brian Battershaw (New York: George Braziller, 1961), pp. 11–22 and passim; Toussaint, "Le dossier de 'L'Atelier' de Courbet"; and James Henry Rubin, "Courbet and Proudhon in 'The Atelier'" (Abstract of a paper

delivered at a colloquium on Courbet, Städelschen Kunstinstitut, Frankfurt am Main, 2–4 March 1979). See also Pierre Georgel, "Les Transformations de la peinture vers 1848, 1855, 1863," *Revue de l'art,* no. 27 (1975); pp. 69–72; Klaus Herding, "Das *Atelier des Malers*— Treffpunkt der Welt und Ort der Versöhnung," in *Realismus als Widerspruch: Die Wirklichkeit in Courbets Malerei,* ed. Klaus Herding (Frankfurt am Main: Suhrkamp, 1978), pp. 223–47; René Huyghe, Germain Bazin, and Hélène Adhémar, *Courbet, L'Atelier du peintre, allégorie réelle, 1855,* Monographies des peintures du Musée du Louvre 3 (Paris: Plon, 1944); Max Kozloff, "Courbet's 'L'Atelier': An Interpretation," *Art and Literature,* no. 3 (1964), pp. 162–83; Lindsay, *Gustave Courbet,* pp. 129–35; Benedict Nicolson, *Courbet: The Studio of the Painter* (London: Allen Lane, 1973); and Linda Nochlin, *Gustave Courbet: A Study of Style and Society,* Ph.D. diss., New York University, 1963 (New York: Garland, 1976), pp. 210–23. I am grateful to Professor Robert Herbert of Yale University for making available to me abstracts of the papers given at the Frankfurt colloquium.

4. Théophile Silvestre, "Gustave Courbet," *Les Artistes français,* 2 vols. (Paris: Les Editions G. Crès, 1926), 2:140.

5. In addition to the *Studio* I am thinking of the *Meeting* (1854), the *Seaside at Palavas* (1854), and the *Quarry* (1857).

6. Michael Fried, "The Beholder in Courbet: His Early Self-Portraits and Their Place in His Art," *Glyph 4: Johns Hopkins Textual Studies* (1978): 85–129. In general the present essay builds on a foundation laid down in the earlier one.

7. The plaster cast appears in an earlier work, the *Draughts Players* (1844), where it faces the beholder; for the identification of the cast as an *écorché* then attributed to Michelangelo, see the catalogue by Marie-Thérèse de Forges, *Autoportraits de Courbet,* Les dossiers du département des peintures 6 (Paris: Louvre, 1973), pp. 31–32, and Toussaint, *Courbet,* p. 90.

8. A second example may be useful here. In the *Wounded Man* (begun ca. 1844, finished ca. 1854; fig. 12), the sitter's left hand loosely grasping a fold of his cloak may be seen as a displaced representation of the painter's left hand gripping his palette, while the presence of a sword just beyond the sitter's right shoulder may be considered a substitute for the painter's brush or knife (and implicitly for his active right hand and arm). This suggests a further analogy between the fictive sword thrust to which the image alludes and the constantly reiterated act of applying paint to canvas by which the painting was produced, as well as between the blood staining the sitter's shirt and paint—pigment—as such. For a detailed discussion of the *Wounded Man* and two related drawings, which stops short of relating those works to the activity of the painter, see Fried, "The Beholder in Courbet," 91–94, 96–101, and 103–6.

9. See for example "Toward a Supreme Fiction: Genre and Beholder in the Art Criticism of Diderot and His Contemporaries," *New Literary History* 6 (1975): 543–85; "Absorption: A Master Theme in Eighteenth-Century French Painting and Criticism," *Eighteenth-Century Studies* 9 (1975–76): 139–77; "The Beholder in Courbet"; and *Absorption and Theatricality: Painting and Beholder in the Age of Diderot* (Berkeley and Los Angeles: University of California Press, 1980). The interpretation of the development of French painting put forward in these writings is adumbrated in "Thomas Couture and the Theatricalization of Action in Nineteenth-Century French Painting," *Artforum* 8, no. 10 (1970): 36–46.

10. See Etienne-Jean Delécluze, *Louis David, son école et son temps* (Paris: Didier, 1855), p. 120. See also Delécluze's recollections of David's remarks on *expression* and *grimace* (p. 112) and on his antitheatrical aims in the *Leonidas at Thermopylae* (pp. 225-27).

11. For a history of the sect see George Levitine, *The Dawn of Bohemianism: The Barbu Rebellion and Primitivism in Neoclassical France* (University Park: Pennsylvania State

124 Michael Fried

Figure 12. Courbet, *Wounded Man,* ca. 1844–ca. 1854. Paris, Louvre. Photo Musées nationaux.

University Press, 1978), and the review of Levitine's book by Peter Walch in the *Art Bulletin* 62 (1980): 670–72.

12. For Stendhal's criticism of David's *Sabines,* see his *Salon de 1824* in *Mélanges d'art* (Paris: Le Divan, 1932), p. 46; for his remarks on the influence of Talma, see that *Salon,* p. 47, and *Des Beaux-Arts et du caractère français,* in the same collection, pp. 159–60.

13. It has been argued that the figure in question, traditionally identified as Courbet, in fact represents his friend Urbain Cuenot (Forges, *Autoportraits de Courbet,* p. 35; Toussaint, *Courbet,* pp. 94–95). I find the visual evidence unpersuasive, as does Alain De Leiris in his review of Forge's catalogue in the *Art Quarterly,* n.s. 1, no. 1 (1977): 138.

14. The structure of the *Burial at Ornans* is more complex than these brief remarks suggest. For example, the perspective of the open grave is such as to place the beholder to its left—more or less directly in front of the man bearing the crucifix, the one figure in the composition who gazes directly and powerfully out from the painting. A little to the left of that figure, however, and further back in space, we recognize the fine head in profile of Courbet's closest friend, Max Buchon, which perhaps suggests that if the crucifix bearer is to be understood (originally, so to speak) as gazing out at the painter-beholder, the latter is in turn to be imagined gazing instead at his friend: as if he wished to effect a separation between the two acts of mutual facing that together constitute the conventional relationship between painting and beholder; or as if he wished to distinguish the *painter's* gaze into

the painting from what might be described as the painting's gaze out at the *beholder,* and thereby to drive a wedge between those two aspects of his compound identity, however narrow the wedge, however unstable its lodgement. The closeness of the relations between Courbet and Buchon is emphasized by T. J. Clark, *Image of the People: Gustave Courbet and the Second French Republic, 1848-51* (Greenwich, Conn.: New York Graphic Society, 1973), pp. 110-13 and passim.

15. The shift is anticipated in the *Demoiselles de village* (1851), which depicts the artist's three sisters giving alms to a peasant girl. It should also be remarked that a painting exhibited by Courbet along with the *Bathers* in the Salon of 1853, the *Wrestlers* (1853), represents two almost grotesquely muscled men contending in a fairground, with spectators in a grandstand in the far distance. It has been suggested that the *Bathers* forms a pendant of sorts to the study of male near-nudity in the *Wrestlers,* and in a fuller discussion of the *Bathers* other points of contrast between the two works would deserve comment. On the *Wrestlers* see Klaus Herding, "*Les Lutteurs* 'détestables': critique de style, critique sociale," *Histoire et critique des arts* 4-5 (1978): 95-122.

16. For Delacroix's comments on the *Bathers* see *Journal de Eugène Delacroix,* ed. André Joubin (Paris: Plon, 1932), 2:18-19. In "Courbet's 'Baigneuses' and the Rhetorical Feminine Image," Beatrice Farwell notes that the pose of the seated companion "suggests ecstatic admiration . . . of a luminous wonder that we cannot see" (in *Woman as Sex Object: Studies in Erotic Art, 1730-1970,* ed. Thomas B. Hess and Linda Nochlin [London: Allen Lane, 1973], p. 67).

17. The somnolent air of the seated wheat sifter recalls the protagonist of another painting by Courbet shown in the Salon of 1853, the *Sleeping Spinner.*

18. This is as good a place as any to cite Delacroix's much-quoted observation that the painting on the easel "creates an ambiguity (*fait amphibologie*): it has the character of a *real sky* in the middle of the painting" (*Journal de Eugène Delacroix,* 2:364; emphasis in the text). Although subsequent commentators have tended a bit too facilely to take the truth of those remarks for granted, Delacroix's implicit recognition that the painted landscape bears a far from conventional relation to the figure of the painter is consistent with my reading of the central group.

A powerful precedent, hitherto unremarked, for the insertion of a brightly illuminated landscape scene into an otherwise somewhat dark interior space is provided by Fra Bartolomeo's Ferry Carondelet Altar (1511-12) in the Cathedral of St. John in Besançon, only fifteen miles from Courbet's native Ornans. Various writers have likened the *Studio,* with its three-part structure, to Renaissance altarpieces, and while I see no strict correspondence between individual figures in the two works, I do suggest that the Besançon panel be added to the possible sources of Courbet's masterpiece. Recent discussions of such sources include: Jeannine Baticle and Pierre Georgel, *Techniques de la peinture: l'atelier,* Les dossiers du département des peintures 12 (Paris: Louvre, 1976); Bowness, *Courbet's 'L'Atelier du peintre',* pp. 15-22; Nicolson, *Courbet: The Studio of the Painter,* pp. 65-71; Toussaint, *Courbet,* pp. 266-69; and Matthias Winner, "Gemalte Kunsttheorie: Zu Gustave Courbets 'Allégorie réelle' und der Tradition," *Jahrbuch der Berliner Museen, 1962* n.f. 4 (1963): 151-85.

19. Cf. Toussaint's statement that Courbet in his landscapes sometimes conferred upon rocks and vegetation "the humorous and clandestine appearance of human faces or heads of animals" (*Courbet,* p. 169). Thus for example in the superb version of *Le Puits noir* in Baltimore (fig. 11), a work discussed briefly in the postscript to this essay, it is possible to see in the rock mass just to the left of center a human head, or at least a nose, mouth, and chin, though whether or not Courbet intended the markings in question to be perceived in those terms, or himself perceived them as such, seems to me unclear. Nor is it clear just how

widespread is this phenomenon in Courbet's *oeuvre*. In any case, only a step separates the deliberate rhyming of model and trees in the central group from the anthropomorphic and animal imagery that Toussaint claims to detect in more than one of Courbet's landscapes.

It is interesting to compare this aspect of Courbet's art with Baudelaire's analysis in *De l'essence du rire* (1855) of "the grotesque," which he defines as "a creation mixed with a certain imitative faculty, imitative of elements preexisting in nature" (in *Curiosités esthétiques, L'Art romantique, et autres oeuvres critiques,* ed. Henri Lemaitre [Paris: Garnier Frères, 1962], p. 254). Baudelaire continues: "I mean that in this case [which he also calls the absolute comic] laughter is the expression of the idea of superiority, not of man over man [as in what he calls the significative comic], but of man over nature" (ibid.). And he goes on to say that "the essence of [the absolute comic] is to appear to be unaware of itself and to produce in the beholder . . . a joy in his own superiority and in the superiority of man over nature" (p. 262). Unawareness of self is, of course, the antitheatrical condition *par excellence,* which suggests that for Baudelaire in 1855 it is precisely the absolute comic that rescues nature from theatricality.

20. On the x-rays of the *Studio* see Lola Faillant-Dumas, "Etude au laboratoire de recherches des Musées de France," in Toussaint, *Courbet,* p. 276. Another point that emerges is that the figure of the model was originally depicted largely from the rear (ibid.). This suggests that Courbet began by conceiving of the model somewhat along the lines of the principal figures in the *Bathers* and the *Wheat Sifters,* and that only when he came to align her with the painter at his easel (the painter *in,* not *of,* the *Studio*) did he feel the need to add another figure—the peasant boy—that would establish a connection of sorts between the painter-beholder and the *Studio* as a whole.

21. One reason for this is that the rock masses surrounding the cave, quite apart from their physiognomic expressiveness (see note 19), suggest a partial human form comprising buttocks and thighs (cf. the principal figure in the *Bathers*).

22. For a more traditional reading of images of caves and flowing water in Courbet, see Werner Hofmann, "Courbets Wirklichkeiten," in *Courbet und Deutschland* (Hamburg, Kunsthalle, October–December 1978; Frankfurt am Main, Städtische Galerie, January–March 1979), pp. 608-10.

23. Cf. the ravishing *Source* (1868; fig. 13), one of the key works of the later 1860s, which recapitulates and in a sense clarifies the central group by (1) eliminating the peasant boy; (2) replacing the picture on the easel by an "actual" forest scene with trees, rocks, waterfalls, a stream, etc.; (3) merging the figures of the painter and the model in that of a seated nude woman seen from the rear; (4) depicting in no uncertain terms the flow of water past that figure toward, and by implication beyond, the surface of the painting; and (5) juxtaposing the woman's apparent absorption in the act of holding her upturned left (palette) hand in falling water with the reflection of her lower body in the surface of the stream in the immediate foreground.

Figure 13. Courbet, *The Source*, 1868. Paris, Louvre. Photo Musées nationaux.

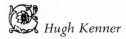 *Hugh Kenner*

The Possum in the Cave

I commence, I was about to say, with an allegory; or not that—
the term has been deconstructed—at any rate with an exemplum,
which means a narrative.

In the early summer of 1919 Tom Eliot, aged 30, joined his compatriot Ezra Pound, aged 33, and Mr. Pound's English wife, Dorothy,
32, at Excideuil in the Dordogne, birthplace of Giraut de Bornelh,
the most Tennysonian of the troubadours, for a walking tour of
which one of the benefits would be celebrating their release from five
years of being shut up in England by war, and another would be
some relief for Mr. Eliot from a three years' marriage already needing
relief. They struck southward, they stayed at inns, and we do not
know what they inspected or talked about.[1] We do know this, that
the Pounds were headed for Montségur, on a northern spur of the
Pyrenees, where seven hundred years earlier the civilization known to
the troubadours had been extinguished by executioners' torches.
Montségur is a castle of white stone, high on a sunlit mountain. We
also know, though we cannot know why, unless Eliot's unpublished
letters someday tell us, that Eliot elected instead to leave them on a
project of his own, which entailed going down into the earth and
inspecting cave paintings. Atop a mountain: down into a cave lit by
torchlight: the antithesis leaps to the mind.

It would be pleasant to know which cave. The map suggests that it
may have been the Grotte de Niaux, where the Missouri Possum
would have been confronted by bison, "d'une pureté de traite éton-
nante." I quote a guidebook because I have not seen those bison myself, though I did manage to see the creatures at Lascaux some years
before it was closed to visitors. In whichever cave it was, Tradition
confronted the Individual Talent, which conceivably felt fairly small
in the first moments of recognizing that the Mind of Europe had
worked in not unfamiliar ways 20,000 years previously. Hands that
could hold a stylus by contracting muscles like those in Eliot's hand
had been prompted by that mind to outline bison—for simplicity let

us posit bison—which Eliot's eye could recognize that day. This fact overrode such 1919 facts as that Tom Eliot wore boots that were giving his feet blisters, and carried an American passport, and had an unstable wife, and worked in a London bank.

It does not do to be naïve about the mimetic eloquence of those creatures someone of whose very language we are wholly ignorant had outlined and pigmented in the flickering torchlight. Such things had been seen many times before, by observers who found it impossible to see them. If you encounter something that is not supposed to be there, your easiest recourse is not to see it. Newton himself, experimenting with the prism by which he broke sunlight into a spectrum, did not see the Fraunhofer absorption lines,[2] which for more than a century have constituted almost the only reason, except freshman instruction, for tinkering with such a piece of apparatus. Being discontinuities in what Newton was talking about, they are omitted from his discourse, and though his eye can scarcely have missed them, he no doubt attributed them to some defect in the prism. They have told later generations of astrophysicists what each star is made of. We must excuse Newton. It is hard to look.

One reason the cave paintings were not supposed to be there was that before anthropology surrounded us with its paradigms there was no conceivable reason for drawing large animals on the walls of a totally dark place that is very troublesome to get inside of. This may be why lore of the caves is not one of the things we have inherited from Roman travelers' archives of curiosities, though in at least one cave the prints of Roman sandals are still to be seen. So they were visited in Roman times; but the drawings were too queer to talk about, or too uninteresting.

The drawings gave trouble to mid-nineteenth-century minds for other reasons, two main ones. That historically minded century had firm paradigms of Art History, and these drawings managed to exist outside of Art History, a way of saying that before a viewer's eyes they managed not to exist. As Remy de Gourmont would note near the century's turn, an *Iliad* newly discovered amid the ruins of Herculaneum would arouse in us only a few archaeological sensations.[3] Also, the century that discovered evolution had no place for gifted cave men in its schemata. One way of coping with the fact that the bison were more convincing than they ought to have been was to judge that they were modern forgeries. Another was to deprecate pictorial accomplishment altogether, as the sort of skill literate people left behind. The draughtsmen were like clever children, or *idiots savants.* One of literature's minor curiosities is the first mention of the cave paintings in an English poem. The date is 1846, by which time four or five caves had been investigated, and the author is William Wordsworth.[4] His occasion is a sonnet deploring the new vogue for illustrated books and newspapers. "A dumb art," he calls Illustration, "that best can suit / The taste of this once-intellectual Land." By "intellectual" he means logocentric: word-centered. For taste now declines, and evolution accordingly runs in reverse; at this rate, he says, we shall soon be back in the cave:

> A backward movement surely have we here,
> From manhood,—back to childhood; for the age—
> Back toward caverned life's first rude career.
> Avaunt this vile abuse of pictured page!
> Must eyes be all in all, the tongue and ear
> Nothing? Heaven keep us from a lower stage!

We must become mid-Victorians to comprehend these lines, noting as we do so that in their premonition of the Village Videot Wordsworth is able to situate the Magdalenian aurochs and bison where we mid-Victorians can live with them: they serve to remind us what a distance Englishmen have come, since their ancestors (or, more precisely, the ancestors of Frenchmen) yielded to the frequent compulsion to scrawl outlines: as, the poet does not note explicitly, Frenchmen still do in studios.

But by 1919 events had provided the individual talent of Tom Eliot with other themes altogether on which to muse, enabling him to commune in the cave with what he subsequently called "that vanished mind of which our own is a continuation."

Art History had absorbed several revolutions, beginning with the Pre-Raphaelite contention that "primitive" Giotto might be a better shaper of taste than accomplished Raphael, some time prior to whom a dissociation of sensibility had set in. (Eliot's Raphael would one day be Milton.) It had next undergone Impressionism and Pointillism, each endeavoring to recover, with the aid of science, the elements of a naïve perception of color, to be simulated without underpainting. Cubists had reminded the eye that the picture plane is after all flat. Picasso (who visited the cave at Altamira in 1902) had been incorporating the most primitive African art into the most advanced European. Correspondingly, Cambridge anthropology had replaced the Homer of Matthew Arnold (rapid, noble, and on the whole biblical) with a Homer remembering mysteries and blood rites, but perhaps decadent to the extent of his removal from these. Gilbert Murray had lectured on the hidden continuities linking Orestes with Hamlet, and Freud had reinstalled Oedipus in the Viennese bedroom. And (Eliot would be writing for *The Egoist* within a few weeks of his vigil in the cave) the poet "must be quite aware of the obvious fact that art never improves, but that the mind of Europe—the mind of his own country—a mind which he learns in time to be much more important than his own private mind—is a mind which changes, and that this change is a development which abandons nothing en route, which does not superannuate either Shakespeare, or Homer or the rock drawing of the Magdalenian draughtsmen. That this development, refinement perhaps, complication certainly, is not, from the point of view of the artist, any improvement. . . . But the difference between the present and the past is that the conscious present is an awareness of the past in a way and to an extent which the past's awareness of itself cannot show."[5]

By 1981 this passage is surely so familiar as to require no gloss. Let us merely observe, before leaving the Possum for a while in communion with graphic bison, that his words encourage us to regard art as the activity of a supracommunal mind, neither improving nor disimproving in its isolated manifestations, and indifferent in some important way to the materials it ingests: the bison perhaps, the madonnas, the princes of Denmark, and the ordinary evenings in New Haven. And if art is mimetic—an "if" that Eliot's formulation does not presume to decide—it will be only secondarily concerned with the objects and the illusion of its mimesis. If poetry, that art will be logocentric.

If we now follow Ezra and Dorothy to Montségur in the expectation of some neat antithesis, we shall be disappointed, though with care a useful antithesis will be discernible. We may ease ourselves toward it by noting a few iconic contrasts: as that Ezra is in the light of his predilection; Tom in an underground domain of the kind that would later feed his imagination during daily travels by tube beneath London.[6] While Tom stands bemused before a manifestation of the Mind of Europe, his compatriot is hiking toward the site of a datable event, the siege of Montségur in 1244 and the execution of two hundred of its defenders, which in extirpating the Cathars at the climax of the Dominican crusade effectively terminated an autonomous Provençal civilization. It would be possible to stand atop Montségur and say, "It happened *here*," and address your companion in the spirit of Byron addressing his reader, "Stop! For thy tread is on an Empire's dust." Not that that was Pound's style.

For to do that is to come as a pilgrim and need not entail *seeing* the landscape. Pound is playful in Canto 24 with fifteenth-century pilgrims to the Holy Land who took note of the school attended by the Virgin Mary and the rock that Christ marked saying, "Hic est medium mundi." Such important places would seem to merit snapshots, but we do not find them so much as described. The pilgrims seemed content to say to themselves what they heard said, "Here it was," a sentiment Pound's own highly topographic poetry seldom indulges. No, what he does is look. What is left here? His wife looks too, and will remember for fifty years that she found a five-leaf clover.

What he saw he never tells us, being on principle averse to description; his is a poetic of enumeration. He sees at once apparently that Montségur is not a fortress, since, contrary to guidebook custom, he nowhere calls it that. Anyone save a guidebook writer might reflect that no fortress has an unprotected main door in its front wall. What prolonged the siege was not fortification nor strength of walls, but the inaccessibility of the site, sheer cliffs on three sides, a narrow uphill path on the fourth. Nor is Montségur a dwelling place. What, for instance, would dwellers do for water, save catch it when they could from the sky? Yet the stone is smooth cut and white. Those huge

blocks have been squared and hoisted to build something of importance to many people. Not stronghold or freehold, then almost
certainly a temple.

As to its god, Pound had seen enough evidence of the cult of the
bull in those parts, notably the bullring at Arles he and Dorothy once
attended, to make the guess that is registered in the *Pisan Cantos*
twenty-six years later, when his mood takes him back to the desolation they had found on the high place:

> and in Mt Segur there is wind space and rain space
>   no more an altar to Mithras. [7]

We may guess that the weather they encountered was bad, though to
be sure we are guessing. What we are told about weather, in adjacent
lines, pertains to two other occasions on that journey:

> and the rain fell all the night long at Ussel
> *cette mauvaiseh venggg* biew over Tolosa

—whereas the wind space and rain space of the lines about Montségur
may be extrapolations formed on a sunny day from the presence of
space. Still, it is surprising how much hard information readers of the
Cantos can recover; thus when "mauvaise vent" is deformed phoneti-
cally, we may deduce that they heard a regional voice comment on
the evil wind.

Nine years after the *Pisan Cantos* were written, Ferdinand Niel's
careful researches were being published, [8] with their demonstration
of Montségur's orientation to the solstices, and of how the shadow of
the doorpost bisects the threshold stone corner to corner at precisely
noon on precisely midsummer day, the same day at the dawning of
which light entering eastward slits cut into walls at the north end of
the temple leaves again through westward slits, grazing no stone; so
that in *Rock Drill* (1956) we read of

> Mont Ségur, sacred to Helios. [9]

Unless Helios is somehow an alternate guise of Mithras, this makes
for an inconsistency in the poem, should anyone choose to correlate
details more than a hundred pages apart: an inconsistency that could

have been avoided by omitting the *Rock Drill* line or revising the Pisan one. The *Cantos* contain many such inconsistencies. Truth, they tell us by their mutual jar, is cumulative, subject to revision, and attained by a collective process; there are authorities one must trust, and they correct their predecessors, or impose new conventions. The Chinese names in Canto 13 have the French spelling of M. G. Pauthier (Paris, 1841), in much later ones the Anglicized convention of Mathews's dictionary (Harvard University Press, 1943); this says, among other things, that there was a time when one's only source for Confucian maxims was a Frenchman who had inherited the enlightenment, but that Harvard has since caught up.

So goes what we may call for the moment the poetic of sunlight, a denotative extreme. Its facts are out there in the light, and it proceeds by a naming, which is a pointing. "Mont Ségur, sacred to Helios" does little on the linguistic plane save shape an affirmative cadence around the joining of a French word to a Greek one with the aid of an English adjective and an English preposition. If we are intent on explicit grammar, we shall not even locate a verb. The cadence, and the word "sacred," say that something here is good; Helios the sun-god rhymes with numerous affirmations of light hereabouts and elsewhere in the poem. Montségur then is receiving benediction, but what is Montségur? Person, place, or thing? The name of a place, a large Larousse may tell us. A place of historic significance, we may learn from history of Catharism. A solar temple, we shall be told if we chance upon the book of Mons. Niel. Other data, its remoteness, its elevation, its whiteness atop its peak against the deep sky in the hard Pyreneean light, we may best collect by going there. On how much, outside itself, that brief line depends! And it makes, does that line, no effort to assemble these particulars. It names and points.

We may provisionally describe this poetic in the following way. Ezra Pound's effort, here and typically, is to move the sources of difficulty out of his text and into the extratextual domain of things we can see with our eyes: Montségur, its temple, to which pertain other things we may read of in books, its cult and history. Pound's unit of obscurity, so to speak, is the single word, and much obscurity is resolved when we locate a referent. "If you have never

seen an elephant," he would remark, "naturally the word is obscure."[10]

Return now to the cave, to be instructed by Eliot on cave poetic.
It will be logocentric as we might expect, the continuities of the
Mind of Europe being accessible chiefly through the language and the
linguistic knowledge each person carries in the hollow round of his
skull. Thus, when Pound makes an imagined survivor of the wreck of
Montségur complain that "they hadn't left even the stair,"[11] the
word "stair" points insistently outward, to a stair in ruins of which I
could show you a photograph; but when Eliot in *Ash Wednesday*
evokes what there was to be seen "at the first turning of the second
stair," we do not expect to be able to find that stair anywhere save in
Dante; in St. John of the Cross; in a tradition of poetic iconography
so diffuse as to be difficult to specify; and, most pertinently, throughout Eliot's poetry itself, where we begin by noting the stair J. Alfred
Prufrock thinks of climbing toward the room where women walk; to
turn back, he thinks, will be to disturb the universe.

For Eliot is "a postsymbolist poet," which is a brief way of saying
that he invites you to compile an ad hoc dictionary of his key words,
and most of the entries in that dictionary refer you to other poetic
occasions, some his, some not his, some ambiguous. Thus, one entry
under "stair" would be the line "que vos guida al som de l'escalina,"
and it would be hard to decide whether this line pertains more to
Dante or to Eliot's note on line 428 of *The Waste Land*, where
Dante's line becomes part of Eliot's canon. One is inclined to guess
that had Eliot written enough poetry, he would have contrived to
incorporate within his canon, somewhere or other, all the literary
occasions to which his lines refer: would have succeeded for instance
in citing Cavalcanti's "Perch' io non spero," to which the opening
line of *Ash Wednesday* points: "Because I do not hope to turn again."
The world, said Mallarmé, exists to end in a book; and, at the asymp-
tote toward which Eliot's poetry seems to tend, we discern but *one*
book, Eliot's own, containing everything in an echo chamber of self-
referentiality. It could thus be the only book on our shelves, and I
am not sure how we might learn to read a book like that.

We may discern some of its features in the incomplete version we have, the volume called *Complete Poems and Plays*. Thus *Ash Wednesday*'s use of the definitive article—"The vanished power of the usual reign"; "The infirm glory of the positive hour"—stimulates the referential "the" of everyday language—"Have you put out the cat?" —to stipulate a power, a reign, a glory, an hour, which are only at this instant becoming objects of attention though the regnant convention is that we know all about them. Thus too, many cardinal events of the first part of *Ash Wednesday* turn out to be purely syntactic happenings, such as the change in the number of pronoun—

> Because I do not hope to turn again
> Let these words answer
> For what is done, not to be done again
> May the judgment not be too heavy upon us

—which in substituting "us" for "me" installs the speaker in a place prepared for him by religious tradition, amid the imperfectly behaving human race. And in these four lines we find no punctuation save one comma, one of the four commas, the two marks of interrogation, and the single pair of parentheses that constitute the entire punctuation of the poem's first thirty-eight lines. There is no irony in describing as a genuine event the termination of the thirty-ninth line by a full stop.

Finally, when Eliot says,

> Because these wings are no longer wings to fly
> But merely vans to beat the air
> The air which is now thoroughly small and dry

—we have sense enough not to inspect human shoulders for wings. We look back instead to the line about the eagle

> (Why should the agèd eagle stretch his wings?)

and outward, probably, to Matthew Arnold's trope about Shelley, "a beautiful but ineffectual angel, beating in the void his luminous wings in vain"; which trope in turn exploits many Romantic tropes wherein a poet is capable of flight, notwithstanding that bird he never was. If we need some assurance that Eliot had Arnold's trope stored somewhere in his mind, even though it is not cited in his essay "Pater and

Arnold," we may turn to a brief review in a 1918 *Egoist,* where he called an otherwise forgettable poet "A beautiful but ineffectual aeroplane, beating its propellor vainly in a tree."[12]

To establish bounds of interpretative relevance with the aid of a poet's prose is a familiar procedure among commentators on twentieth-century poets. Work with *Finnegans Wake* entails sifting Joyce's three volumes of *Letters* and even the undergraduate essays that have survived; the Stevens *Letters* and *The Necessary Angel* are indispensible for Wallace Stevens; Eliot exegetes feel responsible for many hundred pages of uncollected prose, in addition to *Selected Essays* and the other formal collections; and most of what has been usefully written on Pound has either originated in or been controlled by the *Literary Essays,* the published and unpublished letters, the *Guide to Kulchur,* and more.

If we subscribe to the Mallarmé model I have evoked, we may even regard such prose passages as drafts of poems that never got written, human life being short; ideally, everything needful would be in the book of poems, which would then be seen to refer wholly to itself, mirror on mirror mirroring all the show. For by now we are too shrewd to expect the writer to tell us in prose what he *really* meant, which his literary craft disguises, we who routinely take undergraduates aside to disabuse them concerning "meaning." Rather, what the prose tends to do is set bounds to the otherwise boundless, assuring us that our man had indeed *read* this or that book, *known* this or that fact, to which it is consequently appropriate to appeal. Our habit of devoting our attention to single authors implies a sense that the limit of relevance is defined by what we can know the authors' mind contained. It is helpful to know that Eliot did study Sanskrit.

We also know, without reference to letters, that Alexander Pope did not study anything comparable—a way of saying that the boundaries of relevance, which we now refer to someone's skull and define with the aid of every scrap of writing and anecdotage we can find, were once public and cultural, located by a common system of discourse and education. When Pope in *The Rape of the Lock* departs from the public tradition of the mock epic (itself validated by the pseudo-Homeric *Margites*) and fetches his supernatural beings (needful for epic) from Rosicrucian lore, he is careful to tell us so, explicitly, by printing a dedicatory letter at the head of the poem in which these rare matters are explained to Lady Arabella Fermor: knowing well that no unscholarly lady would read it half so carefully as the coffee-house literatti. In that oblique "note" of Pope's we may discern a precursor for the prose of Eliot, Pound, Stevens, Joyce, Yeats, systematically consulted by scholars today.

It has been, then, a working hypothesis of considerable value that each poet aspires toward his own closed world of discourse, to compile and apply the lexicon of which is the agendum of explicative criticism. And yet there are differences in this respect among the writers I have listed, and among almost as many more as might be cited. In lieu of a minute calibration for which this occasion is inappropriate, I shall revert to my extreme cases, Pound hiking toward the mountain top, Eliot in the cave.

Here we need two longer passages. This is Eliot:

> At the first turning of the second stair
> I turned and saw below
> The same shape twisted on the banister
> Struggling with the devil of the stairs who wears
> The deceitful face of hope and of despair.

We have already remarked upon "stair," and nothing we said is in conflict with F. R. Leavis's observation of its equivocal immediacy: it has a "banister,"[13] such as a poet simply moving allegorical counters would not have supplied. Yet the fetid air, the devil of the stairs, the twisted shape, these without having assignable sources evoke an iconic system with which we are comfortable, pertaining both to nightmare and to evil spirits. Commentary on such lines becomes lexical; it notes the enclosing, iterated sounds, stair-banister-air-stairs-wear-despair, a phoneme system from which there seems no escaping; it notes the implications of "twisted," as much moral as corporeal, and of "vapour," anticipating the vowel of "air"—

> Under the vapour in the fetid air

—and substantializing fetor, since it is something a shape can be
discernibly "under": matters like that. "Hope" and "despair" seem
inescapably binary, attributes of the same "deceitful face," deceiving
whichever demeanor it wears.

Here is Pound for comparison:

> From Val Cabrere, were two miles of roofs to San Bertrand
> so that a cat need not set foot in the road
> where now is an inn, and bare rafters,
> where they scratch six feet deep to reach pavement,
> where now is a wheat field, and a milestone,
> an altar to Terminus, with arms crossed
> back of the stone
> Where sun cuts light against evening;
> where light shaves grass into emerald. . . .[14]

Like Montségur with its wind space and rain space, this is a recognizable topos of loss: once two miles of roofs, now a solitary inn, and
the very road buried from long disuse. The names say we are in
France, in a place that flourished when it was Roman (the "altar to
Terminus" survives from that time) and exists now in desuetude
beneath unaltered light, the sole thing that goes on exactly as always.
The rhetoric of patient monosyllabic exactness—"so that a cat need
not set foot in the road"—bespeaks an austere imaginative space in
which a slow voice is finding the evocative image, taking care to
place each small word exactly so.

Though it is situated in the *Cantos*, this passage belongs to a genre
with which Pound had commenced to familiarize his readers before
the Cantos were commenced. It is the kind of landscape we find in
"Provincia Deserta,"[15] subsisting now in a melancholy emptied of
public deeds, its terms as proper to Pound's poetic lexicon as stairs
and fetid vapors are to Eliot's.

And yet it surely matters that the words send us out toward the
verifiable. For we can find the tiny crossroads of Val Cabrere on the
map, two miles more or less from San Bertrand de Comminges
(present population 318). By going there, if we choose, we can verify
that the road between them is bleak now, though it once ran through
a town of 60,000 inhabitants; that an inn is visible; that wheat fields

are in sight; that objects archaeologists discovered in the course of scratching six feet deep to find Roman pavement are now deposited in the village museum in San Bertran: including now, presumably, the altar to Terminus which would seem to have been still *in situ* in 1919 when Pound visited, and is literally the only item in the passage I did not see with my own eyes on a half-day twelve years ago, because the man with the keys to the museum could not be located. I am even able to testify to the light.

I repeat that it matters. This is not the poetic of the cave, the post-symbolist signification of ineffabilities, controlled by allusion and acoustic nuance. It is mimetic in one of the old senses of mimesis: its referents exist "out there," in a place to which a Michelin map will guide you, perhaps two hours by car from Montségur. A system of words denotes that verifiable landscape. The landscape in turn denotes urban decline, as surely as Pope's

> Another age shall see the golden ear
> Embrown the slope, and nod on the parterre.

—and denotes it not simply by having the right look and feel, but by being a place with a history rich enough to have made antiquarians dig six feet deep amid a landscape where little now stirs. Urban decline in turn denotes the decline of Provence after the Montségur calamity, and the Roman decline before that. San Bertrand de Comminges was where Herod of Galilee was rusticated after the historic mess he made there, and it was where his wife died, the Hérodiade of Flaubert and Mallarmé. If we are familiar with Pound's long poem, it is easy to move into larger areas of concern that inform it: the decline of the Mystery Religions, pagan and Christian, their enemy in the poem being always sheer calculating Power; the decline of Rome through economic overstress: Usura.

The words point, point, and the arranger of the words works in trust that we shall find their connections validated outside the poem: connections he imitates on the page by rhythmic and acoustic binding. John Steven Childs[16] has remarked that Imagism (ca. 1913-14) "sought to curtail the proliferation of connotative Signifieds engendered by Symbolism," and that the Chinese ideograms were installed in the *Cantos* to exemplify the possibility of signs whose relation to the signified is not arbitrary but motivated. Such a sign will be a picture, as much the calligrapher's picture of a horse, which is the horse radical, called *ma,* as the cave painter's picture of a bison, which points to no spoken language, but instead to the Western language of the visual arts.

Looking at ideograms in Fenollosa's manuscripts, Pound saw a confirmation of one of the earliest "Don'ts for Imagists," which may be paraphrased, Don't pile up verbiage to the end that a symbol may be incanted, for "the natural object is always the adequate symbol."[17] Looking at the bison in the cave, Eliot saw a confirmation of something else, the continuity of the Mind of Europe, its latest manifestations both burdened and enabled by superincumbent memories of its earlier ones. In one mood, Eliot found it inspiriting to consider how in "not only the best, but the most individual parts" of a poet's work, "the dead poets, his ancestors, assert their immortality most vigorously," and in another mood he could rhyme the Mind of Europe with the weary answer of Cumae's exhausted Sibyl, "I want to die." The deceitful face of hope and of despair: the Mind of Europe, like any mind, is duple.

It may be that nowadays only physicists and biologists share Ezra Pound's faith that the universe is configured according to the configurations of human understanding. The Double Helix is a sort of ideogram, a natural symbol that is also a simplified image of the very thing it denotes. DNA really *is* doubly helical and conveys genetic information to successor cells as efficaciously as its likeness on the blackboard conveys information to our minds. Exactly so, a description of deserted terrain between Val Cabrere and San Bertrand conveys desolation to our minds in a poem that examines causes of desolation, and the terrain itself exemplifies the working of those causes, verifiable outside the poem. The universe, says Bucky Fuller, that profound *faux-naif,* is "all that is not me, and me," and though I can only know what the "me" of it encounters, aided by my language, which was not of my making, still "all that is not me" subsists, knowable, a very great deal.

In his contribution to the recent *Deconstruction and Criticism,*
J. Hillis Miller reflects on nihilism, metaphysics' alien guest.[18]
"Nihilism," he notes, is not its own name for itself, but "the name
given to it by metaphysics, as the term 'unconscious' is given by
consciousness to that part of itself which it cannot face directly."
Metaphysics has been struggling to expel nihilism for centuries: "to
cover over the unhealable by annihilating the nothingness hidden
within itself."

Would it be possible, Miller asks, to reverse the relationship, to
"make nihilism the host of which metaphysics is the alien guest, so
giving new names to both? Nihilism would then not be nihilism but
something else, something without a melodramatic aura, something
perhaps so innocent-sounding as 'rhetoric,' or 'philology,' or 'the
study of tropes,' or even 'the trivium.' Metaphysics might then be
redefined from the point of view of this trivium, as an inevitable
rhetorical or tropological effect. It would not be a cause but a
phantom generated within the house of language by the play of language. 'Deconstruction' is one current name for this reversal.'"

I have no quarrel with the clarity of this, or with its good temper,
or even with its logic. Nor do I propose to shed tears for whichever
metaphysical spook Professor Miller wishes to exorcize—Hegelian,
Husserlian, it is all the same. I shall even be glad to endorse his
premise that "Nihilism is the latent ghost encrypted within any
expression of a logocentric system": his example is Shelley's *Triumph
of Life.*

It is true: logocentric systems are haunted. One name for the
ghost in such a system is The Mind of Europe, apt to discover suddenly that it wants to die: at which moment, or even beforehand, a
host of clever people stand ready with axes. "It is necessary," said
Roland Barthes in 1971, "to attempt to split, not signs, not signifiers
on one side and signifieds on the other, but the very idea of the sign:
an operation one might call a semioclasty. It is Western discourse
as such, in its foundations, its elementary forms, that one must today
attempt to split."[19] Since this alarming proposal is uttered in the
forms of Western discourse, one suspects an instance of such discourse

getting very tired of itself. You would too, if you lived in a logo-centric system (words, words). No voice, not even one's own, can enchant for ever.

Not the metaphysical then but the physical seems worth affirm-ing: the possibility of signs that point, of a "Mont Ségur, sacred to Helios" that points to a demonstrable solar temple that mimes in its configurations a demonstrable sun; of problems shifted to the world of the visible, where we can literally see what we are dealing with and, in meditating on why other men have valued it, refresh our meditations at need with what is enmeshed with language but not logocentric: not enclosed in the cave where the pictures, though they enchant, are no more than pictures, and if you lift your voice you hear its own echo, transcribed by E. M. Forster as "ou boum." Was that what everything came to, asked Mrs. Moore in the Marabar Caves: nothing at all to all that men had valued save "ou boum"?

Uncle Remus's Possum, you will remember, just lay there an' said nuffin' and in saying nothing did not hear "ou boum." Saying nuffin' has made no Possum a poet. T. S. Eliot made poetry by tuning "ou boum," modulating its murmurs, adjusting his voice to its feedback, straining his ear amid its rustle for the voices

> Of children in the apple tree
> Unseen because not looked for
> But heard, half heard in the stillness
> Between two waves of the sea.

His poetry is incomparable of its kind, as is Valéry's poetry and Wallace Stevens's and, for that matter, Mallarmé's. No more than *Little Gidding* is *Sunday Morning* or *Toast Funèbre* something you can argue with. There remains, it is merely necessary to remember, a poetry of light and of the eye, not less sophisticated than these in eschewing logocentrality: the poetry of what is "sacred to Helios,"

> the sound a gemmed light. . . .
> form is cut in the lute's neck, tone is from the bowl[20]

—which happens to be a verifiable fact, if you will look at a lutanist.

NOTES

1. Details of this tour from Dorothy Pound, conversation, 1969, and letter, 16 January 1970.

2. Horace Freeland Judson, *The Search for Solutions* (New York: Holt, Rinehart & Winston, 1980), p. 171.

3. Glenn S. Burne, ed., *Remy de Gourmont: Selected Writings* (Ann Arbor: University of Michigan Press, 1966), p. 97.

4. Wordsworth, "Illustrated Books and Newspapers."

5. T. S. Eliot, "Tradition and the Individual Talent," often reprinted.

6. See *Burnt Norton* 3. Its unstated locale, as Eliot indicated in a copy that he annotated for his brother, is the Gloucester Road station of the London underground.

7. Canto 76, *The Cantos of Ezra Pound* (New York: New Directions, 1970), p. 452.

8. Fernand Niel, *Montségur, Temple et Forteresse des Cathares d'Occitanie* (Grenoble: Imprimerie Allier, 1967); Niel first disclosed his findings concerning solar orientation in *Montségur, la Montagne inspirée* (Paris: La Colombe, 1954).

9. Canto 87, p. 574.

10. See D. D. Paige, ed., *The Letters of Ezra Pound* (New York: Harcourt Brace, 1950), p. 251.

11. Canto 23, p. 109.

12. *Egoist* 5, no. 3 (1918): 44.

13. F. R. Leavis, *New Bearings in English Poetry* (London: Chatto & Windus, 1932), p. 125.

14. Canto 48, p. 243.

15. In *Personae of Ezra Pound* (New York: Boni & Liveright, 1926), pp. 121-23. The poem was first published in 1915.

16. John Steven Childs, "Larvatus Prodeo; Semiotic Aspects of the Ideogram in Pound's *Cantos*," *Paideuma* 9, no. 3: 289-307. See esp. 293, 296 ff.

17. See *The Literary Essays of Ezra Pound* (New York: New Directions, 1954), p. 5. The "Don'ts" were compiled in 1913.

18. J. Hillis Miller, "The Critic as Host," in Harold Bloom, Paul De Man, Jacques Derrida, Geoffrey H. Hartman, and J. Hillis Miller, *Deconstruction and Criticism* (New York: Seabury Press, 1979), pp. 217-53.

19. Quoted in Josué V. Harari, *Textual Strategies* (Ithaca: Cornell University Press, 1979), p. 30.

20. Conflated from Canto C, p. 716, and Canto 109, p. 774.

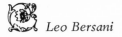

Leo Bersani

Representation and Its Discontents

I wish to examine texts that propose and that resist the following proposition: sexual excitement and even sexual violence are functions of mimetic representations. In *The 120 Days of Sodom*—to take a case of scandalously marginal exemplarity—Curval and the Duke impulsively rape their daughters after hearing the story of a man who is sexually aroused by the sight of female corpses and by fantasies of murder. "And the scoundrel," Sade writes of Curval, "while fucking Adelaide [the more precise French expression is "en enconnant Adélaïde"—and in this area precision is, of course, necessary in Sade], imagined, like the Duke, that he was screwing his murdered daughter. What incredible mental abberation: the libertine cannot hear or see anything without wanting to imitate it at once." But this "égarement" is perfectly consistent with the dominant Sadean view of sexual excitement as a shared commotion. Sade comes close to suggesting, in *The 120 Days,* that we do not have sex with others *because* they excite us; excitement is the consequence of sex rather than its motive. This is because it is essentially a replay in the libertine of the agitation he produces on the other's body. In the funny physiological terms in which Sade sums up the Duke's ideas: "He noticed that a violent commotion inflicted upon any kind of an adversary is answered by a vibrant thrill in our own nervous system; the effect of this vibration, arousing the animal spirits which flow within these nerves' concavities, obliges them to exert pressure on the erector nerves and to produce in accordance with this perturbation [*ébranlement*] what is termed a lubricious sensation."[1] The missing link here would seem to be the means of transport from the other's "commotion" to the libertine's "vibration." The latter can, however, only be the agitated perception of the former. The "vibration" that produces recognizable signs of sexual excitement is the spectacle of the other person's commotion. Sexual excitement must be represented before it can be felt; or, more exactly, it *is* the representation of an alienated commotion. Sadism is a logical

consequence of this view of sexuality. If erotic stimulation depends
on the perceived or fantasized commotion of others, it becomes
reasonable to put others into a state of maximal commotion. In
Sade, the libertine's erection-provoking vibrations increase in direct
proportion to the visible intensification of his victim's suffering.

These remarks bring me back to two psychoanalytic texts that I
continue to find extremely suggestive: Freud's genealogy of sado-
masochism in the 1915 essay "Instincts and Their Vicissitudes," and
Jean Laplanche's reading of that passage in *Life and Death in
Psychoanalysis.* I hope to reach some new conclusions about these
passages by submitting them to the speculative pressures of other
texts: *The 120 Days of Sodom,* Pasolini's filmic reading of that work,
a poem by Mallarmé, and another essay by Freud himself.

Let us begin with a brief summary of the passage in "Instincts and
Their Vicissitudes" with which some readers will undoubtedly be
familiar. In that essay, Freud uses sadism and masochism in order to
illustrate transformations in the objects and aims of instincts. He
begins with a three-step process. The first step, which is somewhat
confusingly called "sadism," is the "exercise of violence or power
upon some other person or object." In step two, both the object and
the aim change: the impulse to master is turned upon the self and its
aim also changes from active to passive. Finally, the instinct returns
to an object in the world, but since its aim has become passive,
another person "has to take over the role of the subject"—that is, the
dominant role of step one. This last case, Freud points out, is what is
usually called masochism, but he then goes on to make distinctions
that profoundly modify the entire scheme just proposed. The conception of sadism is made more complicated, .Freud suggests, by "the
circumstance that this instinct, side by side with its general aim, (or
perhaps, rather, within it) seems to strive towards the accomplishment
of a quite special aim—not only to humiliate and master, but, in
addition, to inflict pains."

How does this happen? The "sadistic" child of step one is
indifferent to causing pain; he wants only to master the world (or
one "object" in it: his mother). But, Freud writes, once the
masochistic stage has been reached in the three-step process, the

instinctual aim may change from that of being mastered to that of experiencing pain. This is possible because (and I will return to this in a moment) "we have every reason to believe that sensations of pain, like other unpleasurable sensations, spill over into or encroach upon sexuality [*auf die Sexualerregung übergreifen*] and produce a pleasurable condition for the sake of which the subject will even willingly experience the unpleasure of pain." Freud concludes that "once feeling pains has become a masochistic aim, the sadistic aim of *causing* pains can arise also, retrogressively; for"—and we begin our return to Sade here—"while these pains are being inflicted on other people, they are enjoyed masochistically by the subject through his identification of himself with the suffering object." Thus sadism ends up in this development by becoming secondary, a masochistic identification with the suffering object. We would seem, then, to have two quite different kinds of sadism existing simultaneously once the infliction of pain has become an instinctual aim: "an original," non-sexual sadism, which seeks to master the world, and a derived, sexual sadism, which is actually a pleasurable fantasy-identification with the intense (sexualized) pain of the victim. The sadist has introjected the self projected into the suffering position of the other. In his later work—and especially after the elaboration of his theory of the death instinct—Freud will be ever more emphatic about the priority of masochism. In "The Economic Problem of Masochism" (1924), for instance, he speaks of the libidinal life instincts attempting to make the death instincts harmless; they do this by directing our impulse to destroy toward objects in the external world, and this impulse "is then called the destructive instinct, the instinct for mastery, or the will to power." Thus step one in "Instincts and Their Vicissitudes" turns out to be a sadism derived from masochism in somewhat the same way as sexual sadism in the earlier essay was described as a projected masochism.

The implications of this shift are crucial for the nature of sexuality itself in psychoanalytic thought. As we saw a moment ago, Freud moves toward the notion of specifically sexual masochism and sadism in "Instincts and Their Vicissitudes" by speaking of sensations of pain "spilling over" or extending into pleasurable sexuality—that is, by suggesting that sexual pleasure may be a component of all sensations that go beyond a certain threshold of intensity. We find the same idea in *Three Essays on the Theory of Sexuality,* where Freud writes: "It may well be that nothing of considerable importance can occur in the organism without contributing some component to the excitation of the sexual instinct." Pleasure and pain are therefore both experienced as *sexual* pleasure when they are strong enough to shatter a certain stability or equilibrium of the self. In passages such as these, Freud somewhat tentatively argues that the pleasurable excitement of sexuality occurs when the body's normal range of sensation is exceeded and when the organization of the self is momentarily disturbed by sensations somehow "beyond" those compatible with psychic organization. Sexuality would be that which is intolerable to the structured self.

I am now inclined to think that the conclusion to which all this points is that sexual excitement is a function of masochistic agitation. That is, in speaking about the presumably limited, even marginal structure of sado-masochistic sexuality, Freud unexpectedly proposes an ontology of sexuality itself. Jean Laplanche has noted, in his discussion of "Instincts and Their Vicissitudes," that "sexual pleasure [in Freud's scheme] resides in the suffering position."[2] He explains this by the nature of fantasizing, assuming, I believe, that what Freud calls the sadist's "identification of himself with the suffering object" is conceivable only as a mental representation of that suffering. In fantasy, an object of desire is introjected; the pleasant or the unpleasant effect that the individual wishes to have on that object is therefore felt by the desiring subject himself. The restlessness of human desire is not only a function of the absence of the object of desire; desire is restless also because it perhaps always includes, within itself, the disruptive effect on the *other*'s equilibrium, which is now an effect on an internalized other. This seems to me to be the gist of Laplanche's argument, and one consequence I would draw from this argument is that sexuality should be understood in terms of the reflexive pleasure of desire's representations; *desire produces sexuality*.

Sexuality would be desire satisfied *as* a disruption or destabilization of the self. It would therefore not be originally an exchange of intensities between individuals, but rather a condition of broken negotiations with the world. The movement to satisfy a need (the "sadistic aim of inflicting pain," for example) becomes a desiring fantasy in which the psychic apparatus is more or less gravely "shaken" by an exceptional convergence between need and satisfaction. Perhaps the "threshold of intensity" of which Freud speaks is passed whenever this kind of *dédoublement* takes place. The excess intrinsic to sexuality would have to do with the excessive expenditure involved whenever the imagined effect of our appetites on the world is internalized.

I realize that these suggestions involve an extraordinary generalizing *and* limiting of sexuality. They are, however, an attempt not to describe empirically what people "feel" in sexual contacts, but rather to account for the very *constituting of* sexuality, and this leads to a certain displacement of the entire notion of sexual pleasure. Sexuality would no longer describe a particular type of encounter; rather, it would be definable in terms of the quantity of excitement (Freud) generated by the introjection of objects in desiring fantasy (Laplanche). If, as Laplanche writes, "fantasy *is in itself* a sexual perturbation [*ébranlement*]," it is "intimately related, in its origin, to the emergence of the masochistic sexual drive." The activity of fantasmatic representation, which constitutes sexuality in human beings, is inherently an experience of "psychic pain." If we understand fantasy here as the imaginary expression and fulfillment of a desire, then the psychic disturbance produced by fantasy is an experience of pleasure *as* pain—that is, as a masochistic sexual excitement. Sexuality—at least in the mode in which it is constituted—might even be thought of as a tautology for masochism.

Thus the genealogy of sado-masochism has somewhat startling consequences. In order to account for the mystery of sadistic sexuality—that is, how we can be sexually aroused by the suffering of others, as distinct from the easier question of why we wish to exercise power over others—Freud is led to suggest that the spectacle of pain stimulates a mimetic representation that, so to speak, shatters the subject into sexual excitement. Mimetic sexuality would therefore

be, constitutively, sado-masochistic sexuality. More generally, we
might ask to what extent the fantasy-identifications outlined by
Freud are crucial to *all* sympathetic responses to suffering. Ironically
enough, Sade's sadism is consistent with the theories of benevolent
sympathy which he scornfully rejects. For what Sade rejects is not
the mechanism of sympathetic projection assumed by theories of
benevolence, but rather the pious view that we are stirred by *virtuous*
identifications with others. Virtue is irrelevant to the agitation
induced by the suffering of others. It is the identification itself—that
is, a fantasmatic introjection of the other—which appears to be
intrinsically sexual. Such introjections make us "vibrate." They
destroy psychic inertia and shatter psychic equilibrium. Both Sade
and Laplanche use the word *ébranlement* to describe this psychic
shattering, which produces what Sade calls "une sensation lubrique"
and which for Laplanche characterizes our inescapably fantasmatic
sexuality.

The value of our capacity to identify sympathetically with the pain
or suffering of others has, of course, generally been taken for granted.
It has been assumed that this capacity is central both to our responses
to art and to our capacity for moral behavior. But a reading of
Laplanche's reading of Freud may suggest to us that "sympathy"
always includes a trace of sexual pleasure, and that this pleasure is,
inescapably, masochistic. If this is the case, there is a certain risk in all
sympathetic projections: the pleasure that accompanies them promotes a secret attachment to scenes of suffering or violence. The
very operation of sympathy partially undermines the moral solidarity
that we like to think of as its primary effect. I am not, it should be
said, arguing (absurdly) "against" sympathy. Rather, I wish to
suggest that the psychic mechanism that allows for what are rightly
called humane or morally liberal responses to scenes of suffering or
violence is, intrinsically, somewhat dysfunctional. The dysfunctional
aspect of that mechanism is, of course, evident not only in our
reactions to scenes of suffering. An imitative sympathy is crucial to
our ability to learn, and in the context of a more general epistemological investigation, one might speculate about the effects on our
presumed knowledge of the world of a learning process that

destabilizes the relations between subject and object and transforms the world into an excessive, sexualizing psychic expenditure.

I would now like to propose a model of fantasmatic sexuality supplemental to, and subversive of, the model just derived from Laplanche's reading of Freud. I have used *The 120 Days of Sodom* as a "pure" or radical exemplification of the mimetic violence outlined in "Instincts and Their Vicissitudes." Let us first consider an alternative to that violence not in theoretical Freudian terms, but rather in terms of an effort to duplicate the violence of Sade's work in a film. I refer to Pasolini's *Salò*. (What I have to say about *Salò* is the result of work done in collaboration with Ulysse Dutoit.) In spite of the changes that Pasolini has made in his treatment of *The 120 Days of Sodom* (principally, the transposition of the story to a fascist enclave in northern Italy toward the end of World War II), his adherence to Sade is striking. He almost succeeds in making sadistic violence part of an entertaining spectacle, and, in so doing, Pasolini appears to have accepted an extraordinary degree of complicity with his fascistic libertines. *Salò* diminishes the grotesqueness of the literary text; indeed, what I take to be Pasolini's mistrust of the alienating aspects of *The 120 Days* even leads him to a certain embellishment of Sade's work. No one in *Salò*, for example, has the physical grotesqueness of Sade's characters. The acceptable appearances of Pasolini's libertines and women narrators make it impossible for us to ignore their considerable intelligence and their considerable elegance—both of which, while they also characterize Sade's friends, are somewhat obscured (and may therefore even be dismissed) by all the reminders in the book of their sensationally repellent bodies. By making his libertines presentable, Pasolini corrects Sade's own willingness to allow us not to recognize them. Furthermore, violence in *Salò* is at once served and kept at bay by a minor festival of the arts: in addition to the Sadean narratives, we have some dancing, music (a pianist accompanies the narratives, and we also hear "serious" and popular music over a radio), and a small gallery of modern painting. Horror is almost constantly forestalled by a multiplication of esthetic appeals. The lateral divertissements of dance, music, and painting allow for an easy and radically frivolous turning away from torture and murder. By pleasantly scattering our esthetic attention, *Salò* keeps us from focusing for very long on narrative centers of violence, and the ease with which we move to and from these centers *could* be interpreted as a consequence of our already having been seduced into a certain sympathy for their content.

I wish to suggest something quite different: Pasolini distances himself from his Sadean protagonists *by going along with them.* There is no Brechtian distancing from Sade; the relation of *Salò* to the literary text is one of subversive passivity. Pasolini duplicates that from which he wants to separate himself. The duplicating intent of his film is pointed to by several curious repetitions within the film itself. *Salò* frequently displays a kind of mimetic attachment to its own devices. The music during the two boys' dancing at the end, for example, is the same song that accompanies the titles at the beginning. The boys' dancing also reminds us of the sequence during which the Monsignore and Signora Maggi dance. In the earlier scene, the camera itself seems to be imitating the dancers' steps as it moves with them around the room. And in one of the most curious touches in the film, Pasolini has placed a statuette of a woman fixing her stockings in front of the table mirror in the room where Signora Maggi dresses before going downstairs to start her narratives The object is reflected in the mirror, and the scene it depicts is repeated by Signora Maggi, who stops near the dressing table to arrange her stockings. Finally, the Sadean libertines' habit of acting out the passions that excite them, after they are narratively described by one of the women storytellers, is, toward the end of the film, adhered to in a manner that makes the subversive intent of all these repetitions, duplications, and symmetries especially clear. I refer to the pianist's suicide: her death leap from a window into the courtyard "illustrates" Signora Castelli's anecdote about girls being brutally pushed across a room and out of a window into a cellar torture chamber. More exactly, the pianist's leap refers us to Signora Castelli's story, but the two are, so to speak, imperfectly symmetrical. One event evokes the other, but with a disquieting difference—in somewhat the same way as the cross-eyed president reminds us of the symmetry of the human face by virtue of that which violates it, a comically displaced eye.

Pasolini's brilliant trick in *Salò* is to use repetition and replication as distancing rather than imitative techniques. It is as if a fascinated adherence—to Sade, to Pasolini's own cinematic libertines, to the techniques of his film—were, finally, identical to a certain detachment. Pasolini exploits film's potential for a vertiginous passivity (its eagerness merely to *register*) and then, having allowed his work to abandon itself to all sorts of submissive doublings and pacifying symmetries, he creates a type of nonimitative recognition which is his distance from Sade and sadistic violence. What we recognize is, however, nothing more than our pleasure at being carried along as spectators. It is as if the ease with which we "go along" with *Salò*'s sadists included a folding movement of cognition—a *repliage* that constitutes our simply recognizing that ease. Thus the distance Pasolini takes from his subject consists in an excessive indulgence toward his subject; he moves away from images and styles by duplicating them rather than "criticizing" or "opposing" them.

The logic of this strategy could be defined in these terms: *moral consciousness in Salò is the replication of esthetic consciousness.* Or, to put this in another way, the folding back referred to a moment ago is also an *enfolding,* a thorough assuming or taking on of the pleasures of mimetic spectatorship. The Sadean libertines are experts in this type of pleasure, but their activities are also designed to rid them of the very "vibrations" that they seek in torturing others. The appropriation of the other's "commotions" in Sade is meant to serve a narrative denouement that kills excitement: the great test by which all acts are measured in *The 120 Days* is *la perte du foutre*. Sex in Sade is essentially the loss of cum, the coming to a loss, the climactic explosion that confirms the success of an esthetic limited to the madly rigorous schedules of Sade's narrative orders. In the Sadean system of phallic machismo, nothing is viewed more contemptuously than the weak orgasms of modestly endowed males. Sadism is an estheticized erotic, but the esthetic is limited to the controlled movements of narrative progressions. *Salò* multiplies esthetic seductions

and, appropriately almost neglects the orgasm. Pasolini has simply
let all that prideful Sadean *foutre* drop. . . . He makes us into more
willing, less purposeful spectators than his sado-fascistic protagonists.
In a sense, this means that we never tire of being spectators, but it is
the very limitlessness of our estheticism which constitutes the moral
perspective on sadism in *Salò*. The saving frivolity with which we
simply go on looking creates a consciousness of looking as, first, part
of our inescapable implication in the world's violence and, second, a
promiscuous mobility thanks to which our mimetic appropriations
of the world are constantly being continued *elsewhere* and therefore
do not require the satisfyingly climactic destruction of any part of
the world.

In what ways might the limitless and mobile visual interest promoted by *Salò* be made psychoanalytically intelligible? Freud describes an illustrious case of restlessly mobile fantasy in his essay on
Leonardo da Vinci. In some respects, this is surely one of Freud's
least satisfactory performances. Not only does much of the argument
seem to depend on Freud's mistaken translation of *Nibio* as *Geier*, or
vulture, instead of *kite*, and on inadequate, even faulty, biographical
information, but the work is full of patently unscientific conjectures
about, for example, the excessive love lavished by Leonardo's emo-
tionally frustrated unwed mother on her infant son, and the equally
excessive love given to him by his father's mother, who "we will
assume," writes Freud, "was no less tender to him than grandmothers
usually are." Furthermore, the essay ends with a rather sloppy com-
promise according to which Freud, reminding us that normal and
neurotic cannot be sharply distinguished from each other, claims that
he has "never reckoned Leonardo as a neurotic" and yet places him
"close to the type of neurotic that we designate as 'obsessional.'"
More significant is the nearly querulous tone of some of the analysis,
especially in that early section where Freud the man of science
appears to be scolding Leonardo for abandoning art for science in his
later years, and for combining genius with inactivity, indifference,
and especially an inability to conclude investigations. In saying this,
we approach what I take to be the theoretical turbulence of the
Leonardo essay: Freud's own inability to be theoretically conclusive

(and even consistent), his divided feelings about conclusiveness and consistency, and what I can only call his unarticulated sense of the enormous theoretical consequences of what he has to say about both the origins and the value of the radically inconclusive mind. Freud's study of the "psychosexuality" of Leonardo enacts as a major theoretical crisis of psychoanalysis itself what it officially presents as nothing more or less than an exceptionally interesting case history.

What, after all, could be more compelling to the founder of psychoanalysis than the question of how, and why, one concludes, or fails to conclude, an investigation? Leonardo's "problem"—his unsteadiness, his willingness to leave work half-done, his inability to execute many of the projects he imagined—is, Freud argues, the result of his father's absence in his early years. There was no one to inhibit the infantile sexual curiosity, which, sublimated later on into Leonardo's scientific curiosity, keeps the compulsively repetitive, inconclusive nature of the child's questions. But what does it mean to ask questions? The child's sexual curiosity is a form of desire, and, in Leonardo's case, this means that his investigations carry the mark of his having been kissed by his mother, as Freud strikingly puts it, "into precocious sexual maturity." "His mother's tenderness," Freud writes, "determined [Leonardo's] destiny" and that destiny is characterized by an extraordinary degree of indeterminacy and mobility in Leonardo's thought. The mother's "excessive" love for the child initiates him into sexuality, and this should be taken to mean that she seduces him into ontologically traumatic fantasy. Leonardo seeks to possess his mother by imitating her possession of him. His homosexuality is, according to Freud, the disguised expression of a precociously intense heterosexuality: he continues to enjoy his mother's love by moving into her position and loving boys as she loved him. The vulture fantasy is less important in Freud's text as indicating a "truth about" Leonardo than it is as an exemplification of traumatic sexuality (and it should now be clear that this is a tautology) *as* continuously shifting positions. In that fantasy, Leonardo is at once being nursed and nursing; he is both being kissed and being nursed by his mother; it is Leonardo's own penis that the vulture-mother thrusts into his mouth; and the bird itself is at once the mysterious, loving mother and the child experiencing, in flight, the sexual satisfaction of his desire to be sexually satisfied. . . . In these self-shattering fantasies, Leonardo is nowhere except in a certain readiness always to begin again his experimental representations of how, by whom, and by what he has been shattered.

Freud thus seems to be moving toward the position that to put an end to this mobility would be to put an end to sexuality itself. Freud himself is, however, continuously shifting positions on the question of shifting positions. The traits of infantile investigations are presented as both harmful and beneficial; they are at once responsible for Leonardo's inability to execute so many of his projects *and* for the richly undecidable figures in his paintings. Freud scolds Leonardo for his inability to conclude, at the same time that he eloquently describes the "beautiful youths of feminine delicacy" in Leonardo's art, the boys in whose mysteriously triumphant gaze Freud reads knowledge of a "secret of love," of "a great achievement of happiness, about which silence must be kept," but which we already know to be the issue of sexuality as the suspension, even the death, of identity.

Freud's own inability to conclude is even more visible in the peculiarly unsettled roles attributed to the father in the study of Leonardo. Leonardo's work simultaneously suffers and profits from his imitating his father, from his resisting the father, and also from his having been neglected by him in his early years. On the one hand, Leonardo is said to be imitating his father when he leaves work uncompleted: "He created [works of art] and then cared no more about them, just as his father had not cared for him." On the other hand, inhibited execution is the result of the father's not having put an end to the infantile investigations initiated by the mother's traumatizing love for the child. Furthermore, if Leonardo is copying his father by being indifferent to his own paintings, Freud also tells us that when he took his father for a model, Leonardo "passed through a period of masculine creative power and artistic productiveness in Milan," where he found a substitute for his father in Lodovico Sforza. And yet, if Leonardo's art suffers from the loss of his patron, it begins to flourish again not when another father substitute is found, but when he regresses to the earliest period of happy union with his mother. Finally, Freud has even called Leonardo's "rebellion against his father . . . the infantile determinant of his . . . sublime achievement in the field of scientific research." To resist the father is to resist authority and to assert an independence fruitful for both artistic and scientific investigations—although why this independence is not fruitful and necessary for art too, and what the exact relation is between the independence of Leonardo's investigations and their incomplete character are by no means clear. Thus (1) to imitate the father promotes manly creativity *and* Leonardo's indifference to his art; (2) to resist the father promotes a productive independence in his work; (3) to regress to the period of maternal seduction is, for Leonardo, to find the source of inspiration for his greatest art; although (4) the father's failure to inhibit the excited curiosity sustained by the mother's love has the negative effect of making Leonardo abandon his art and multiply uncompleted investigations into the "maternal body" of nature.

What I have called the theoretical turbulence of Freud's essay on Leonardo can perhaps be traced to Freud's resistance to the implications of his traumatic (maternal) model of sexuality. The trauma by which the infant is kissed into sexual prematurity immediately produces fantasmatic energies, energies that, as Freud shows, involve an immensely productive play of representations. In Leonardo's case, the persistence of his attempted identification with the mysterious, shattering, "excessively" loving mother led him not only to multiply his scientific investigations but also to paint figures of a troubling and powerful indeterminancy of being. I suggest that the maternally derived traumatic model of sexuality moves Freud toward a view of cultural symbolization as a continuation rather than a repressive substitute for sexual fantasy. Or, in other terms, it provides the genetic basis for a view of sublimation as coextensive with sexuality, as an appropriation and elaboration of sexual impulses rather than as a special form of renunciation of such impulses. (This view of sublimation has been proposed in a recent series of articles by Laplanche, who emphasizes Freud's startling parenthetical remark, in the Leonardo essay, that in sublimation the libido accompanying infantile sexual investigations escapes from the fate of repression and is transformed "from the very beginning" [*von Anfang an*] into intellectual curiosity.) Freud is clearly reluctant, however, to accept the psychic and social consequences of the sexual and ontological floating that he describes in his study of Leonardo, and as a result he moves, in somewhat incoherent fashion, between the trauma of maternal love and a paternally centered account of Leonardo's sexual, artistic, and scientific life. The role of the father in the argument of the essay could lead us to conclude—and this would obviously require further development—that the Oedipal father in Freud's work is the fantasmatic agent responsible for the repression not only of desire for the mother but also, in a sense, of sexuality itself. In the Oedipal fantasies of the male child, the paternal phallus is not merely placed between the mother and the child in order to prevent their sexual union. More profoundly, that phallus first of all allows the child to conclude his investigations (or to arrest his representations and mimetic appropriations) of the mother's being (he now "knows" that the father castrated the mother), and, most importantly, it keeps the identities of mother and child distinct and therefore binds or puts an end to the radically mobile sexuality initiated by the mother's earlier, traumatizing love.

The Oedipal triangle is an immobilizing structure of affective and sexual representations. If, as I have argued, sexuality originates in the masochistic excitement of fantasy, the immobilization of fantasmatic structure can only have a violent denouement. That is, the oppressive, excessive, destablizing, exciting representation must be evacuated; the masochistic origin of sexuality means that the extreme logic of sexual pleasure is its explosive end. Masochism is both relieved and fulfilled by death, and to stop the play of representations perhaps condemns fantasy to the climactic and suicidal pleasure of mere self-annulment. The violence of the Oedipal structure is not merely that of an imagined rivalry between child and parent; by inhibiting fantasmatic mobility, the Oedipal father promotes a self-destructing sexuality and therefore vindicates Freud's melancholy opposition between sexuality and civilization. The sublimation produced by the Oedipal stage is nearly indistinguishable from repression, whereas in the Leonardo essay Freud actually proposes another type of sublimation in which cultural forms would be the productively mistaken replications of sexual fantasy, the proliferations of fantasmatic shocks. One might therefore look forward to a reworking of psychoanalytic theory in which the paternal figure would no longer play the role of the inhibiting law, but would rather provide the opportunity for a socializing of the traumatic loving initially experienced at the mother's breast. The father would then function as a duplicating generalization of that love, not as its repudiation. This de-Oedipalizing of the father in the psychological mythology of our culture might also be an important step in the removal of paranoia as a dominant social structure. In literature, Stendhal's fiction could be studied both as a corroboration of the intrinsically paranoid nature of Oedipal sexuality and, astonishingly enough, as an effort to re-create the father, in the milieu of the Stendhalian *salon,* as the agent of an affectionately ironic generalizing of the mother's love.

I will, however, conclude not with Stendhal, but with a literary example closer to the Leonardo essay in that, like Freud's work, it deals with the relation between esthetic sublimations and unconcluded investigations. I refer to Mallarmé's "L'Après-midi d'un faune," in which the faun's uncertainty about whether the nymphs really existed, far from crippling his inventiveness, turns out to be the condition for an intensification of both erotic and esthetic power. Let's look at a passage that has been called a description of artistic sublimation. I propose that the interest of the following lines lies in the suggestion that sublimation is not a transcendence of desire, but rather a kind of extending of desire that has taken the form of a productive receding of consciousness:

> Mais, bast! arcane tel élut pour confident
> Le jonc vaste et jumeau dont sous l'azur on joue:
> Qui, détournant à soi le trouble de la joue,
> Rêve, dans un solo long, que nous amusions
> La beauté d'alentour par des confusions
> Fausses entre elle-même et notre chant crédule;
> Et de faire aussi haut que l'amour se module
> Evanouir du songe ordinaire de dos
> Ou de flanc pur suivis avec mes regards clos,
> Une sonore, vaine et monotone ligne.[3]

The faun's reed turns away from, replicates, supplements, and modulates his sensuality. And yet the "long solo" of his musical dream is not the fictive "line" of music which could be read as the esthetic distillation of his sensual fantasies of a nymph's back of "flanc pur." His solo *dreams of* making that distillation take place. In other words, the faun's art is not the metamorphic replication of bodily lines as lines of music, but rather the suspension and deferral of that esthetic distraction in an anticipatory consciousness of it. The possibility of treating art as symbolic equivalents or disguises of sensual impulses is therefore ruined by the agitations of the "symbolizing" consciousness itself. More precisely, the sublimating consciousness described by the faun operates on what might be called a principle of accelerating supplementarity. The consequence of this process of acceleration is that symbolic equivalences are never more than a step in the supplemental movements of thought. The faun profoundly suggests that the reflection of his erotic fantasies in his music is a mobilizing *project* of his art rather than its actual sense. That reflection may be the purpose of his art, but his performance of art depends on the suspension of its purpose, on a slippage of sense from the evoked, unperformed, and oppressively significant "line" to the space between it and the "dream," which has actually already retreated from any such settled sense in dismissively anticipating it.

The faun moves from wondering if he desired a mere dream to dreaming, in the long solo of his music, that Nature was amused by his confusion between his dream and her. During the "prélude lent où naissent les pipeaux," he had seen "ce vol de cygnes, non! de naïades." But to remember them is to wonder if he really saw them. But to doubt their reality is to wish to paint them, and to paint them is to return to his desires, and to confuse, once again, what he desires with what may really be there. In this pseudo-circle, which appears to return the faun to his musical point of departure, but which really moves him from an art of entrapped realism to an art of happily mobile ironies, the faun "revises" his having been seduced by his own art by including, within that art, nature's gentle mockery of his credulous song's confusions. In one sense, that mockery is the faun's ironic snapping away from his own naïveté. It is the reservation hidden within the subsequent account of the faun's sexual assault on the nymphs, the potentially annihilating awareness of that assault as mere illusion. And yet nothing is annihilated. The faun's "remembered" erotic violence is somewhat modified by our own uncertainty about where or who the faun is. He is the perpetrator of violence, but he is also Nature's amusement at the emptiness of that violence. The irony of "L'Après-midi d'un faune" is additive rather than corrosive. It both removes the faun from the nymphs and returns him to them, and, far from undermining his desire, it makes the objects of desire productively unlocatable.

"L'Après-midi d'un faune" performs sublimation as a mode of Mallarmé's irony. Mallarmé encourages us to view sublimation not as a mechanism by which desire is denied but rather as a self-reflexive activity by which desire multiplies and diversifies its representations. There is, to be sure, a certain purification of the desiring impulse, but purification should be understood here as an abstracting rather than a desexualizing process. The faun's sexual brutality is modulated by the doubt inherent in the account of his brutality; his attack is both negativized and enjoyed once again by an analytic and critical recitation of the attack. In reading that the nymphs try to escape from the faun's arms, "Pour fuir ma lèvre en feu buvant, comme un éclair / Tressaille! la frayeur secrète de la chair [To flee my lip on fire drinking, as a flash of lightning/Quivers! the secret terror of the flesh]," we may—inappropriately yet also aptly—remember the etymological sense of sublimation: a transformation by fire of a solid into a gas. The quivering flame of the faun's lips explodes the still unity of the nymphs' sleeping bodies, but the faun himself is divided and devoured by the ironic passion of Mallarmé's poem. In his willful re-creation of scenes that never have taken place, the faun narcissistically indulges a self already burned away. Desire purifies the faun of his identity. It "drinks" the "secret fright" of a person, just as the poet's sublimating speech divides the writer from himself, dissipates the oppressive themes of his being in the exuberant irony of his work. With a sophistication worthy of his creator, Mallarmé's faun ironically offers us the coolness of art in his surely mistaken memories of the terror inspired by a tongue on fire.

NOTES

1. The translation of the Marquis de Sade's *The 120 Days of Sodom and Other Writings* is by Austryn Wainhouse and Richard Seaver (New York: Grove Press, 1966).

2. See the chapter "Aggressiveness and Sadomasochism," in Jean Laplanche, *Life and Death in Psychoanalysis*, trans. Jeffrey Mehlman (Baltimore: Johns Hopkins University Press, 1976).

3. But, enough! such a secret chose for confident / The vast and twin reed on which one plays under the blue sky: / Which, diverting to itself the cheek's unease; / Dreams, in a long solo, that we were charming / The surrounding beauty by fictive / Confusions between itself and our credulous song; / And [dreams] of making—as high as love modulates—/ Flee from the everyday dream of a back / Or of a pure thigh followed by my closed eyes. / A sonorous, empty and monotonous line.

Translation by the author.

 *Michael Holquist*

The Politics of Representation

But the social order is a sacred right which serves as a foundation for all others. This right however, does not come from nature. It is therefore based on convention—The question is to know what these conventions are . . .

Rousseau, *The Social Contract*

We meet under the aegis of the English Institute. As an outsider, I am aware that departments of English have recently demonstrated a quite remarkable openness to non-Anglo-Saxon ideas about the nature of literary study. However, this new cosmopolitanism has not been all-inclusive; it has stretched to Paris, but such places as Prague and Tartu still seem a bit exotic. As someone, then, who comes out of neither an English nor a French background—and who is yet anxious not to be perceived as coming out of left field—I would like to make a few preliminary observations about the assumptive world from which I have come here as a visitor.

The one thing we would now all appear to have in common is an overriding interest in the nature of language. But each different national tradition seems to have a different idea as to what that nature might be: the word *language* is in danger of losing its status as a noun as it shades more and more into the category of what Jakobson calls shifters, a word such as a pronoun, that indicates nothing more than position in discourse. From the no doubt slightly skewed perspective of an American Slavist, there would seem to be at least three such positions, three different conceptions of language abroad in the academy today (I begin by excluding a fourth conception— the one reigning in departments of linguistics—which is arguably the most outlandish of all).

In departments of literature, the three dominant ways language has come to be understood may most economically (if not responsibly) be characterized according to how each conceives the ownership of meaning. A first conception, which I shall call *Personalist,* has been associated on the continent with names like Wilhelm Wundt, Karl Vossler, Benedetto Croce, and Edmund Husserl. But, in less evident forms, it has long been regnant in English studies as a more or less unspoken first principle. This view holds that "*I* own meaning." A close bond is felt between the sense I have of myself as a unique being and the being of my language.

Such a view, with its heavy investment in the personhood of individuals, is deeply implicated in the Western Humanist tradition. As such, it is at the opposite pole from another view of language which has recently come to dominate departments of French and comparative literature, as well as many English departments. This second, or *Deconstructionist* view, holds that "*No one* owns meaning": the very conception of meaning, to say nothing of persons, invoked in most traditional epistemologies, begins by illicitly assuming a presence whose end Nietzsche really was announcing when he let it be known that God had died in history.

A third conception of language, which I shall call *Dialogism,* is one found increasingly in Slavic departments. Like the second, it has roots in Geneva. By analogy with leftist and rightist Hegelianism, we might say that it is a right-wing Saussurianism, as opposed to Deconstructionist leftism. If the Left has evolved ever increasingly radical implications of *Langue* and text, the Right has continued to mediate the complexities of *Parole* and context. The Slavic view holds that "*We* own meaning." Or—as I am reaching more familiar ground, I feel the need to be more precise—"If we do not own it, we may at least *rent* meaning." If Personalists maintain that the ground of meaning is in the unique individual, and Deconstructivists locate it in the structure of difference itself, this third view holds that meaning is rooted in the social, but the social conceived in a particular way.

The contention here is that meaning comes about *not* as the lonely product of an intention willed by a sovereign or transcendent ego. Nor is meaning ultimately *impossible* to achieve because of the arbitrary play of differences between signs. In the first instance, meaning would give itself as an immediate presence; as such, it would be subject to all the powerful criticisms Deconstructivists have mounted since at least Derrida's 1967 attack on Husserl.[1] In the second instance, such criticisms may (partially) be avoided, or at least robbed of their worst sting, through the deference one pays

them in ordering his own discourse. But the price of such tact—
which can be very impressive in its stoic way—is the perpetual elusive-
ness of meaning as it fades away in the phantom relay of the signifying chain.

The Personalist view is simultaneoulsy logo- and phono-centric:
the assumption is that I can by *speaking* appropriate to my own use
the impersonal structure of signs, which is always already there. The
breath of my life is the material of words; my voice welds me to
language. The second view goes to the opposite extreme: in it, the
human voice is conceived merely as another means for registering
differences—one, moreover, not necessarily privileged: it is far less
powerful than writing.

Russians, Poles, and Czechs such as Baudouin de Courtenay,
Nikolai Kruszevski, Mikhail Bakhtin, Lev Vygotsky, Sergej Karcevskij,
Jan Mukařovský, and of course, Roman Jakobson himself have sought
since at least the early 1920s to avoid both these extremes. They
would argue that the apparently mutual contradiction between
phonocentrism on the one hand, and grammatology on the other—
the *tertium non datur* of an overconfident monolog, or an excessively
ascetic silence—obscures a third possibility for conceiving language. It
is the one that maintains: I can mean what I say, but only *indirectly,*
at a second remove, in words I take and give back to the community
according to the protocols it establishes. My voice can mean, but only
with others: at times in chorus, but at the best of times in a dialogue.

Meaning in this view is made as a product, much as a work of
folklore is "made" in societies that strictly hold to their traditions:
"A work of folklore comes into existence only at the moment it is
accepted by a particular community."[2] There may be many versions
put forth, but only one will be capable of resisting the structural
amnesia of the group. Its acceptance by the community is the actual
—if chronologically secondary—birth of the text. As metaphor for an
account of meaning, this process is, of course, extremely crude; but
it has at least the virtue of highlighting what is of central importance
in East European philosophy of language from Kruszevski up to and
including the work of such people as Jury Lotman: that my words
will always come already wrapped in contextual layers sedimented by

the many intralanguages, various social patois, the sum of which will constitute "the" language of my culture system.

If we were to compare current ideas about language in terms of the semantic space characteristic of each, it might be said that for Personalists it is inner; for Deconstructivists elsewhere; and for East Europeans somewhere in-between: I emphasize "in-between" here not only to suggest meaning's need always to be shared, but to underline as well the degree to which multiplicity and struggle characterize this heteroglot view of language. At the highest level of abstraction, the contest may be conceived as a Manichean struggle. On the one side are ranged those forces that serve to unify and centralize meaning, that conduce to a structuredness that is indispensible if a text is to manifest system. On the opposing side stand tendencies fostering the diversity and randomness needed to keep open paths to the constantly fluctuating contextual world surrounding any utterance. The normative, systemic aspects of language have attracted the attention of most linguists, whether New Grammarians or Structuralists, and until quite recently the same could be said of most students of literature as well. It is this imbalance that the Russians seek to redress by devoting the majority of their considerable energies to studying the centrifugal forces in language, particularly as they are made specific in the various professional, class, generational, period, and other patois that the academic fiction (a necessary fiction) of a unitary national language seeks to contain. "This stratification, diversity and randomness [which Russians call *raznorečie,* or heteroglossia] is not only a static invariant in the life of language, but also what insures its dynamics. . . . Alongside centripetal forces, the centrifugal impulses of language carry on their ceaseless work. Alongside . . . centralization and unification the uninterrupted processes of decentralization and disunification go forward."[3]

Stated in such general terms, the struggle must appear a bloodless clash of abstractions; however, this is far from being the case. This conflict animates every concrete utterance made by any speaking subject: "The utterance not only answers the requirements of its own language, as an individualized embodiment of a speech act, but it answers the requirements of heteroglossia as well—indeed, any

particular utterance is an active participant in such speech diversity"
—a fact that determines the linguistic profile and style of the utterance to no less a degree than its inclusion in any normative centralizing system of a unitary language."[4]

The most comprehensive statement of the dialogic exchange
between static signs and a constantly fluctuating reality was made in
1929 by Saussure's Russian student (and respectful opponent) Sergej
Karcevskij (1888–1955): "the signifier (sound) and the signified
(meaning) slide continually on the 'slope of reality.' Each one "over-
flows' the member assigned to it by its partner: the signifier seeks to
express itself by means other than by its sign . . . it is thanks to the
asymmetric dualism of the structure of its signs that a linguistic
system can evolve: the 'adequate' position of the sign is continuously
displaced through its adaptation to the exigencies of the concrete
situation."[5] Or, as Edward Sapir never tired of repeating, "All systems
leak."

Instead of a neo-Platonic gap between *langue*'s dream of order and
parole's necessary deviance, Dialogists propose a continuum between
system and performance, the complimentarity of both. The common
element connecting both levels is the never-ending contest between
canonization and heteroglossia, which is fought out at each level. The
process is fairly obvious at the highest levels of generalization, if only
because there the struggle has served as traditional subject for
philology, which has always studied the victory of one language over
another, the supplanting of one normative dialect by another—indeed,
the life and death of whole languages. Philology, of course, has
emphasized the role of the great centralizing forces as it pursued its
utopian quest for a single *Ursprache,* a tendency that finds its comic
extreme in August Schleicher's short story *avis akvāsas ka,* "The
Sheep and the Horses" (1868), a work written in a totally concocted
proto-Indo-European.

It bears repeating that the contest is present as well in individual
utterances. It is more difficult to perceive at the most immediate
levels because neither traditional linguistics nor stylistics, as it is
usually practiced, has provided units of study adequate to the struggle's complexities. The concentration of linguists on such invariant

features as grammatical or phonemic markers misses the point
because so much of the battle is prosecuted through the interplay of
codes, each of which may be socially distinct, but all of which
employ the same grammatical and sound system (a point used by
Stalin in his 1950 *Pravda* attack on the hapless Nikolai Marr, a
linguist who argued language was a phenomenon of ideological super-
structure rather than economic base). The attention stylistics has
devoted to units such as whole sentences and paragraphs fails to take
into account that the contest may be fought out as a duel of two
social codes within a single sentence—indeed, within a single word.

For this reason, Bakhtin has proposed as a more sensitive stylistic
unit of study what he calls hybrid constructions, that is, "an
utterance which belongs, by virtue of its grammatical (synactic)
and compositional markers to a single speaker, but which actually
contains mixed within it *two* 'languages,' two semantic and axiological
belief systems." As an example, he cites a passage from Dickens's
Little Dorritt: "That illustrious man and great national ornament, Mr.
Merdle, continued his shining course. It began to be widely understood that one who had done society the admirable service of *making
so much money out of it,* could not be suffered to remain a com-
moner. A baronetcy was spoken of with confidence; a peerage was
frequently mentioned."[6]

In this passage there is first of all the author's fictive solidarity with

the hypocritically ceremonial general opinion [held by most people] of
Merdle. All epithets referring to Merdle in the first sentences derive from [such
a] general opinion, that is, they are the concealed speech of another. The
second sentence—"it began to be widely understood" etc.—is kept within the
bounds of an emphatically objective style, representing not subjective opinion,
but the admission of a . . . completely indisputable fact. [However,] the
phrase "who had done society the admirable service" is completely at the level
[once again] of common opinion, repeating its official glorification; but the
subordinate clause attached to that glorification ("of making so much money
out of it") is made up of the author's words (as *if* put into parenthesis) [but
actually without any distinguishing punctuation at all]. The last sentence then
picks up again at the level of common opinion. [This is] a typical hybrid con-
struction, where the subordinate clause is in an authorial speech that is
relatively *direct* [by contrast with] the main clause [which is] in someone

else's speech. The main and subordinate clauses are constructed in different semantic and axiological conceptual systems. [7]

Dialogism argues that what in the English comic novel is often written off as mere irony, actually constitutes a paradigm for all utterance: I can appropriate meaning to my own purposes only by ventriloquating others.

A first implication of this principle is that as speakers we all participate in the rigors of authorship: we bend language to represent by representing languages. As an illustration of this process, I would like once again to use Bakhtin as an example; this time, the example provided by the relation he himself bears to certain texts he authored. In order to proceed in this way, some historical context will be necessary.

In the year 1929, three important events occurred in Bakhtin's life. The first was publication of his book *Marxism and the Philosophy of Language;* the second was his arrest and subsequent exile to Kazakhstan; the third was publication of another of his books, *Problems of Dostoevsky's Poetics.* Each of these events had its curious twist. The arrest and exile were never officialized: there were never any formal charges brought and no trial. The only procedures involved were lengthy interrogation (which Bakhtin found quite interesting) and a certain amount of uniquely Soviet plea bargaining; that is, should he be sent to certain death in the forced labor camps of the Solovki islands, or merely exiled to a remote area for a fixed period? In the end he got off with six years exile, but because the whole thing was officially a nonevent, Bakhtin could never officially be rehabilitated. The Dostoevsky book appeared while Bakhtin was already in jail undergoing questioning. It was highly praised when it came out, by, among others, a leading member of the government, Anatoly Lunacharsky, who made strong claims for the work in a long review article. Thus you have a book written by a man who at that very moment was being held in the Lyubyanka prison being advanced as a model by the Soviet minister for education.

Strangest of all, however, are the facts surrounding the other book Bakhtin published that year, *Marxism and the Philosophy of Language.*

I wish to dwell on the eccentric textology of this book, but let me first quickly recapitulate its main thesis. My reason for doing so is that I hope to apply some of its own dicta about the nature of representation in general to the specific act of representation constituted by the text itself.

Anticipating George Herbert Mead's and C. Wright Mills's concept of the "generalized other," Bakhtin points out that

> the word is always oriented toward an addressee, toward who that addressee might be . . . each person's inner world and thought has its stabilized *social audience* that comprises the environment in which reasons, motives, values and so on are fashioned . . . the word is a two-sided act. It is determined equally by whose word it is and for whom it is meant. As word it is precisely the product of the reciprocal relationship between speaker and listener, addresser and addressee. Each and every word expresses the one relation to the other. I give myself verbal shape from another's point of view, ultimately from the point of view of the community to which I belong. A word is territory *shared* by both addresser and addressee, by the speaker and his interlocutor. [8]

It is this territorial concept of the word which necessitates a politics of representation: How is the territory governed? What legislates the way meaning is parcelled out in any given utterance?

In order to take up these questions, let me return to the peculiarities surrounding the appearance of *Marxism and the Philosophy of Language* in 1929. A first irregularity concerns the fact that the book, although written by Bakhtin, was actually published under the name of his friend Valentin Nikolaevič Vološinov. This is not the only case of plagiarism in reverse to be laid at Bakhtin's door during the 1920s. He published another book (*Freudianism: A Critical Sketch,* 1927) and an article ("Discourse in Life and Discourse in Art," *Zvezda,* no. 6 (1926), pp. 244–67) under Vološinov's name; a book attacking the Formalists under the name of his friend P. N. Medvedev (*The Formal Method in Literature Study*) in 1928, plus an article on Vitalism in a science journal in 1926 under the name of another friend, the eminent biologist I. I. Kanaev.

This is not the place to rehearse the long and complex proofs of Bakhtin's authorship of these books and articles. Suffice it to say that there is no doubt that he is their actual begetter (I do not say "onlie," because in Bakhtin's theory there are no "onlie" begetters). It is germane to our argument, however, to pause for a moment on his reasons for entering into what might be called, in his own terminology, such a *polyphonic* arrangement with his friends. These reasons are complex, and different in the case of each book or article involved, but essentially they all boil down to expedience: Bakhtin was notorious in Leningrad intellectual circles as a *cerkovnik,* a devout Orthodox Christian (of the unorthodox sort Russian intellectuals become when they give themselves to the Russian Orthodox Church). He was associated with the *Vosskresenie* group, which gathered weekly for prayer and discussion. From early on (1918–24) in his career, while still living in Byelorussia, in retreat from the capital, Bakhtin had been working on a magnum opus that he hoped would succeed in doing for the Russian religious tradition what Hermann Cohen had failed to do in his last book, *Religion der Vernunft,* (1918), for Judaism: that is, to completely rethink West European metaphysics in the light of religious thought; to show, as it were, that philosophy had in a sense always been anticipated by religion. The problems metaphysics had not solved within *its* categories could be shown to avail themselves to theology. This intention took the shape of an enormous book Bakhtin wrote during the early 1920s in the area of moral philosophy.

Only portions of the manuscript have survived, written out in pencil on crumbling student note pads. It bears no title, but internal evidence suggests it might be called *The Architectonics of Responsibility.* [9] It is a full-blown axiological theory having clear ties with both Neo-Kantianism and Husserlian phenomenology. The theory is couched in its own highly idiosyncratic language, which exploits Russian for its unique coining capacities—much as Heidegger plays with German and Greek.

We shall not have time to dwell on this work, but in order to proceed it must be kept in mind that *it contains, in embryonic form, every major idea Bakhtin was to have for the rest of his long life.* The whole conception of the work (a kind of phenomenological meditation on Christ's injunction to treat others as you would yourself be

treated), to say nothing of its lyrico-metaphysical style, was wildly at
odds with the time and place in which Bakhtin lived. He attempted
to publish a watered-down version of one section in 1924, but the
journal that had been foolhardy enough to accept it was closed down
before the fragment could be published. Bakhtin's problem, then, was
to find ways he could translate his idiosyncratic religious ideas into a
language and a genre that would be publicly acceptable in the Soviet
Union at a time when that country had already begun its march into
the dark night of the 1930s.

The problem became even more urgent in the latter half of the
1920s, since Bakhtin could find no work. He and his wife lived the
most ascetic of lives, existing for long periods on little more than
strong tea, and smoking endless, even stronger cigarettes in an effort
to keep warm. At this point, the theoretical epicenter of his work—
how to reconcile modern linguistics with the biblical assurance that
the Word became flesh—overlapped with his own most pressing
practical needs: How was he to find an appropriate ideological flesh
for the spirit of his own words so that he could sell his work before
wasting completely away?

His answer was to conceive a number of books, each of which
would convey one or another aspect of the general theory of his
Architectonics, but all of which could be presented in the Marxist
idiom of the day. Thus a major thesis of his axiology had been that
human existence is the interaction between a given world that is
always already there (*uže stavšee bytie*) and a mind that is conjoined
(*priobščën*) to this world through the deed (*postupok*) of enacting
values. What Bakhtin does in *Marxism and the Philosophy of Language,* for instance, is to define the always-already-there aspect of the
world as the "socioeconomic base." A central obsession in the axiology had been the relation between the "I" and "the other," an
irreducible duality conceived in terms of the need to *share* being.
Bakhtin's term for the distinctiveness of human existence is *sobytije
bytija,* a pun implying that such existence is both a coexisting
(*sobytie*) and an event (*sobytie*). In the Vološinov books, Bakhtin
continues to foreground the primacy of shared being, but this time in
terms of social existence. In his book on Freud, Bakhtin says

"dialectical materialism demands that . . . human psychology be socialized."[10] We might add this is not only the demand of "dialectical materialism," but of Bakhtin's own system of ethics as well, in which there is no "I" without "the other."

Marx is sometimes present in the works published in the late twenties as an honored philosopher who very early saw the systematic implications of man's social being. Thus his *Sixth Thesis of Feuerbach* can be quoted with approval: "The essence of man is not an abstraction inherent in each separate individual. In its reality it is the aggregate of social relationship."[11] This emphasis on the collective and social dimension in human beings is not, of course, an exclusively Marxist attitude (another area where such a position is an enabling a priori is, obviously, the study of language: Zellig Harris relates that after Leonard Bloomfield read *Capital* in the thirties he "was impressed above all with the similarity between Marx's statement of social behavior and that of linguistics").

Marxist terms are, however, most often present in Bakhtin's books from this period as a kind of *convenient,* in the abstract, not necessarily *inimical*—but above all, *necessary*—flag under which to advance his own views: If the Christian word were to take on Soviet flesh it had to clothe itself in ideological disguise.

It would have been impossible, of course, for Bakhtin himself, in the tight circle of the Leningrad intelligentsia, to publish self-dramatizingly Marxist works, even had he wished to; everyone knew of his religious beliefs. Two of his *friends,* however, could publish such works without straining credulity: Vološinov because of his relative obscurity—he was a minor poet, amateur musicologist, and student of linguistics, about whose personal convictions very little was generally known;[12] and Medvedev, because he was not only a Marxist, but a well-known and energetic member of the party, former chairman of the Central Committee in Vitebsk province, and, in Leningrad, a frequent go-between in the party's dealings with people in the theater and other intellectuals. Each of these men had his own reasons for entering the deception: Vološinov, because he wanted to help his beloved friend and mentor; Medvedev, because he felt such a book might raise his stock both in the party and among the ranks of the intelligentsia. So it was that the three books were published as if they were contributions to Marxist theory put forward by committed Soviet Marxists. The parts Vološinov and Medvedev were assigned required both actors to have well-established *emplois.*

Did Bakhtin—as did so many others—have to completely *misrepresent* his personally held beliefs in order to publish in the unusual conditions obtaining in the Soviet Union? The answer, while it must, of course, be highly qualified, is that he did *not.* The Vološinov and Medvedev books are, among other things, investigations into the mystery of the voice. They probe the surprising complexities that lie hidden in the apparently elementary question, "*Who* is talking?" When discussing the phenomenon of "reported or indirect speech" (*čužaja reč;* literally the "speech of another"), there is a point in each of the books where Bakhtin leaves an opening in the manifest rhetoric he has woven around his argument. He creates a kind of authorial loophole (*lazejka*), in which he describes exactly what he is doing.

In *Marxism and the Philosophy of Language,* one such loophole is constituted by his discussion of the situation that occurs in fiction when the character and author speak with a *single* voice:

> The absolute of acting out we understand to be not only a change of expressive intonation—a change logically possible within the confines of a single voice, a single consciousness—but also a change in voice in terms of the whole set of features individualizing that voice, a change of persona ("mask") in terms of a whole set of individualizing traits of facial expression and gesticulation, and finally, the complete self-consistency of this voice and persona throughout the entire acting out of the role.[13]

In other words, the text of *Marxism and the Philosophy of Language* itself constitutes the kind of dialogic space Bakhtin is talking about within it. Bakhtin, as author, manipulates the *persona* of Vološinov, using his Marxist voice to ventriloquate a meaning not specific to Marxism, even when conceived as only a discourse.

The recurring motifs of *Marxism and the Philosophy of Language*—"the concrete utterance," "the living word," and "the word in the word"—bespeak in their Marxist context an emphasis on the here and now, on the intensely immediate exchange between living people in actual historical and social encounters. Does not this emphasis on the material world of the present preclude any religious interpretation? Some background is necessary here. Such motifs are present in the Russian religious tradition as well, even the insistence on materialism (Nicolas Zernov has recently pointed out that "the fundamental conviction of the Russian religious mind is the potential holiness of matter").[14]

This concern for the materiality of things is nowhere more insistently present in Orthodoxy than in its ancient obsession with the corporeality of Christ, the emptying out of spirit, *kenosis*, when the Word took on flesh during the life of Jesus. From the time of their conversion as a nation, the Russians have venerated Christ not as the Byzantine Pantocrator, but as a humble man, a tradition that continued to live in the twentieth century in the fascination exercised by "God-Manhood," not only on such would-be mystics as Merezkòvsky, but even on political radicals such as Gorky, who preached God-building (*bogostroitel'stvo*) from the rostrum of the Writers' Union Congresses as late as the thirties.

There is no time to trace this "kenotic" tradition in any detail, but we should keep in mind that the first Russian saints, Boris and Gleb, were canonized not because they were martyrs for the faith. Their deaths were cold-bloodedly political; they were assassinated by their brother Sviatopolk and his followers to insure Sviatopolk's inheritance of his father's throne. They submitted humbly and meekly to the knives of their attackers, and it was this humility, this following of Christ's example (Russians shy away from the idea of "imitatio") that served as grounds for their being made saints. G. P. Fedotov, a member of the *Vosskresenie* group that Bakhtin frequented, in his history of the Russian religious mind (written after Fedotov's emigration) points out that St. Theodosius, founder of the greatest of the old Russian monasteries, was opposed to any mysticism. In this, he "is the spokesman of ancient Russia. . . . The terms in which he speaks of his love for Christ are quite remarkable: the Eucharistic bread speaks to him not only of Christ, but especially of Christ's flesh."[15]

This tradition was kept alive in Russian religious experience throughout the centuries: at times the obsession with Christ's corporeality took extreme forms, such as the sect of the *Khlysty*, an

Orthodox version of Tantrism, in which sexual orgies were an inveterate feature (and whose importance in the twentieth century was highlighted in the central role played by Rasputin at the court of the last Romanov czar).

Bakhtin's work in axiology was a philosophical contribution to this tradition. Its basic thesis was that men define their unique place in existence through the responsibility they enact, the care they exhibit in their deeds for others and the world. Deed is understood as meaning *word* as well as physical act: the deed is how meaning comes into the world, how brute facticity is given significance and form, how the Word becomes flesh.

Marxism and the Philosophy of Language, if treated as an utterance —that is, a statement whose meaning depends on the unrepeatable historical and social context in which it was pronounced, as well as on the repeatable words of the text—is, then, a very complex example of the transcoding possibilities in indirect speech, *čužaja reč,'* the speech of the other: Bakhtin has appropriated the code of one ideology to make public the message of quite another.

One of the more popular accounts of representation imported recently from France has been Pierre Macherey's application of Louis Althusser.[16] It is a highly sophisticated model for mapping the relationship between an individual consciousness and the expressive means a society makes available to such a consciousness. As such, I would like (in passing) to point out why it cannot account for Bakhtin's ideological transcoding. Pierre Macherey still assumes the necessity of bad faith, the inescapability of false consciousness. In this view, authors can never express the actual place they occupy among the reigning myths of their own time and place. It is a Marxist version of "blindness and insight," in which a text is always incomplete insofar as it will always leave out its author's complicity in the web of his own—unavoidable—misrecognitions. Thus, Jules Verne might "figure" the ideology of the Third Republic's colonializing bourgeoisie, but a discerning (subsequent) critic will be able to perceive a gap in his texts where, all unknown to the historical subject Jules Verne, he is actually "representing" a powerful critique of that ideology. There are, as it were, two voices, two ideologies to be found in a single text, but only as it is constituted by the astute reader who can overcome its delusion, the delusion of its author, that it (he) is monologic. Clearly such a theory cannot account for Bakhtin's very consciously wrought creolization of different ideologies in the texts he published as Vološinov. In his case, we get the very opposite of what Macherey proposes: it is precisely the *author* who knew more about the ideologies concealed in the gaps of his text than his "discerning readers" in the office of the Soviet censor.

The theory of representation most capable of accounting for Bakhtin's dialogic practice is, not surprisingly, his own.

In his book on Freud, Bakhtin redefines the distinction between the conscious and the unconscious. This part of the argument is initiated by a bold act of substitution. Bakhtin reformulates the distinction between conscious and unconscious as a difference not between two different kinds of reality, for they are both variants of the same phenomenon: *both* are aspects of consciousness. Instead of positing an ontological difference between the two, Bakhtin perceives the distinction as differing degrees of ideological *sharing:* the unconscious is a suppressed, relatively idiosyncratic ideological realm (insofar as ideology can *ever* be idiosyncratic), whereas the conscious is a public world whose ideologies may be shared openly with others. He calls Freud's *un*conscious the "unofficial conscious," as opposed to the ordinary "official conscious."

The language of unofficial conscious is inner speech, the language of official conscious outward speech, but they both operate according to the general rules of all human verbal behavior. *"The verbal component of behavior is determined in all fundamentals and essentials of its content by objective-social factors. . . .* Therefore nothing verbal in human behaviour (inner and outward speech equally) can under any circumstances be reckoned to the account of the individual subject in isolation; the verbal is not his property but the property of his *social group* (his social milieu)."[17]

There is, of course, a *hierarchy* of causes and effects which stretches from the content of the individual psyche (understood as *individual,* but never isolated) to the content of a large-scale system of culture. The route between the two extremes is, however, a highway governed by the same rules of the road: "At all stages of this route human consciousness operates through *words*."[18] It follows that:

> Any human verbal utterance is an ideological construct in the small. The *motivation* of one's behaviour is *juridical* and *moral* behaviour on a small scale; an exclamation of joy or grief is a primitive *lyric* composition; pragmatic considerations of the causes and consequences of happenings are germinal forms of *scientific* and *philosophical* cognition. . . . The stable, formulated ideological systems of the sciences, the arts, jurisprudence and the like, have sprung and crystallized from that seething ideological element where broad waves of inner and outward speech engulf our every act and our very perception.[19]

But if there are important similarities between the *modus operandi* of individual psyches and whole culture systems, there are also significant differences. In outlining these, we first become aware of the reasons for Bakhtin's substituting unofficial/official consciousness for Freud's unconscious/conscious distinction.

Although the systems of individual psyche and whole societies are both ideological through and through, ideology has a different status in each. The primary difference consists in the achieved, stable quality of official ideologies that are shared by the group as a whole. They are, in Bakhtin's own terminology, "finished off" (*zaveršën*), the source of what he will call, in the thirties' version of the same distinction, the discourse of authority (*'avtoritetnoe slovo*). Because of its rigidity, it is always-already-there, it is "pre-located discourse" (*prednaxodimoe slovo*), the language, then, of the fathers, a past that is still very present.

Against this fixed system of values, Bakhtin poses another system, which he calls behavioral ideology, "that inner and outward speech that permeates our individual, 'personal' behaviour in all its aspects."[20] As opposed to broad-based social values, behavioral ideology is "more sensitive, more responsive, more excitable and livelier" than an ideology that has undergone formulation and become 'official.'" It is *not* finished off, and corresponds to what Bakhtin will call innerly persuasive discourse (*vnutrenno-ubeditel'noe slovo*) in the thirties. It is unfinished, not completely formulated, because it is the world ideologized from the point of view of an individual consciousness who lives in "the absolute future" of still unrealized possibilities.

The opposition Bakhtin sets up here, although carefully camou-
flaged in Marxist terminology and neutral adjectives (i.e., "social,"
"behavorial"), is still the master opposition at the heart of his
Architectonics: the conflict between a set of values grounded in the
self, and a set of values grounded in the other. What Bakhtin is saying
in his distinction between behavorial ideology and social ideology is
that there is a *gap* between the two. Individual consciousness never—
even among the most wholly committed ideologues—fully replicates
the structure of the society's public values. To assume that it *can* is
the great mistake of "vulgar Marxists" who seek a one-to-one
correspondence between individuals and their social origin, who seek
to close the space between individual consciousness and class consciousness.

In his *Architectonics,* Bakhtin had explained the gap in ontological
terms; the self and the other were seen to constitute two different
realities, which could never fuse on a single plane. In the book on
Freud, the explanation for the gap is developmental, that is, behavioral
ideology is conceived as still inchoate, a primitive form of more public
ideologies: when behavioral thought finds its highest expression, it
will be fixed in the *shared* values of an official ideology. The switch
to such developmental categories was a perhaps necessary dissembling
if so radical a distinction was to be maintained at all. But, even so, the
clear implication is that the traffic between the social and the individual is not *all one way.* An ideology, once formulated, has enormous
impact on individuals comprising the society whose values it defines.
The *opposite* is also the case, however, for "in the depths of behavioral
ideology accumulate those contradictions which once having reached
a certain threshold, ultimately burst asunder the system of the
official ideology."[21] (This surely is what Erik Erikson has in mind as
well when he characterizes the collision between the individual
histories of Luther and Gandhi and the collective histories of their
societies as the willingness of such men "to do the dirty work of their
ages.")

What Bakhtin has done is to realize, in a recognizably Russian
scenario, Freud's metaphor of censorship: the *unconscious,* as unofficial *conscious,* operates like a minority political party opposed to

certain aspects of the politics reigning in the surrounding culture. The more of these aspects it opposes, the more "censored" it is, because the difference between its values and those of the majority will be expressed as a difference in the intelligibility of languages; the less the unofficial party has in common with official ideology, the more restricted will be its expressive means. Insofar as the minority cannot *share* its values, it is condemned to a relative silence. It is as if an Eskimo revolutionary group, seeking independence from the United States, were to flood New York City with manifestoes written in Athabaskan—even though *willing* a conflict with the majority culture, the group is condemned to inaction by the structure of communication, the architectonics of value. In a very real sense, what Bakhtin is doing may be likened to the efforts of early Christians to spread their message by parable and allegory. The clandestine church in Leningrad during these years was called "the catacomb church" because its members felt they lived in times very similar to those first-century sectarians who met by night in cellars below the imperial marble of a hostile Rome.

It is here we should seek the reasons Bakhtin feels compelled to revise Freud's scenario of conflict between the official and unofficial conscious. When he writes that "the wider and deeper the breach between the official and unofficial conscious, the more difficult it becomes for motives of inner speech to turn into outward speech . . . wherein they might acquire formulation, clarity and vigor,"[22] he is describing his own dilemma, the increasing gap between his own religious and metaphysical ideas and the Soviet government's ever more militant insistence on adherence to Russian Communism. Bakhtin says that "motives under these conditions begin to . . . lose their verbal countenance, and little by little really do turn into a 'foreign body' in the psyche," but it is clear he also means that they become foreign bodies in the state as well.

His daring insistence on the uniplanar coexistence of rules of governance in the *psyche* with rules for governance in the *state* is not merely one more way to conceive Freudian theory. It also explains Bakhtin's practice of sending out transcoded messages from the catacombs. He has just said that the gap between official and unofficial conscious can become so great that finally the content of the unofficial conscious is snuffed out. But if we remember that the traffic between the terminus of an individual psyche and that of a whole culture moves in *both* directions, a more optimistic scenario may be conceived for unofficial forces; it is not true

> that *every* motive in contradiction with the official ideology must degenerate into indistinct inner speech and then die out—[one of them] might well engage in a struggle with that official ideology [and] . . . if it is not merely the motive of a declassé loner, then it has a chance for a future and perhaps even *a victorious future* . . . at first a motive of this sort will develop within a small social milieu and will depart into the underground—not the psychological underground, but the salutary political underground. [23]

For Russians, utterance has ever been a contest, a struggle. The need to speak indirectly has resulted in a Russian discourse that is always fabular precisely when it is fueled by the most intense desire to mean. Such indirection has resulted in an allegorical mode known as "Aesopic language." Bakhtin's achievement is to refine, out of the particular features that have created such a situation, a synthetic philosophy of language.

If he is correct, utterance cannot avoid contest and struggle. The dictum that "War is the prosecution of diplomacy by other means" may in Bakhtin's case be paraphrased as "Allegory is the prosecution of semantic intention by other means". As such, Bakhtin's example provides at least the beginning of an answer to some troubling questions raised recently by Paul de Man in his reading of Pascal: "From a theoretical point of view," de Man writes, "there ought to be no difficulty in moving from epistemology to persuasion. The very occurrence of allegory, however, indicates a possible complication. Why is it that the furthest reaching truths about ourselves and the world have to be stated in such a lopsided, referentially indirect mode?" (See Chapter 1.)

The answer provided by Bakhtin in both his theory and his practice, although not adequate to all the implications of de Man's question, suffices at least to point us in a further direction. If we begin by assuming that *all* representation must be indirect, that *all* utterance is ventriloquism, then it will be clear—even, or especially, "from a theoretical point of view"—that difficulties *do* exist in moving from epistemology to persuasion. This is because difficulties exist in the very politics of any utterance, difficulties that at their most powerful exist in the politics of culture systems.

If the actual source of prohibition is recognized, however, the possibility of deceiving the censor becomes an option. I would like now, very briefly, to return to the three views of language with which I began. Such a tripartite division is, of course, already overschematized. I hope, however, such categorization will take any further strain put upon it by suggesting that each view of language results in its own characteristic genre. Personalism has a natural affinity with the *Bildungsroman;* it is full of "Great Expectations." Deconstructivism has an affinity with lyric and fragment; it concerns itself with traces such as the message that never gets delivered in Kafka's fragment, "The News of the Building of the Wall."

Dialogism has a taste for carnival and comedy, an affinity perhaps best caught in Bakhtin's lifelong affection for the first story of the *Decameron,* "How Ser Ciapelletto Became Saint Ciapelletto." You will remember it is a funny—but somewhat eerie—tale about an evil merchant who has lied, cheated, and indiscriminately fornicated all his life. He falls ill and recognizes that he is about to die while visiting a strange town where no one knows him. He calls for a priest in order to make his final confession and, by a series of subtle indirections, convinces the priest he has led a life of the most unexampled virtue. After the evil merchant's death, the priest to whom he confessed tells everyone about his discovery of a secret saint. Soon pilgrimages are made to the merchant's tomb, and, before very long, miracles begin to occur on the site.

In conclusion, I would like to suggest that this tale of how subversive intentions get canonized is not only a parabolic expression of Bakhtin's biographical project. It serves as well to remind us that although the politics of representation are vexed, it is still a politics insofar as it is an art of the possible. Paraphrasing Stephen Daedelus, we may say that silence is not mandatory, exile may be overcome, as long as cunning reigns.

NOTES

1. Jacques Derrida, *La Voix et le phénomène* (Paris: Presses universitaires de France), 1967. Translated by David Allison, as *Speech and Phenomena* (Evanston, Ill.: Northwestern University Press, 1973).

2. Roman Jakobson (with P. Bogatyrev), "Die Folklore als eine besondere Form des Schaffens," Selected *Writings* (The Hague: Mouton, 1966), 4:13.

3. M. M. Bakhtin, "Slovo v romane," *Voprosy literatury i estetiki* (Moscow: Xudožeztvennaja literatura, 1975), p. 85. The essay here quoted, "Discourse in the Novel," together with three other pieces on theory of the novel and philosophy of language, will be published in English translation in 1981.

4. Ibid.

5. Sergej Karcevskij, "Du dualisme asymétrique de signe linguistique," *Travaux du Cercle linguistique de Prague* (Prague, 1929), 1:88. See also Wendy Steiner's fine piece comparing Saussure and Karcevskij: "Language as Process: Sergej Karcevskij's Semiotics of Language," *Sound, Sign and Meaning: Quinquagenary of the Prague Linguistic Circle*, ed. L. Matejka (Ann Arbor: University of Michigan Press, 1978).

6. Bakhtin, "Slovo v romane," p. 119.

7. Ibid., p. 120.

8. M. M. Bakhtin, *Marxism and the Philosophy of Language*, trans. Ladislav Matejka and I. R. Titunik (New York: Seminar Press, 1973), pp. 85-86.

9. A longish portion of this work (one of five sections) was published under the calculatedly neutral title of "Author and Hero," in the latest collection of Bakhtin's writings to be published in the Soviet Union. See "Avtor i geroj," *Estetika slovesnogo tvorčestva*, ed. S. Bočarov (Moscow: Isskustvo, 1979), pp. 7-180.

10. M. M. Bakhtin, *Freudianism, a Marxist Critique* (the translator has changed the original title, which was *Marxism: A Critical Sketch*), trans. I. R. Titunik (New York: Academic Press, 1976), p. 22.

11. Ibid., p. 5.

12. There has been a good deal of confusion surrounding Vološinov, due to a rumor that has several times found its way into print in the West. The assumption that Vološinov was arrested in the purges of the 1930s is, however, utterly unfounded. Unlike Bakhtin or Medvedev, Vološinov was never even arrested. He died of tuberculosis in 1936.

13. Bakhtin, *Marxism and the Philosophy of Language*, pp. 156-57.

14. Nicholas Zernov, *The Russian Religious Renaissance of the Twentieth Century* (London: Duckworth, 1963), p. 285.

15. G. P. Fedotov, *The Russian Religious Mind* (Cambridge: Harvard University Press, 1966), 2:317.

16. Pierre Macherey, *A Theory of Literary Production*, trans. Geoffrey Wall (London: Routledge & Kegan Paul, 1978).

17. Bakhtin, *Freudianism*, p. 86.

18. Ibid., p. 87.

19. Ibid., p. 88.

20. Ibid.

21. Ibid.

22. Bakhtin, *Freudianism*, p. 89.

23. Ibid., p. 90.

The English Institute, 1979-80

The Program

Friday, August 29, through Monday, September 1, 1980
  I. Form and Context in Eighteenth Century Narrative
     Directed by Leopold Damrosch, Jr., University of Virgina

Fri. 1:45 P.M.	Providence, Guilt, and the Rise of the Novel *Leopold Damrosch, Jr., University of Virginia*
Sat. 9:30 A.M.	Fielding, Sterne, Austen, and What Figures in a Novel *Michael Rosenblum, Indiana University, Bloomington*
Sat. 11:00 A.M.	Mary Wollstonecraft: The Gender of Genres in Late Eighteenth Century England *Mary Poovey, Swarthmore College*

  II. Beyond Tradition: Projects of American Modernist Poetry
     Directed by Joseph Riddel, University of California–Los Angeles

Fri. 3:15 P.M.	Pound and the Poetics of Loss *Herbert Schneidau, University of California–Santa Barbara*
Sat. 1:45 P.M.	Foreshadowing and Foreshortening: The Prophetic Vision of Origins in Hart Crane's *The Bridge* *John T. Irwin, Johns Hopkins University*
Sat. 3:15 P.M.	Repetition and Vision in Stevens, Ammons, and Ashbery *Helen Reguerio Elam, SUNY–Albany*

  III. Film and Film Criticism
     Directed by William Rothman, Harvard University

Sun. 9:30 A.M.	The Present Condition of Film Criticism; or, The Movie Vanishes *William Rothman, Harvard University*
Sun. 10:00 A.M.	Film Showing: *North by Northwest* (Hitchcock)
Sun. 1:45 P.M.	Symposium: Approaches to *North by Northwest* *Stanley Cavell, Harvard University* *Ann Douglas, Columbia University* *William Rothman, Harvard University* *Geoffrey H. Hartman, Yale University*

IV. Mimesis and Representation
   Directed by Stephen J. Greenblatt, University of California–Berkeley
   Mon. 9:30 A.M.   Representation and Its Discontents
                     Leo Bersani, University of California–Berkeley
   Mon. 11:00 A.M.   The Politics of Representation
                     Michael Holquist, University of Texas–Austin
   Mon. 1:45 P.M.   Courbet's Realism
                     Michael Fried, Johns Hopkins University
   Mon. 3:15 P.M.   The Possum in the Cave
                     Hugh Kenner, Johns Hopkins University

Sponsoring Institutions

Columbia University, Princeton University, Yale University, University of Rochester, Claremont Graduate School, Rutgers University, Michigan State University, Northwestern University, Boston University, University of California–Berkeley, University of Connecticut, Harvard University, University of Pennsylvania, University of Virginia, Amherst College, SUNY–Stony Brook, CUNY–Graduate Center, Brandeis University, Cornell University, Dartmouth College, New York University, Smith College, Johns Hopkins University, Washington University, SUNY–Albany, Temple University, University of Alabama–Birmingham, University of California–San Diego, Boston College, Brigham Young University, University of California–Los Angeles, University of California–Santa Cruz, Massachusetts Institute of Technology, Wellesley College, Indiana University–Bloomington, Tufts University, University of Colorado, Wesleyan University

Registrants, 1979-80

Joseph Adams, SUNY–Binghamton; Ruth M. Adams, Dartmouth College; Janet E. Aikins, University of New Hampshire; Samuel W. Allen, Boston University; Marcia Allentuck, CUNY; Geraldine Anthony, S.C., Mt. St. Vincent University; Jonathan Arac, University of Illinois at Chicago Circle; N. S. Asbridge, Central Connecticut State College; Henry Auster, University of Toronto; James H. Averill, Princeton University

George W. Bahlke, Hamilton College; James E. Barcus, Baylor University; J. Robert Barth, S. J., University of Missouri–Columbia; Adrianne Roberts Baytop, Douglass College, Rutgers University; Jerome Beaty, Emory University; John E. Becker, Fairleigh Dickinson University; Nancy M. Bentley, San Diego City Schools; Leo Bersani, University of California–Berkeley; Warner Berthoff, Harvard University; Walter Bezanson, Rutgers University; Kenneth Bleeth, Connecticut College; Charles R. Blyth; Frank Brady, CUNY–Graduate Center; Leo Braudy, Johns Hopkins University; Laurence A. Breiner, Boston University; Stephen M. Bretzius, Harvard University; Christine Brooke-Rose, University of Paris VIII; Elizabeth Brophy, College of New Rochelle; James Brophy, Iona

College; Peter Brunette, George Mason University; Elizabeth Bruss, Amherst College; Jane Britton Buchanan, Tufts University; Scott Buechler, Virgina Polytechnic Institute and State University; Daniel Burke, F.S.C., La Salle College; John J. Burke, Jr., University of Alabama; Ronald Bush, Harvard University

John Cameron, Amherst College; Jerry W. Carlson, DePaul University; Robert L. Caserio, Yale University; Stanley Cavell, Harvard University; David Cavitch, Tufts University; Lila Chalpin, Massachusetts College of Art; P. S. Chauhan, Beaver College; James T. Clifford, University of California–Santa Cruz; Arthur N. Collins, SUNY–Albany; James M. Cox, Darmouth College; John D. Cox, Hope College; Patricia Craddock, Boston University; G. Armour Craig, Amherst College; Martha A. Craig, Wellesley College; Patricia Cramer; William M. Curtin, University of Connecticut

Emily Dalgarno, Boston University; Timothy J. Dalton, University of California–Berkeley; Leopold Damrosch, Jr., University of Virginia; Susan Dannenbaum, Harvard University; Tom Dargan; Charles T. Davis, Yale University; Robert A. Day, CUNY; Winifred M. Davis, Columbia University; David Diamond, University of Pennsylvania; E. Talbot Donaldson, Indiana University; Deborah Dorfman, SUNY–Albany; Clyde H. Dornbusch, Ohio Northern University; John F. Dornbusch, Ohio Northern University; Ann Douglas, Columbia University

Helen Regueiro Elam, SUNY–Albany; Robert C. Elliott, University of California–San Diego; David Erdman, SUNY–Stony Brook; Elizabeth Ermarth, University of Maryland, Baltimore

Mary Anne Ferguson, University of Massachusetts–Boston; Randy Fertel, Harvard University; Leslie Fiedler, SUNY–Buffalo; Richard Flantz, Tel Aviv University; Ephim Fogel, Cornell University; Leslie D. Foster, Northern Michigan University; Debra Fried, Cornell University; Michael Fried, Johns Hopkins University; Margaretta Fulton, Harvard University Press

Lea Hamaoui, CUNY–Graduate School and University Center; Maryhelen Harmon, University of South Florida; Victor Harris, Brandeis University; Geoffrey H. Hartman, Yale University; Richard Haven, University of Massachusetts–Amherst; Barrie Hayne, University of Toronto; Joan Hedrick, Wesleyan University; Carolyn G. Heilbrun, Columbia University; Margorie H. Hellerstein, Massachusetts College of Art; Suzette Henke, SUNY–Binghamton; Karen S. Henry, Tufts University; Bruce Herzberg; Margaret R. Higonnet, University of Connecticut; William B. Hill, S.J., University of Scranton; Myra Hinman, University of Kansas; Daniel Hoffman, University of Pennsylvania; Steven K. Hoffman, Virginia

Polytechnic Institute; Michael Holquist, Indiana University; Bernard Horn, Northern Essex Community College; Susan R. Horton, University of Massachusetts-Boston; Chaviva M. Hošek, University of Toronto; Pat C. Hoy II, U.S. Military Academy; Dianne Hunter, Trinity College

Marcia Ian; John T. Irwin, Johns Hopkins University ˎ

Nora Crow Jaffe, Smith College; Kenneth Johnston, Indiana University; Sidney Jones, Carroll College

Marjorie Kaufman, Mt. Holyoke College; Carol Kay, Amherst College; Donald Kay, University of Alabama; Robert A. Kelly, Macon Junior College; Hugh Kenner, Johns Hopkins University; Bernard Khieger, University of Haifa; Arthur F. Kinney, University of Massachusetts-Amherst; Rudolf Kirk; Susan S. Klemtner, SUNY-Binghamton; Andrea F. Korval, CUNY-Graduate Center; Murray Krieger, University of California-Irvine and Los Angeles; Joseph G. Kronick, University of California-Los Angeles

G. R. Lair, Delbarton School; Berel Lang, University of Colorado; Nancy Leonard, Bard College; Vivien Leonard, Rensselaer Polytechnic Institute; Richard Leveroni, Schenectady County Community College; Katherine Bailey Linehan, Oberlin College; Joanna Lipking, Northwestern University; Lawrence Lipking, Northwestern University; James T. Livingston, Drury College; Joseph P. Lovering, Canisius College

Howard Mayer, University of Connecticut; Stuart Y. McDougal, University of Michigan; Terence J. McKenzie, U.S. Coast Guard Academy; James R. McNerney, Catholic University; Irving Malin, CUNY; David Marshall, Yale University; Robert K. Martin, Concordia University; Donald C. Mell, Jr., University of Delaware; Ronald Meyers, East Stroudsburg State College; John H. Middendorf, Columbia University; J. Lawrence Mitchell, University of Minnesota; Helen Moglen, University of California-Santa Cruz; Adbul R. Jan Mohamed, Boston University

Rae Ann Nager, Harvard University; Edward Nathan, Harvard University; John M. Nesselhof, Wells College

James Olney, North Carolina Central University; S. K. Orgel, Johns Hopkins University; Chas. A. Owen, Jr., University of Connecticut

Stanley R. Palombo, Washington School of Psychiatry; Coleman O. Parsons,

CUNY–Graduate School; June Parsons, CUNY–Graduate School; Annabelle Patterson, University of Maryland; John Pattinson, New Jersey Institute of Technology; Richard Pearce; Roy Harvey Pearce, University of California–San Diego; Donald Pease, Dartmouth College; Ellen Peel, Yale University; Dale E. Peterson, Amherst College; Linda H. Peterson, Yale University; Burton Pike, CUNY–Graduate School; Mary Poovey, Swarthmore College; Thomas Postlewait, M.I.T.; Robert O. Preyer, Brandeis University; Robert P. Price, Ohio Northern University; Wyatt Prunty, Virginia Polytechnic Institute and State University

Melinda Alliker Rabb, M.I.T.; Rubin Rabinovitz, University of Colorado–Boulder; Jon Ramsey, Skidmore College; Donald Reiman, Carl Pforzheimer Library; Eleanor N. Richwine, Western Maryland College; Keith N. Richwine, Western Maryland College; Joseph N. Riddel, University of California–Los Angeles; Bruce Robbins, University of Geneva; Jeffrey C. Robinson, University of Colorado–Boulder; Mark Rose, University of California–Santa Barbara; Ruth Rosenberg, Brooklyn College; Michael Rosenblum, Indiana University; Adena Rosmarin, Harvard University; William Rothman, Harvard University; Marylea Rudnik, University of Amsterdam

Elaine B. Safer, University of Delaware; Dorothy I. J. Samuel, Tennessee State University; Elaine Scarry, University of Pennsylvania; Daniel Schenker, Brandeis University; Herbert N. Schneidau, University of Arizona; Joseph Leondar Schneider, Curry College; Sue W. Schopf, Harvard University; Samuel E. Schulman, Boston University; Mary Anne Shea, New York University; Marc Shell, SUNY–Buffalo; Carol Shloss, Wesleyan University; Myron Simon, University of California–Irvine; John L. Simons, Colorado College; Patricia L. Skarda, Smith College; Barbara Herrnstein Smith, University of Pennsylvania; Marc Trevor Smith; Sarah W. R. Smith, Tufts University; Thomas R. Smith, Rutgers University; Edward A. Snow, George Mason University; Janice Sokoloff, University of Massachusetts; George Soule, Carleton College; Patricia Meyer Spacks, Yale University; William Spanos, SUNY–Binghamton; Robert Spiller, University of Pennsylvania; Robert Sprich, Bentley College; Michael Sprinker, Oregon State University; John D. Stahl, University of Connecticut; Richard Stamelman, Wesleyan University; Susan Staves, Brandeis University; Holly Stevens; Fred Stockholder, University of British Columbia; Albert Stone, Jr., Hellenic College; Rudolf F. Storch, Tufts University; William W. Stowe, Wesleyan University; Marcia Stubbs, Wellesley College; Jean Sudrann, Mount Holyoke College; Sara Suleri, Indiana University

Stephen L. Tanner, Brigham Young University; Irene Tayler, M.I.T.; Dennis Taylor, Boston College; R. Z. Temple, CUNY–Graduate School; Elizabeth Tenenbaum, M.I.T.; J. J. M. Tobin, Boston State College; Lewis A. Turlish, Bates College

Thomas Vargish, Dartmouth College; Helen Vendler, Boston University

Eugene M. Waith, Yale University; Emily M. Wallace, Curtis Institute of Music; Melissa Walker, Mercer University–Atlanta; Aileen Ward, New York University; Grant Webster, SUNY-Binghamton; Sister Mary Anthony Weinig, Rosemont College; Laura J. Wexler, Amherst College; Hayden White, University of California–Santa Cruz; Epi Wiese; Carolyn Williams, Boston University; Marilyn L. Williamson, Wayne State University; Hugh Witemeyer, University of New Mexico; Cynthia Griffin Wolff, M.I.T.

Curt Zimansky; Carol Zuses, Middlebury College

DATE			